IS FEMINIST PHILOSOPHY PHILOSOPHY?

Northwestern University

Studies in Phenomenology

and

Existential Philosophy

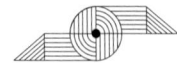

IS FEMINIST PHILOSOPHY PHILOSOPHY?

Edited by
Emanuela Bianchi

Northwestern University Press
Evanston, Illinois

Northwestern University Press
Evanston, Illinois 60208-4210

Compilation copyright © 1999 by Northwestern University Press.
Published 1999. All rights reserved.

Printed in the United States of America

ISBN 0-8101-1594-8 (cloth)
ISBN 0-8101-1595-6 (paper)

Library of Congress Cataloging-in-Publication Data

Is feminist philosophy philosophy? / edited by Emanuela Bianchi
     p. cm.—(Northwestern University studies in phenomenology and exis-
tential philosophy)
  Includes bibliographical references.
  ISBN 0–8101-1594–8 (cloth : alk. paper)—ISBN 0–8101-1595–6 (pbk. : alk.
paper)
    1. Feminist theory.   2. Feminism—Philosophy.   I. Bianchi, Emanuela.
II. Northwestern University studies in phenomenology & existential
philosophy.
HQ1190.I77 1999
305.42'01—dc21   99–046794
                                                     CIP

For my mother, Lorenza Bianchi

Contents

Acknowledgments

The editor would like to thank the following for permission to reprint the following articles: *differences: A Journal of Feminist Cultural Studies* for Alys Eve Weinbaum, "Marx, Irigaray, and the Politics of Reproduction" from *differences: A Journal of Feminist Cultural Studies* 6.1 (1994): 98–128; the University of Chicago Press for Iris Marion Young, "Mothers, Citizenship, and Independence: A Critique of Pure Family Values" from *Ethics* 105, no. 3 (1995): 535–55; Blackwell Publishers for Teresa Brennan, "Essence against Identity" from *Metaphilosophy* 27 (1996): 92–103; and Virginia Held for "Feminist Interpretations of Social and Political Thought" revised from Virginia Held, *Feminist Interpretations of Social and Political Thought*.

This volume has come to fruition only through the hard work, assistance, and guidance of numerous individuals and organizations. First, thanks to the members of Graduate Faculty Women in Philosophy who organized the original conference from which this volume has grown; Camille Atkinson, Shana Mahaffey, Kelly Stoner, Lynn Taddeo, and especially Rachael Cayley worked tirelessly and with excellent humor to make it happen. The Department of Philosophy, the Committee on Gender Studies, and the Office of Student Affairs at the Graduate Faculty, New School for Social Research provided much needed and much appreciated financial assistance. Kitty Holland's astute advice on many aspects of the conference process was invaluable, as was that of Drucilla Cornell.

The production of the book itself was vastly aided by my original coeditor, Falguni (Tina) A. Sheth, whose untimely withdrawal from the project was much regretted and to whom I owe an enormous debt of gratitude. Thanks too to Judith Friedlander, whose skillful editorial work on Jacques Derrida's remarks has made his words so readable. The advice and support during different stages of editing and publication from Drucilla Cornell, Teresa Brennan, and Judith Butler has been much appreciated. Every contributor to this volume has abided through this somewhat lengthy process with patience and grace, and it has been an easy pleasure to work with each one of them, for which I am very grateful.

Much headway was made on this volume during the tenure of an International Fellowship from the American Association of University Women, and during the tenure of the List Holocaust Fellowship from the Graduate Faculty, New School for Social Research. A visiting scholarship at the Department of Rhetoric at the University of California, Berkeley, has provided an institutional base for this project. The partners at my part-time law firm job, Penelope Chronis and Elizabeth Kreher, willingly donated copying and printing facilities, and I thank them kindly for this and for their daily commitment to feminism.

Lastly, immense gratitude must go to those people in my life who on a daily basis have been involved in the long and sometimes difficult process of the production of this book, namely, Tim Watson, David Kazanjian, Nicolai Meador, and Neon Weiss.

Introduction

Emanuela Bianchi

This collection of essays arose out of a conference, held at the Graduate Faculty of Political and Social Science, New School for Social Research, in the fall of 1993, entitled "Is Feminist Philosophy Philosophy?" The conference was organized by a group of graduate students, Graduate Faculty Women in Philosophy, as a way of raising, in an audible and far-reaching way, the question of the legitimacy of feminist philosophy in the discipline of philosophy as a whole. Although not intending to detract from nor disregard in any way the important gains that feminist scholars have made throughout the humanities as a whole, the conference organizers wished to address the question of feminist philosophy in the specific context of the traditionalist discipline and institution of philosophy, what Christine Battersby has memorably termed "the recalcitrant discipline."[1]

Philosophy has the dubious distinction of attracting the least women students and scholars of any humanities or social science field,[2] which is perhaps all the more surprising because feminist theory in the last two decades has provided the academy with debates of exemplary vibrancy and rigor—debates which in large part answer to, resonate with, and often draw their conceptual underpinnings and vocabularies from writings in the philosophical canon. Upon closer inspection, however, many of the voices in such feminist theoretical scholarship have their institutional locations elsewhere: in English departments, history, sociology, anthropology, political science, and the newer disciplines of women's studies and ethnic studies. Why should this be the case? Why have comparatively few feminist theorists received their training within philosophy, and why has the philosophical establishment been relatively slow to welcome feminist practitioners and ideas within its institutional purview?

The intention of the conference, and of the present volume, is to turn the mirror back toward that institution and to inquire, in a spirit both feminist and philosophical, into the reasons for philosophy's particular resistance to the inroads of scholarship represented by feminist theory. How do the questions that feminist theorists are interested in throw into question the already questionable boundaries of philosophy's traditional self-definition? Do they threaten or expand philosophy, or both? How are feminist philosophers altering the landscape of philosophical inquiry? In what sense, if any, is philosophy itself *at issue* in the questions that feminist philosophers are wont to ask?

The question that is the title of this volume—*Is Feminist Philosophy Philosophy?*—has, then, both an ironic and a serious sense. The ironic sense assumes that of course there exist, quite self-evidently, feminist philosophers and theorists, and what indeed do they do, if not feminist philosophy? And what is feminist philosophy, if not a species of the genus "philosophy"? Asking the question in this light is both ironic and provocative; it assumes that those who would ask this question seriously must quite wrongly contest the self-evident existence of feminist philosophy, and must contradictorily and quite egregiously question the subsumption of the species "feminist philosophy" under the genus "philosophy."

The serious sense of this question, however, is not that in which it might demand or elicit a simple yes-or-no answer. It rather marks a desire to inquire into the reasons for, to understand as fully as possible, the structures underlying and the motivations behind the tangible lack of communication between feminism and philosophy. It is only when, this volume contends, we have sufficiently understood the depth of this problem and its character and topology that we may begin to move beyond it to a more fruitful and productive dialogue.

The collection also represents, at the same time, a significant sally into that dialogue itself. It is not the first collection of this type, of course. Volumes such as Sandra Harding and Merrill B. Hintikka's *Discovering Reality* (Dordrecht, Holland: D. Reidel Publishing Company, 1983), and Ann Garry and Marilyn Pearsall's *Women, Knowledge and Reality* (Winchester, Mass.: Unwin Hyman, 1989) have established themselves as canonical texts of feminist philosophy whose many essays demonstrate the range, depth, and fruitfulness of the alliance between feminism and philosophy. The present volume continues and adds to that tradition, revealing many of the philosophical dimensions of feminist thinking and the feminist possibilities dwelling in the traditions of Western philosophy, while also explicitly thematizing the difficulty of this relation between feminism and philosophy.

One of the chief issues thematized in various ways and in various vocabularies throughout this volume is what one might designate as the general paradox of feminist philosophy. In its most schematic terms, it can be described as follows: Feminism is a historically situated liberation movement, taking as its concern a specific subject position or set of concrete persons—women—and subsuming its conceptual and theoretical apparatuses to the ends of articulating the specifics of the oppression undergone by women and exploring and acting upon possible means of overcoming that oppression. Philosophy, on the other hand (and by "philosophy" here I am referring to a specific tradition, peculiar to the Western world, whose roots lie in Ancient Greece and whose legacy is preserved today in Western philosophy departments), in its most traditional and schematic formulation, abstracts itself out of the complicated mess of everyday life and seeks truths of universal and eternal validity concerning ultimate reality and human existence. Based on these definitions, a clear set of oppositions thus presents itself—concrete versus abstract, historical versus eternal, particular versus universal, situated rather than seeking a "view from nowhere"—in which "feminism" falls on the side of the former and "philosophy" falls on the side of the latter.

Indeed from its birth, most explicitly with Pythagoras, the Western philosophical tradition has defined itself, in fact has thrived upon, thematizing oppositions such as these and has consistently valorized the latter over the former. In Plato's *Phaedo,* in Aristotle's *Politics,* indeed throughout the canon, women, or woman representing a "female principle," are placed on a side hostile to rationality, hostile to abstraction, and thus hostile to philosophy itself. In more recent times philosophers critical of the metaphysical tradition have put this theme to work in strange inversions; witness, for example, Nietzsche's ambivalent deployment of the figure of woman both as dissimulation *and* as truth.[3] Recent critical developments notwithstanding, it is easy to see how, given the immense force of tradition, feminism and philosophy may be set in antipathy to one another.

Looking more closely at this schematic presentation of the problem, however, almost immediately a somewhat different story begs to be told. Feminism, in its least controversial definition, claims to work in favor of women. Instantly, questions are raised: What women? Where? How is this "woman" in whose name feminism exists to be defined? In terms of biology as the "weaker sex" or as reproducers? In terms of economic position as forming the great proportion of the world's low-wage and no-wage workforce? In her social or familial role in the private or domestic sphere? As having a particular character or psychological profile? As occupying a certain place in kinship structures? By simply being an identification or subject position with which one identifies *as a woman?* Does feminism indeed *require* at all a fixed definition of "woman" in order to coherently establish itself? These questions have given rise to many debates within feminist philosophy, perhaps most notably to what are now known as the "essentialism debates" which took place through the eighties and early nineties in journals such as *differences* and *Feminist Studies,* and which have been helpfully summarized by Diana Fuss in her key text, *Essentially Speaking.*[4]

Further questions also present themselves in even the most simple definition of feminism: What is the "end" or telos of feminist movements —formal and abstract equality with men, or articulating and valorizing what is said to be specific to women, such as a nurturing ethos? This question and its ramifications are explored in an extensive literature in feminist political philosophy and ethics. Can feminist projects and theorizing be framed in the same language, terms, and criteria of legitimacy as traditional theorizing, or is the latter itself framed by criteria of discourse that are inimical to women's styles of thinking (whatever they may be) and to the articulation of women's issues? Does the historical fact of women's oppression arise from an ideological or symbolic context with respect to which the categories and structures of traditional philosophy are themselves not innocent?

All these are questions which raise specifically philosophical issues, employ philosophical language and rhetoric, and which use concepts such as essence and identity which have a respectable provenance in the history of philosophy. They challenge the taken-for-granted valorization of the public sphere over the private in traditional political philosophy; they ask to what extent the philosophical tradition is itself implicated in the conditions which have produced the particular kinds of oppression experienced by women. To these various extents it is clear that philosophical terms, thinking, and history are irreducible and indispensable elements in feminist thought; that philosophy cannot possibly be thought of as either an addendum or a counterpoint to feminism, because it is in play as soon as feminism even attempts to articulate itself.

What, then, of philosophy and the Platonic dream which (perhaps still) haunts it of casting away the exigencies of embodiment, of emotion, of particular interests, history, and situation? First, it should be noted that, at least since the nineteenth century if not before, philosophers both male and female have been actively critical of this philosophical dream and have been concerned to incorporate history and situation into their thinking.

Feminists have raised this question systematically *for* philosophy in an unprecedented way, reading the exclusions of gender as deeply interwoven into the metaphysical tradition and giving new insights on the history of philosophy which mark precisely the mechanisms by which philosophy has effected these exclusions. Feminism's avowed particularity and interestedness have exposed the supposed universality and objectivity of philosophy as themselves particular and interested. Feminism has forced philosophy to examine the extent to which at its heart it contains historically locatable, concrete interests, which are put into play in the very act of their disavowal. Feminism raises *par excellence* questions concerning philosophy's self-definition in late modernity, in an intervention which, in raising such questions, is also *par excellence* philosophical.

This volume (and feminist philosophy in general) brings together in one place many strands of philosophizing not usually seen in the same place. Essays on essentialism, on pedagogy, on social and political phenomena, and on reproductive ethics sit side by side with essays exploring facets of analytic philosophy, psychoanalysis, Heidegger, and the dawn of metaphysics in Ancient Greece. The split between philosophers who are analytically trained and those working in continental traditions is infamously well-entrenched in the discipline, and the relations between them range from blatant hostility, to a studied silence, to tentative gestures of dialogue and reconciliation. Feminist philosophers, however, bring their varied backgrounds to bear on a common problematic, one that is at once historical and philosophical, and in doing so prepare the ground for the possibility of an authentic dialogue between traditions. That is not to say that such a dialogue has genuinely come to pass, nor that the disciplinary divisions that exist between us will, or even should, somehow be miraculously overcome. Nor is it to assert that significant differences should not exist between feminist philosophers of different theoretical stripes, nor are in any case these differences mitigated by the feminist commitments of participants in the field.

However, in the process of engaging with a common and urgent concern, the necessity of listening to and engaging unfamiliar discursive approaches—a necessity both pragmatic and ethicopolitical—arises in a distinctive and potentially productive fashion in feminist philosophy. The mere fact of their juxtaposition in this volume encourages the reader to consider the merits of distinct approaches side-by-side, as well as emphasizing the value of a broad church in political theoretical enterprises. Not only does one set of "master's tools" (which, *pace* Audre Lorde,[5] in the process of their deployment come to look less and less as if they belong to "master") work to dismantle the master's house but different sets with different kinds of capacities do different kinds of jobs.

It has become a credo of the Third Wave of feminism that it is impossible to divorce feminist struggles from those of other oppressed groups. Discussion of feminist issues must take place alongside and in conjunction with discussion of other modalities of oppression such as race, class, sexual orientation, and disability. This position is well-taken, in that it is the same hegemonic structure, at once patriarchal, white supremacist, capitalist, heterosexist, and ablist, which produces these various modes of oppression, and in that the divisions produced by these modalities work to serve the interests of power.

In addition, movements addressing one modality, such as the first and second-wave women's movements or trade unionism, have been historically governed by power dynamics which have reproduced within their ranks the hegemonic hierarchizing of the dominant culture. Critiques of these institutions by people of color, queers, and other excluded groups have begun altering the landscapes of such liberation movements in numerous ways: new alliances have formed in many grass-roots organizations which have challenged the old order of things.[6] In certain disciplines in certain portions of the academy, such as English or anthropology, hiring and curriculum committees have taken a commitment to diversity seriously, and the result has been, in some cases, a major shift in the makeup and emphasis of departments. In one of the essays in this volume, Patricia S. Mann argues that retaining an emphasis on feminism *tout court* is in fact outmoded and detrimental to the development of dialogues of resistance which are sensitive to this changing landscape.

Feminist philosophy, when one considers the characteristic recalcitrance of philosophy, has significant ground to gain here too, to say the very least. It is no credit to this volume that there are no women of color represented among its authors, despite solicitations by the conference organizers of papers from some of the very few women of color in philosophy departments and those doing feminist philosophical work in other disciplines.

As feminist theory increasingly intersects with theories of sexuality, race, class, and postcoloniality and bodily ability in dialogues which seek to do justice to the multiplicity and complexity of the ways in which lives are lived and power is distributed, there is still, this volume contends, a place for theorizing gender and feminism qua gender and feminism. The aspiration to do justice to complexity and specificity requires that modalities of power be examined both in their complexity and their specificity. To the extent to which feminism itself, within philosophy, stands in for and is marked by "particularity," it is also a particular kind of particularity, which cannot and should not be subsumed among other kinds. Every modality of power deserves to be examined in its own specific topology. This volume contrives to do just that, to examine the specificity of the juncture between feminism and philosophy, providing a snapshot of its complex historical development toward the end of the twentieth century.

The selection of essays presented here represents a marked variety of responses to our original question. Ranging from debates in contemporary continental philosophy and psychoanalytic feminism, to feminist readings of historical philosophers, to feminist inroads into analytic philosophy, to discussions of identity and the private/public distinction endogenous to feminist theory in the 1990s, these essays span the range of positions and approaches coexisting today under the general rubric of feminist philosophy.

The opening plenary, which presents remarks and a discussion among Drucilla Cornell, Jacques Derrida, and Teresa Brennan, illuminates some difficult terrain in contemporary continental philosophy, delving into the question of gender and the feminine as it can be traced through the work of Heidegger and Lacan. Cornell examines metaphors of Being, of "nothing," and of "time" in Heideggerian thought, revealing how these conceptions, for Heidegger prior to the contingencies of embodiment or gender, are themselves produced and expressed via unconscious structures of sexual difference. The unconscious imagining of feminine sexual differences as lack, she argues, will subtend any attempt, within the Western philosophical framework, to disclose a "neutral" ground of being. Derrida, by way of response, argues that although the Western philosophical imagination is, of course, deeply entrenched in patriarchal structures, it is nonetheless sometimes important to make this gesture of "neutralization." Such a gesture might represent movement toward opening up a space in which we might get beyond a merely dual or "duel" determination of sexual difference, in which a masculinist metaphysics is pitted against women or the "feminine," or feminist critique, and is thereby locked into an immovable conflict or impasse.

Teresa Brennan, in turn, asserts the necessity of a historical approach in order to think of sexual difference in relation to Heidegger's ontology. Heidegger, she reminds us, citing both Spivak and Derrida, ignores Nietzsche's statements on the relation between woman and truth as veiled. *Dasein* then becomes counterposed to the feminine, which remains beyond, outside representability, outside temporality. It is via this genealogy that Lacan is then able to locate both femininity and psychosis beyond and outside the symbolic order, in the Real. According to Lacan (and Freud before him), woman cannot speak her desire; it is identified with psychosis. But, Brennan argues, in the case of female mystics there is to be found a complex illumination of this claim, in which female desire is spoken, along with a phenomenology of temporality a reading of which might tell a very different story from the Heideggerian one. In the exchange that ensues, the panelists discuss each other's pieces and develop the concepts of courage and of temporality and its relationship to sex and gender as raised by Derrida and Brennan.

Part 2, "Essence, Identity, and Feminist Philosophy," examines the key feminist questions of woman's essence and women's identities within the context of a discussion of feminist philosophy itself. As Marjorie C. Miller notes, in "Women, Identity, and Philosophy," there have been some quite serious philosophical difficulties with identifying the category "woman," and she claims the ground of philosophy as a space for clarification of these issues. Is there such thing, she asks, as an adequate ontology of identity and difference that is at the same time philosophical and feminist? Using a vocabulary of complexes and integrities borrowed from Justus Buchler, she argues for a version of philosophical and personal identification involving links and relatedness. Moving to a discussion of the social effects of gender identification, Ruth Ginzberg argues that one of the significantly harmful upshots of the traditional identification of women with nature is that women have been seen as not requiring acculturation and therefore not requiring education. She explores Sandra Bartky's claim that shame is a part of women's experience of learning and that the stake of getting caught learning is the very social construction of gender itself. She warns that feminist philosophers must approach the ideological ground of knowledge production with a consciousness of its fundamental genderedness.

In a polemical piece, Patricia S. Mann makes the case for philosophy in a "postfeminist" era. She cites the third-wave insight that struggles around gender are never waged in a vacuum but take place in the context of many other social hierarchies, as well as noting the shifts in gender-role and expectations brought about by both economic shifts and as a result of the women's movement. Mann's controversial claim is that feminist philosophers should maintain a commitment to gendered analyses in theoretical work but should not be overly wedded to "feminist philosophy" as a valuable theoretical or institutional location. Creating institutions such as "feminist philosophy" carries the unacceptable risk of re-entrenching other kinds of hierarchy even as it foregrounds, and perhaps substantializes, the specific configuration of gender hierarchy. By contrast, and in conclusion of this section, Teresa Brennan offers a psychoanalytic reading of "essence," in particular "women's essence," in which it is understood as a "fixed point" which enables us to crystallize our commonalities. Such an essence, contra Mann, need not result in the ossification of rigid identities. Essence, according to Brennan, in an analysis clearly inflected by Hegel, is rather a fundamental aspect of a "moving life-drive" through which we can move ahead against static and substantializing identities, and thereby transform ourselves and our world in a dynamic interplay of motion and fixity.

In part 3, entitled "Engendering the Sociopolitical Body," each of the papers takes as its starting point a feminist critique of classical liberal conceptions of equality and freedom. These abstract, modern, political values have been subject to thorough-going feminist critique by virtue of their historical rootedness in a conception of a public political sphere comprising abstractly equal, autonomous, and presumably male subjects, explicitly distinguished from the private, domestic, or familial spheres, traditionally the sphere of women. As the papers here show, complicating this picture by examining the political sphere from a feminist perspective or by interpreting the kinds of relationships usually thought of as either "domestic" or "natural" as deeply social and political is a productive and telling exercise.

Virginia Held undertakes an ambitious survey in which she examines the consequences for liberty and equality of a feminist ethics of care, in which relationality is valued over autonomy. The kinds of relationships that primarily exist in a domestic or familial context are offered as alternative or additional models for conceptualizing the interactions, currently based on conflict and ego-satisfaction, that take place in the public or political arena. If "public" relationships reflected "private" values more and were judged by the same kind of criteria, Held argues, the democratic culture would be immeasurably enriched. Tackling the current and concrete issue of the legitimacy of different family forms in contemporary American life, Iris Marion Young's paper, "Mothers, Citizenship, and Independence: A Critique of Pure Family Values" fleshes out and develops some of the themes introduced by Held's paper. Young demonstrates how citizenship itself is bound up with an ideal of independence which is impossible to live up to for those involved in relationships and networks of dependence and care, including mothers, older people, sick people, children, and their caretakers. This notion of citizenship implicitly devalues this group of people, the majority of whom are women. Teasing apart the different historical meanings of "independence," and the undesirable "dependence" against which it is defined, Young argues for a redrawing of the notion of citizenship to include dependents and their caretakers. To this end, she recommends de-emphasizing the nuclear family form which supports male "independent" subjects at the expense of dependents and their caretakers, and a revaluation of a plurality of family forms, in which extended families, lesbian and gay families, and other kinds of family arrangements would not only be tolerated but appreciated as part of the citizenry in a plural society.

Turning to the historical development of the private/public split, Lew R. Silliman examines John Locke's largely neglected treatment of the family. Coming as it does from one of the "fathers" of modern democratic liberalism, this account is instructive because it in the last instance shows how Locke's liberal political subject has its provenance in a generalization of the former privileges and prerogatives of kings and feudal lords, who have become private citizens but who remain masters in their own private realms. By bringing to light the authoritarian paternalism of Locke's account of the family, Silliman reveals how the equality and liberty of Locke's public sphere is founded upon a deeply hierarchical familial context. Political relationships among subjects involving equality and respect do not extend to relations with or among women. This "domestic abuse," argues Silliman, might thus be seen to function as a measure of the failure of the modern liberal project.

A somewhat different configuration of the relationship between familial relations and political struggle is drafted in Alys Eve Weinbaum's Marxist intervention into contemporary discourses of abortion rights and surrogate motherhood. Noting that within the economy of surrogacy women are both buyers and sellers, and that the baby itself has become the commodity or object of exchange in which social relations are congealed, Weinbaum argues that abortion can be reconceived as a right to remove one's labor from the circulation of economic exchange. In doing so she demonstrates how typical pro-abortion stances naturalize and essentialize the maternal body. The risk of this argument, however, is to subsume reproductive relations under the abstract rational relations of capitalist economics. Countering this risk, Weinbaum looks to the work of Luce Irigaray, suggesting a paradigm shift in reproductive ethics in which the relational situation between mother and fetus becomes the model for the ethical relation, rather than a problematic or limit situation in which women's rights are pitted against the putative rights of the so-called unborn child.

The essays in part 4, "Analytic Approaches and Feminist Theory," explore how feminists might inhabit the language of and employ the tools of analytic philosophy, as well as how those tools might be refined or transformed by feminist insights and critique. Lynn Hankinson Nelson considers the ways in which the very idea of feminist epistemology has come under fire from different ends of the philosophical spectrum: from epistemologists who find the notion of historically located, politically informed, or gendered viewpoints irrelevant in the pursuit of conditions for truth and knowability, and from feminists who find the pursuit of epistemology and its analytic framework deeply conditioned by and inseparable from the interests of the white, patriarchal nexus of power in which the discipline itself is hopelessly entrenched.

Such a conflict strikes at the heart of one of the issues addressed by this volume: the separation of the "search for truth" as philosophy's central mission from the historical and political contexts of its production. Nelson contends that the stakes of abandoning epistemological inquiry to the mainstream are simply too high. She argues eloquently that any viable theory of knowledge or science must be able to countenance the relation between knowledge and power; feminists, above all (and this is their strength), should not accept an unbridgeable distinction between questions of evidence, justification, and warrantability on the one hand, and questions concerning material, historical, and cultural circumstances of knowers and their interests on the other. In doing so she also shines a light on the possibility of dialogue between those on either side of perhaps the most entrenched division in philosophy today—the analytic/continental divide—while remaining firmly within the analytic discursive universe herself.

The question of logic, that most abstract level of discourse and argumentation in philosophy and arguably the most hegemonically entrenched, comes under feminist scrutiny in Marjorie Hass's essay, "Can There Be a Feminist Logic?" Hass examines a number of different feminist perspectives on logic: the critique that it violently totalizes complex and untotalizable circumstances and states of affairs, as well as the critique that its very abstraction and decontextualization enacts a split from the realm of emotions and desires and embodiment that is a part of a larger picture in which maleness is identified with rationality and abstraction and femaleness with emotionality and concreteness. Hass, however, points out that abstraction is also necessary to the process of critique, that using and forming generalities is an irreducible feature of the way we use language, and that therefore to dismiss it out of hand would be not only a mistake but a mistake antipathetical to feminist ends.

Hass also examines research in the field of feminist logic which has sought to identify and construct different kinds of approaches to logic. She carefully separates Gilligan-inspired attempts to articulate "women's logic" as opposed to "male logic" from approaches which seek to recraft logical structures in ways which pay attention to concreteness and context, in particular citing Val Plumwood's "relevance logic" as a possible model for feminist logic. Accepting the value-ladenness involved in dividing the world up into a proposition and its negation, rendering what is not included absent, nullified, and dominated, this logic rather seeks to specify what is excluded as merely different, rather than as negated and therefore devalued. Bringing to logic an analysis of its implicit hierarchies of value, as well as demanding that it pay attention to context and the concrete, such feminist approaches, contends Hass, enhance and enrich our understanding of the mechanisms and the possibilities of logic and logical analysis.

The huge and popular subfield within analytic philosophy of philosophy of mind is an area which has, historically, been particularly resistant to feminist insight and critique. David Golumbia asks the question of both why so few feminists have sought to engage with it and why feminist philosophers of mind have exerted so little influence in the field. Citing first some institutional reasons for this situation, Golumbia then examines some of the underlying factors circulating in major philosophy of mind debates, including the status of the individual and the relationship to scientific realism, that might deter or welcome feminist engagement with the issues. He argues that Hilary Putnam's insistence that social and environmental factors contribute to the shaping and fixing of meanings, rather than just minds trapped inside the heads of individuals, provides a philosophy of mind framework less inimical to the concerns and aims of feminists in philosophy than that, for example, of Jerry Fodor. Golumbia calls, on this basis, for an increased dialogue between feminists and the philosophy of mind subject matter which might, hopefully, result in something of an institutional detente.

In a formal shift which returns us to the dialogic scene of the conference itself, Nickolas Pappas concludes this section with a pair of commentaries fleshing out the issues in and answering both Hass's and Golumbia's papers. Pappas first asks of Hass at what point, if pushed, a logic can still be said to be a logic, or is no longer a logic. He reflects on the possibility that incorporating the concrete and the contextual into logic might make it no longer function as a logic in any meaningful sense, because it may be just part of what it is to be a logic to be, or to aspire to be, abstract, general, and universal. He does, however, consider Hass's suggestion that feminist logic should explore what is involved in the assertion of presuppositions as well as structures of entailment to be an extremely fruitful line of inquiry. Suspecting that logic's exclusionary mechanisms may be endemic and irreducible to the field, Pappas further suggests that rather than attempting to revalue what logic excludes, feminist logicians should perhaps assist in demoting logic from its historically foundational role and replace it alongside, on a more equal footing with, other subject areas in philosophy.

Turning to Golumbia's paper, Pappas expresses reservations concerning Golumbia's search for feminist "friends" in the philosophy of mind debates. Taking Golumbia's analysis a few steps further, Pappas argues that Putnam's ultimate determinants of meaning are the facts of the physical, rather than the social world, and that in this he commits the same universalism of which Golumbia accuses Fodor. Pappas also points out that fixing meaning in the social world is not necessarily any more liberatory or progressive than looking inside the head of an individual, because although shifting the scene of meaning production to the social world does allow for the possibility of socially driven change in those meanings, social facts or mores can themselves be conservative just as easily as they can be liberal or radical. Looking for figures sympathetic to feminism in these analytic debates might unfortunately, he concludes, be harder than we thought.

In the final section of the volume, part 5 returns to an examination of feminism in the historical frame of Western metaphysics characteristic of continental approaches to philosophy. Using feminist insights to examine the assumptions and limits of metaphysics as a whole, might it be possible to forge models of philosophical thinking that go beyond the dominative and exclusionary philosophical practices of metaphysics? Leslie A. MacAvoy takes up this theme, employing a distinction derived from Heidegger between "leaping in" and "leaping ahead." "Leaping in" denotes an attitude toward another human being in which one as it were "stands in another's shoes," taking over the tasks of another, speaking for the person, and acting for him or her. "Leaping ahead," on the other hand, involves encouraging another to speak and act for himself or herself. The appropriative attitude involved in "leaping in," argues MacAvoy, is all too characteristic of many aspects of traditional philosophy. It can be observed in metaphysics, in epistemological positions, in social and political theory, and in ethics. Not only that, but as the Third Wave of feminism has shown, the history of feminist thought can also be seen to have reenacted a kind of "leaping in," in which mainly white, middle-class feminists have spoken, erroneously, in the name of "all women," ignoring the fundamental differences in race, class, sexuality, physical ability, culture, and so on, among women. Instead, philosophy should strive to understand the world, ourselves, each other, and the interrelations among these entities in a way that rejects dominative determination, and in a spirit of respect for the alterity of what is other. And philosophical feminism must strive to foster many voices, to offer tools and opportunities for disclosure and self-determination among women rather than playing a determinative, and ultimately paternalistic, role.

Finally, Cornelia A. Tsakiridou's paper turns to the dawn of Western metaphysics in Ancient Greece and traces how, with the rise of literacy, figures of femininity became excluded from the philosophical enterprise. She examines how philosophical language repeats and reinforces a move toward abstraction and neutrality engendered by the rise of literacy, and shows how this is exemplified in the Platonic corpus. Feminist engagements with philosophy as currently conceived, argues Tsakiridou, will always run into an impasse; they can exert critical force, but any attempt to articulate specifically "feminine" philosophical discourses, as attempted by, for example Luce Irigaray and Julia Kristeva, will issue in dispersed, fragmentary, and self-contradictory trajectories which render them irrefutable and unamenable to reason or logic, traditionally conceived. Returning to an examination of pre-Socratic philosophers Heraclitus and Parmenides, Tsakiridou demonstrates how analogies of orality, of action and lived gesture in which "feminine" truth or wisdom might lie are at work in their writings, but how they become progressively and systematically subsumed by the abstract, neutral concepts characterized by literacy.

This argument, Irigarayan in inspiration, separating forms of discourse into oral and literate, feminine and masculine, is fraught with difficulties as it seems to naturalize and essentialize an originary femininity, superseded by the masculine *technē* of writing. But taken allegorically or metaphorically, the argument is instructive in that it reveals the extent and depth of reach of categories of gender in Western philosophy, and in so doing points beyond and before philosophy, to the realm of allegory and myth. In the final section of the essay, therefore, Tsakiridou sketches the banishment of the "feminine" in a number of examples of early theogony and tragedy. The "feminine," having been exiled, returns in the figure of the goddess Aphrodite, a cipher of masculine desire rather than a figure of originary, fecund, femininity. Tsakiridou intimates, therefore, that it is through a mythical, prephilosophical understanding of the exile of femininity from the Symbolic order that we can grasp the depth and pervasiveness of the masculinism of our metaphysical discourses, and it is only when this has been understood that feminist philosophy, a kind of philosophizing that has always been, if we had known where to look, can take its rightful place.

Notes

1. Christine Battersby, "Philosophy: The Recalcitrant Discipline," *Women: A Cultural Review* 3, no. 2 (1992).

2. National Research Council, *Humanities Doctorates in the U.S.* (Office of Science and Engineering Personnel, National Academy Press: Washington, D.C., 1997).

3. See Peter J. Burgard, ed., *Nietzsche and the Feminine* (Charlottesville, Va.: University Press of Virginia, 1994) for various developments of this point.

4. Diana Fuss, *Essentially Speaking* (New York: Routledge, 1989). See also Naomi Schor and Elizabeth Weed, eds., *Feminism Meets Queer Theory* (Bloomington: Indiana University Press, 1997).

5. Audre Lorde, "The Master's Tools Will Never Dismantle the Master's House" in *Sister Outsider* (Trumansburg, N.Y.: The Crossing Press, 1984).

6. For an excellent and entertaining example, see the documentary examining the alliance between gay politics and workplace politics, "Out at Work: Lesbians and Gay Men on the Job," Kelly Anderson and Tami Gold, prod. and directors (New York: AndersonGold Films, 1997).

PART 1

OPENING PLENARY:
IS FEMINIST PHILOSOPHY
PHILOSOPHY?

What follows is a lightly edited transcript of the conference's opening plenary.

Prior to the conference, the participants, Drucilla Cornell, Jacques Derrida, and Teresa Brennan, had been provided with a number of questions that they were each asked to consider in turn. After these presentations, a short discussion ensued among the participants, which has also been reproduced here. The questions were devised by Drucilla Cornell in conjunction with Reiner Schürmann, who had also been asked to participate in the plenary. Professor Schürmann, sadly, passed away during the summer prior to the conference. The shock of his death was tangible to all at the New School and in the broader philosophical community at the time of this meeting, and it is to his memory that the transcription of this session is dedicated.

The questions, read to the conference by way of introduction, are as follows:

1. Is the question of sexual difference a philosophical question?
2. Is the philosophical thinking of sexual difference separate from feminist aspirations more broadly?
3. Does the psychoanalytic understanding of gender raise the question of sexual difference as a philosophical one?
4. How does Derrida interrogate the linkage of the question of sexual difference with *es gibt*, Heidegger's "it gives" or "there is"?

1

Opening Remarks

Drucilla Cornell

T hank you very much. I am honored to be part of this conference, particularly because it has been organized by graduate students. For me, personally, there is an implicit legacy in the title of the conference, and it is cheering to us older girls who have been around for a while to know that when we pass on there will be daughters who are relentlessly struggling for the recognition of the philosophical significance of feminism.

I have to begin on a sad note because the four questions which I will answer were not written by me alone but were written in March 1993 with Professor Reiner Schürmann. Professor Schürmann and I had run a seminar with Jacques Derrida in the fall of 1991, and we had intended to adopt the same format for this seminar. Our process then was as follows: Reiner and I met regularly, almost every other day, for a period of five weeks, to formulate and debate our own positions on the issue set before us. At that time it was whether the question of the ethical was a philosophical one. For this seminar we had hoped that we would work in the same manner. Reiner said at the time that he did not believe that he would be with us at this seminar and jokingly made me promise to try, if he were not, to present his side of the debate. I was unable to face at that time and am unable to face now that Reiner is not with us today, and I am in no position to represent his position adequately. So, as you can imagine, my audience today is the absent other. No one pushed me more to think about the questions before us today than did Reiner Schürmann.

So let me begin with my promise to Reiner, although all that Derrida has written about not being able to fulfill promises is with me today as I begin speaking. I will try to present a response to a set of questions, Heideggerian in spirit, that may be asked of any feminist who says that both the thinking of sexual difference and feminist aspirations have philosophical standing.

The Heideggerian position might run, broadly, as follows: Questions of sexual difference cannot follow directly from an analytic of finitude, because the marking of *Dasein* as differentiated by sex is a secondary phenomenon. An analytic of finitude that would proceed along the lines of *Being and Time*[1] must not include secondary characteristics in its analysis because these would involve the philosopher in engaging with ontic and not ontological questions—questions of anthropology, in Heidegger's sense, rather than questions of philosophy. An analytic of finitude addresses the confrontation of *Dasein* with the most fundamental horizon, the horizon of death, and what can be deduced from engagement with that horizon.

The question, then, to someone insisting that the question of sexual difference is a philosophical question is: Is it necessitated by the thinking of Being? Reiner Schürmann and I read several essays by Derrida on precisely this problem, in which he specifically questions the implicit assumption inherent in that mode of inquiry. He questions, in other words, whether sexual difference can be reduced to a secondary characteristic of *Dasein*.

Let me take up that question now. Is sexual difference a secondary characteristic? And if in turn it is a secondary characteristic, would that necessarily mean that, being an ontic question, it is not a philosophical one? Do we abide by, or invest in, the ontic/ontological distinction as it has been given by Heidegger, if indeed this is a true reading of Heidegger, so as to make sexual difference a matter of anthropology and not philosophy? We also need to recognize that even if one decided that sexual difference might be thought of as a philosophical question in the Heideggerian sense, an important question would still remain. It would not necessarily follow from the acceptance of sexual difference as philosophically important that feminist political aspirations be part of that questioning of sexual difference. A feminism that accepts that we are divided into two genders, and that feminism is the struggle for the empowerment of women, would insist that we fight, not philosophize. Within such a feminism, we identify as women, and we fight for power as women. This kind of feminism would seem to simply replicate and inhabit on a structural level the gender hierarchy it challenges, and would not therefore be adequate to a philosophical positioning that would want to challenge the very basis of the gender hierarchy as such.

I wish to return now to the specific question that Reiner demanded I address, as my answer informs my own philosophical understanding of ethical feminism. I put the question in Schürmann's terms thus: Can we so radically think anarchy, in the sense that the very idea of principles to guide us in our political behavior can no longer be thought, at least in a traditional way, without undermining all arguments on behalf of feminist political positions?

I argued with Reiner that in fact ethical feminists are the best kind of anarchists, in his sense, and I will try to explain how this can be. My own answer to the issue of whether the question of sexual difference is a philosophical question is yes. I answer that question affirmatively in the first instance because it is impossible for us to separate out the way in which sexual difference has informed what Jacques Derrida calls "phallogocentrism" and thus our very understanding of what philosophy is. The metaphors of Being, the metaphors of non-Being or nothing, and indeed the answers to the question, "Why is there something rather than nothing?" have, throughout the history of Western philosophy, been couched in the language of "lack." The lack is feminized, and as a result feminine sexual difference and its lack are implicated at every level of philosophy. If you were to approach this issue as something like a continental ordinary-language philosopher, you would have to begin a long struggle, undoubtedly an impossible struggle, to separate out the metaphors of being, nothing, and time, clearly fundamental concepts of philosophy, from the way they have been thought through the unconscious structures designated by sexual difference and more precisely those designated by the definition of the feminine sex or gender as lack. Given the language in which they have been addressed philosophically, the questions of Being, of non-Being, and of time implicate the question of sexual difference and the unconscious identification of the feminine sex as lack.

Thus we are turned to the third question, which is whether psychoanalysis can be read as having philosophical import. I will answer this question with a focus on the writings of Jacques Lacan. Let's look at Lacan's three fundamental concepts, the Imaginary, the Symbolic, and the Real, and the interconnections among them. The entire structure of the unconscious is grounded in the Oedipus complex, which in turn enforces the repression of feminine sexual difference. Feminine sexual difference exists for Lacan only as the Real, which for him is the site of impossibility. I have argued that there is a contradiction inherent in Lacan's designation of the impossible Real as feminine, because the feminine is unconsciously identified as what "is not." If you say that the

Real is absolutely unknowable, is that which is beyond the meaning of the Symbolic, that there is something other that we cannot know; how can that something other that we cannot know have a causal effect that makes feminine lack determinative of all of our sublimations? On a more humorous note, why does Lacan endlessly express absolute terror of some giant vulva in the sky that's going to eat him up? Lacan and his followers are always warning us that the scariest thing that can happen to a man is to be trapped in that spaceship with those awful, yucky, abject things—the Aliens One, Two, and Three. Alien Four should surely swallow him right up!

For the early Lacan, this projection of the feminine onto the Real, and the terror that comes with it, was the result of the projection of the terror of the phallic mother: the mother that had to be repressed into the unconscious and abjected because she herself could not be the longed-for fantasy figure existing only for the infant. Her desire for another, designated as the Father—Real or Symbolic—renders the infant insecure because of its dependence on her. The infant therefore turns to the symbolic Father who can provide the child, as he provides the mother, with a name and the goal of security that the name is fantasized as providing. This potent Father is always Imaginary in Lacan, and unfortunately, as Lacan tells us, he is a castrating father. He is the one who can always "take it away," symbolically, and turn the little boy into a little girl.

There's no real penis envy for girls, in Lacan, because the penis paradoxically stands in itself as the very mark of masculine castration. In the unconscious, every man knows that he does not have the phallus and lives in a state of constant anxiety about it. He therefore obviously feels that his identity is extremely precarious. For the early Lacan that meant that woman becomes the symptom of the man's lack. Every time a man sees a woman he realizes that his poor little penis isn't the phallus and he feels awful about himself. As a result we have a range of structures of defensive reaction, from the horrific reality of rape to violent pornography; because if you can't deal with a woman as a whole being, you are forced to reduce her to her parts, so that in popular parlance we have "breast men," "leg men," "little-finger men," and the like. In the later Lacan, after the so-called turn, the repression of the phallic mother is no longer projected onto the Real, but, surprise surprise, the Real still carries all of the characteristics of nothingness, of lack, and of the masculine horror of lack. I have recently argued that there is no "turn" in Lacan, that his later emphasis on the Real is once again based on the repression of the phallic mother and the horror man has of woman as his symptom.

Now we can ask whether this reading of the Real, and Lacan tells us it is a reading of the Real, answers the philosophical question of the nature of Being and of ourselves as existents. I have argued that indeed he is attempting something of a Kantian analysis, in the sense that he offers his own analytic of finitude that gives us the limit of experience, which he calls the Real. For Lacan, however, unlike Kant, experience is limited by the logic of castration—which clearly brings the question of sexual difference to the forefront of the question of Being. But to make explicit the contrast with Derrida here; as I see it, the central difference between Derrida and Lacan is that for Derrida, the limit cannot be known solely as the logic of castration, and ironically, therefore, the positions are exactly the opposite of those that the Lacanians tell us are taken by the Lacanians and the Derrideans. It's the Derrideans, and in particular the Derridean feminists, who are "true" to the problematic of the beyond, and to the remains, and particularly to what gets reduced to refuse by the symbolic order, governed as it is by the logic of castration.

After all, if we women are reduced to refuse, we already possess a potential gentleness and tenderness toward everything and everyone that's been thrown out of the system. The rethinking of the philosophical categories of Being and non-Being implied by phallogocentrism is inseparable from the rethinking of the meaning, or more precisely the enforced lack of meaning, of feminine sexual difference. Thus, Lacan raises the question of sexual difference and its lack to the level of a philosophical question, and his own work shows us just how strong the law of the Oedipus complex is within at least Western culture. Derrida throws into relief the question of the possibilities of thinking the impossible Real, without locking out feminine sexual difference necessarily, for once and for all.

I now come to the question of how one might think and engage with the Real if one accepts that there must be a feminist deconstruction of phallogocentrism. How can one understand the limits of symbolic meaning? How can one understand gender identity and its potential transformation? First, I would like to differentiate the kind of feminism that I think grows out of this insistence on the need to deconstruct phallogocentrism, from a project that would be grounded in object-relations theory. Object-relations theory makes the simple mistake of conflating real familial objects with unconscious objects. In the traditional object-relations story, the mother cannot be the object of identificatory love because she is locked into a dyadic relationship with the infant. The third term breaking up the dyad becomes the figure who offers freedom and thus an identity independent from the mother, so it then becomes the daddy who ultimately confers upon children of both sexes an individual identity. Identity problems in both female and male children will therefore result from the absence of the father, and traditional gender stereotypes are either reinforced by, or come into being as result of—the theory is never quite clear on this point—the different kinds of relation that the father, as the object of identificatory love, will have with boy and girl children, respectively. The phallus is completely identified with this object and is longed for because it is inseparable from the freedom that the father symbolizes.

For a Lacanian, this story is not true but is rather itself a fantasy. It assumes that real familial objects can be identified with unconscious objects. For Lacan, the longed-for father is always an imaginary father. The imaginary father is the Big Other represented in the symbolic order, whose power is enforced through patrilineal kinship structures. Not one woman in this room can pass on her own name to her daughter: That's what it means to have to live with the stamp of the father's name on our backs at all times. It means that women are denied equality at the level of the kinship system. Lacan tells us that without a challenge to this inequality nothing will change at a fundamental level even if fathers try to give the same quality of attention to little girls that they give to little boys.

A feminism that challenges this inequality finds itself fundamentally allied with queer politics. A feminism that challenges phallogocentrism involves the complete shattering, dismantling, deconstruction, and disruption of the very notion of gender hierarchy itself in the name of equality of kinship systems. Its implicit demand is a demand for an end to the very idea of the "normal" family and with it our conceptions of gender, and to the structures of sexuality formed in and through those conceptions. This feminism would argue that the normalization of heterosexuality is part of the very gender system that limits the play and possibilities of a new choreography of sexual difference. It would demand that any feminism that is true to this effort to challenge phallogocentrism would have to undermine the very structures upon which it has been based and would endlessly engage in the questioning of its structures. This is why Jacques Derrida has said we do not need a new concept of "woman." In fact, I've argued in *Beyond Accommodation*[2] that it is the impossibility of our ever arriving at an adequate structure of "woman" that allows this kind of radical feminism room to get off the ground.

This does not mean that we cannot act in terms of identification: We can take on what I call "mimetic identifications" for any purpose, for any struggle. But the idea that feminism requires our reducing ourselves to our gender identity as women, and our empowerment as such, as opposed to the dismantling of the very symbolic bases of gender is, to me, to turn feminism into a conservative movement—a movement that is not true to the radicalism of its promise. And I mean "radicalism" here in its old-fashioned sense, in which feminism demands that we go all the way back to the deepest structures of the psyche. In this way, feminism is utopian, not in that it promises a utopia or dreams of a utopia but in that it always returns us to the problematic of what is beyond the symbolic order and our accommodation to it. And such a question is inseparable from what we might call the question of Being, because the demand for the deconstruction of the symbolic bases of gender hierarchy is not separable from the demand for the deconstruction of the question of Being.

A feminism that accommodates to gender and accommodates to the symbolic order will only replicate the structures that it should challenge. It will separate "white" women from African American women, separate upper-class women from women of working-class origins, and will take us away from the whole struggle of postcolonialism to redefine the very boundaries of what we call "Western" philosophy. The alliance with deconstruction is decisive, for me, because Jacques Derrida has been relentless in his interrogation of the fundamental philosophical questions as they have been ordered, structured, and thought within phallogocentrism. Thank you.

Notes

1. Martin Heidegger, *Being and Time,* J. Macquarrie and E. Robinson, trans. (Oxford: Basil Blackwell, 1967). See especially section 10.

2. Drucilla Cornell, *Beyond Accommodation* (New York: Routledge, 1991). See especially chapter 2, "The Feminist Alliance with Deconstruction" and chapter 3, "Feminism Always Modified: The Affirmation of Feminine Difference Rethought."

2

Opening Remarks

Jacques Derrida
Edited by Judith Friedlander and Emanuela Bianchi

As I was listening to Drucilla and thinking about her wonderful daughter, I thought about the fact that I have no daughter. I used to dream sometimes of having a daughter. . . . I could have adopted one. And the question I'll leave unanswered is this: Because one's relationship to children is not natural, but symbolically constructed—and this is so even when children are not adopted—would my relationship to my daughter have been the same as Drucilla's? I don't know. I have no daughter; I have missed having a daughter; I've only dreamed about having adopted one. So who knows?

I share Drucilla's feelings about the absence of Reiner Schürmann at this conference, and for many reasons. I can't address the questions we are trying to raise here, however imperfectly, timidly, and insufficiently, without thinking that in philosophy Reiner was the author of these questions. And so, to some extent, we are answering him. We should not forget this and I won't. This is all the more true, given that we are addressing these problematics with reference to Heidegger.

I remember the first time I met Reiner. It was in Paris and he had just published his book in French on the principle of anarchy.[1] We had a discussion about Heidegger in a cafe. For me, this is a vivid memory, very sad and very happy at the same time. Let's remember, then, that Reiner thought of these questions, the questions we are trying to discuss this morning. Now the questions themselves are numerous and difficult. They are so numerous and so difficult that, as Drucilla indicated, we are constantly forgetting even the most insignificant of them. It's a way of repressing them; it's too difficult. I was thinking of the courage we men and women need to address all these questions.

Why do I speak of courage? First, the questions are complicated, theoretically complicated; they take us through difficult texts, and so on. This takes courage, then, because these are not only theoretical questions, but questions we have to answer in life, practical and political questions concerned with making alliances and strategies; and this is always risky; this too takes courage.

Drucilla referred to the alliance between deconstruction and what she thinks feminism should be. Well, as you know, such an alliance is often not accepted. A number of women think that deconstruction should be opposed for this reason or that; or be partially opposed and partially accepted. The system of alliance is always risky, and we have to be very cautious. What feminism are we talking about? What deconstruction? What feminist discourse? What deconstruction of the discourse? With whom? And so on and so forth. Because you can never be sure you are making the right strategic choice, making the choice at all demands courage.

To oppose a hegemonic discourse demands courage. This is particularly true when you know you have to confront even your allies, to say to them that you want to discuss the matter in more detail. They may think you are in agreement, but you know it's more complicated than that. It takes courage to run the risk of breaking with your allies, because you insist upon asking difficult questions over and over again.

Courage itself, the very value placed on courage, is also at stake in this discussion. In another context, I have tried to indicate the phallogocentric way in which Heidegger identifies courage with virility, with a virile virtue, as if courage were a manly thing, something masculine. So if we really, courageously, want to open this discussion without phallogocentric assumptions, we must understand courage in another way; not simply as heroic, military, masculine bravado. This will obviously be a very strange kind of courage, but it is the kind I shall try to adopt as I attempt to address the terribly difficult questions we raised a few moments ago.

I start with Heidegger because, given the way he questions these things, he is an important strategic lever. It is true that on one level of his discourse Heidegger has neutralized sexual difference. As Drucilla noted, he has made sexual difference secondary, made it anthropological. The motivations of this gesture are strong: they involve gaining access to universal structures of *Dasein*, to structures which must be considered universal and which are not therefore limited by race, nation, blood, language, country, or even by sex. And because Heidegger did this in a very powerful and new way, we have to pay attention to the necessity, at a certain level, of his neutralizing gesture. But, as we know, this gesture repeats at a very deep level an old metaphysical gesture, which consists precisely in neutralizing sexual difference, in effacing it or putting it into brackets. And then, thanks to this neutralization, the masculine is empowered in this apparently neuter space.

Thus, in asking once again whether sexual difference is or is not a philosophical question, for me or for others, I answer: yes and no. It has always been a philosophical question. You can find traces of it in Aristotle, in Descartes, in Kant. So the question before us is not whether sexual difference is a philosophical question, but whether it can be asked in such a way that would unlock or displace the neutralization, the neutralization and creation of hierarchies I was just referring to. From this point of view, sexual difference has been a philosophical question only to the extent that it has been made secondary and treated as marginal: as a question which would have no effect on the main fundamental concepts that have structured the philosophical tradition from the very beginning, from Plato on.

Thus, on a certain level, Heidegger was repeating the same gesture of neutralization. What I tried to show in a text I wrote on the question of *Geschlecht*, on this question of sexual difference in Heidegger—in a tentative and risky interpretive gesture—is that perhaps what Heidegger neutralized or wanted to put in parentheses was not sexual difference as such, but a certain determination of sexual difference as an opposition, or duality.[2]

I can't go back to that text now. But what I tried to raise as a question in that text, if not to show, is the possibility that perhaps Heidegger's gesture leaves room for some freedom, an opening of a space in which sexual difference would *have a chance,* so to speak, without being reduced to, locked into, a duality or opposition.

The question then becomes: Why is sexual difference a difference between two, and not three, four, five, and more? I tried to address this question in "Choreographies," an interview with Christie MacDonald.[3] There may be a way to think about history, a hidden kind of history, in which sexual difference is not determined as a war, as conflict, a duel between two parties. This hidden history *is* a history; it *has* a history. Perhaps Heidegger and Levinas too (who is also "guilty" of neutralizing or making secondary sexual difference)[4] are looking for a way out of this dual/duel determination of difference when they make the neutralizing gesture. If that is the case, we should not reject every attempt to neutralize sexual difference.

Neutralizing differences may be just and helpful in some struggles, in some situations. Sometimes feminists have to say "no" to sexual difference. "We want equality. We struggle for equality, for the same dignity as men," and so on and so forth. From that point of view, difference does not count. So, it depends on context. It depends on the givens of the particular conflict, of the war, so strategy here is an important matter. That's what makes the relationship between deconstruction and feminism difficult.

I would say, as I hope is well known, that I share the same convictions as a number of feminists. But then, when I see these feminists reproducing phallogocentric presuppositions, I have to challenge them or ask them to put brackets around these assumptions by saying either, "Well, no," or "Well, okay, in this context I think it's useful for you to behave in this way and use such a discourse." Which is exactly the phallogocentric discourse.

But one has to do this provisionally and in context. So for me, that's the quick answer to the question: Is feminist philosophy a philosophy? For me, feminism should only be a provisional strategy using philosophical tools in a given situation—even if the situation lasts a very long time, has lasted for centuries. It cannot be, should not be the end point. For me, rather, it is a flag. This doesn't mean it has no philosophical value. It is philosophical and it has to be philosophical. A feminism without philosophical training, an inexperienced, innocent, or ignorant feminism, would be weak, all the weaker. So it has to be philosophical. It has to be as philosophical as possible, to be able to analyze philosophical discourses expertly, to explicate the way philosophical presuppositions work in every rhetorical form, in all discourses in society, in academia.

Feminism has to be philosophical. But I do not consider it a philosophy, nor do I think it should be a philosophy. It should not be a philosophy, if by philosophy one understands precisely a history which has been programmed, structured, by fundamental concepts—which were phallogocentric from the very beginning. From my point of view, feminism should be philosophical, powerfully philosophical, but not *a* philosophy.

Now, to turn to Lacan, who, like Heidegger, is an important point of reference in this debate. To have courage—I told you that by courage, here, I mean being shy, prudent, rather than having bravado—with that kind of courage in mind, I have to say that it wouldn't be fair to claim that Lacan thinks or says such-and-such in general about women, feminism, and so on. I must say, rather, that Lacan's discourse is heterogeneous. It is the result of thirty or forty years of teaching, of many difficult texts, and so on. It would be unfair to limit his thought on the subject to a single statement on women. He has made a number of statements about women.

Instead of trying to represent Lacan in general or psychoanalysis in general, I tried a long time ago to enter into dialogue with a certain stage in Lacan's pedagogical and theoretical development. This was the stage represented by a number of important texts, such as the "Rome Discourse," or the "Seminar on 'The Purloined Letter.' "[5] Looking at this stage, and this stage alone, I would agree with everything Drucilla said concerning Lacan's determination of the symbolic in terms of lack, the lack of the phallus, the role of the phallic mother here, and so on. I won't repeat what Drucilla carefully reviewed for us before.

I would simply say that when looked at from the point of view of this stage, Lacan was *too* philosophical—too much of a philosopher. In his own original way, he was repeating a very old and very powerful philosophical discourse. At least that's what I tried to show. Later on, in the seminars that followed, he made other statements that complicated a number of things. For example, he finally dropped, or gave up, the triangle of the Symbolic, the Real, and the Imaginary. And so everything became more complicated.

To have courage, here, would be to read Lacan, among others, and to respect the difficulty and the heterogeneity of his works. It would involve isolating the layers in which he repeats phallogocentric presuppositions while giving him credit for having opened up a closed system elsewhere in his writings.

The same holds for the works of those we call traditional philosophers. I'm sure that if you read in a certain way the works of some of the most phallogocentric philosophers, at some point, even in the writings of the most aggressively phallogocentric, you will find that things get reversed. That something else is being uttered more or less discreetly in his discourse. In other words, if we read these texts with an ear to their symptoms, we can see, we already know, that the most violently phallogocentric discourse undermines itself and says something else which precisely challenges what is apparently being said. You can find this even in Aristotle, who has been one of the main targets of feminists interested in philosophy. Given the time, I could show you how in Aristotle's work there is something that in fact contradicts and undermines his own massively phallogocentric statements.

And so courage, in this context, consists of saying, "Well, things are not simple." Even sexual difference is not simple. We may, on the one hand, want to continue to struggle, to remain at war where war is needed, but at the same time look for a horizon, a space where sexual difference isn't simply a duel between two adversarial camps; to do this is itself to struggle in a war. From that point of view, we are indeed soldiers. As soldiers at war, we have the obligation to think about what we are fighting for: sexual difference which wouldn't simply be opposition and conflict. And this, I think, is what makes possible alliances among a number of partners.

Just one more word because, as usual, I am speaking too long. I will tie Heidegger and Lacan together as indicators, indicative references, for the question raised referring to the *es gibt*. You find in Lacan, who doesn't quote Heidegger, and in Heidegger, who doesn't quote Plotinus, references to a gift which consists of giving what one doesn't have.

In his own way, Lacan says that love consists of giving the other what one doesn't have and what the other refuses. He then immediately identifies this gift of love with the phallus. Before Lacan, Heidegger had already asked the same question in *Early Greek Thinking:* How is it possible to give something one doesn't have? And this in a text about justice!

This question actually comes from Plotinus, whom Heidegger never mentions in this context, concerning the Good: the Good, which is beyond Being, beyond the limit of Being. The Good, which gives what it *is* not—because the Good *is* not, is not present—and what it *has* not. The Good is not and it has not. So, the Good gives something, which is not a thing, not a present; it gives what it doesn't have, and what it is not.

Now, let's take this abstract schema of the gift which consists of giving what one doesn't have. This matters a lot to me. I am trying to build toward, but "build" is not the right word, saying things that matter a lot to me. Such a gift is a possibility, but I'm not sure that it has ever happened, that someone has given to another something that he or she didn't have. A gift, that which exceeds the circle of restitution, reappropriation, and economy. . . . I'm not sure that you can prove that such an event has ever taken place.

Nevertheless, we can think it can happen, desire it—and we have and we do. It's thinkable, even if it's not knowable. That's Kant's famous distinction. You have to read Kant on the distinction between knowing and thinking. So, even if we don't know of any gift that in actuality exceeds the circle of economy and reappropriation, or of a situation in which somebody gave something he or she didn't have, and have that something be accepted by the other—even if we don't *know* this, we can certainly think it.

And this thinking is important. It is an event. It takes place, perhaps not in space and time, but it still takes place. I desire this: to give or receive something that extends beyond the circle of reappropriation.

Now what happens when one identifies this kind of gift the way Lacan does, as the phallus, as something absolutely determined by the relationship between man and woman, with its implications of lack, castration, and the entire system of concepts that Lacan introduces at this point? I think it's a rephilosophization, a phallogocentric rephilosophization of a schema, but the schema is not necessarily rooted in this particular situation of sexual difference.

That's why neutralization is sometimes important. I think we need to be able to think of a gift which extends beyond economy and beyond sexual difference as we understand it. To desire going beyond sexual difference doesn't mean effacing it. Nor does it necessarily mean repeating or reconstituting phallogocentric structures.

I would love to think that this gift beyond being, beyond the present, the gift which is not a present, which is beyond restitution, can happen between two men, two women; between father and son, father and daughter, mother and daughter—even in our relationship with animals.

And so, from this point of view, the question of sexual difference requires some neutralization but not the traditional kind of philosophical neutralization. We should keep this point in mind, or in the heart, I don't know where. We have to keep thinking of this possibility, not as guiding a strategy or plan, but as the possibility for thinking all the possible givens of a complicated strategy.

I think that only by thinking this *es gibt* . . . "there is," but *not* "there is"—the "is" here, the translation of *es gibt* to mean "there is," is already erasing what's at stake—only by this reference to the *es gibt*, to the gift beyond being, beyond economy and even beyond pleasure, can we have the courage to face these complicated struggles, alliances, and questions. Again, I am talking about the kind of courage I defined at the beginning: a very unique, specific kind of courage, which is not simply male bravado, male heroic courage. I'm talking about another kind of courage, and that is what we need in order to address questions such as these.

Notes

1. Reiner Schürmann, *Le principe d'anarchie: Heidegger et la question de l'agir* (Paris: Seuil, 1982); translated as *Heidegger on Being and Acting: From Principles to Anarchy,* trans. Christine-Marie Gros in collaboration with the author (Bloomington: Indiana University Press, 1987).

2. Jacques Derrida, *"Geschlecht:* Sexual Difference, Ontological Difference," *Research in Phenomenology* 13 (1983): 65–83.

3. Jacques Derrida and Christie V. MacDonald, "Choreographies," *Diacritics* 12 (1982): 66–76.

4. See ibid. Also, see Jacques Derrida, "At This Very Moment in This Work Here I Am," in *Re-Reading Levinas,* Robert Bernasconi and Simon Critchley, eds., Ruben Berezdivin, trans. (Bloomington: Indiana University Press, 1991).

5. Jacques Lacan, "The Function and Field of Speech and Language in Psychoanalysis," in *Ecrits: A Selection,* Alan Sheridan, trans. (New York: W. W. Norton, 1977); Jacques Lacan, "Seminar on 'The Purloined Letter,' " *Yale French Studies* 48 (1972).

3

Opening Remarks:
Timing Is All

Teresa Brennan

BIANCHI: Professor Brennan, would you like me to repeat the questions before you start?

BRENNAN: No, please don't, Emma. Emma, our noble chair, rang me a couple of nights ago before I flew across to tell me what the questions were. I felt filled with a kind of preexamination dread, the sort I have not had for many years. I thought, "I can't answer these questions." And I can't. But what I'd like to do is to build on themes that Professors Cornell and Derrida have introduced, and move toward some sort of synthesis of ideas in this discussion. Maybe through that synthesis the questions will reemerge in different forms.

I think one of the most important things that I have heard for some time was Derrida's statement, in this highly specific context, that sexual difference has a history. Of course, he did not mean that sexual difference has a history in the received sense (which it obviously does). Derrida did not mean the history of sexual difference as such, or that sexual difference is sociohistorically constituted. It is. Rather, I take it that Jacques Derrida means that the concept of sexual difference—in relation to Heidegger's ontology—needs to be thought historically.

Now, I want to unpack that a bit. What I see in the significance of rethinking ontology in this way, placed alongside the other statement that some attempt at rethinking the neutral might be helpful (that it is not always negative and tacitly aligned with masculinity), is that this is a revolutionary statement from Derrida. He has spent much of his life trying to go beyond duality and insisting on the necessity of going beyond it. I want to cross-reference this insistence to Drucilla Cornell's beginning with the idea that sexual markings were in some way, for the Heideggerian, secondary rather than prior; ontic rather than ontological.

The way I will try to tie these things together lies in an essay that some of you may still use. It is one of the best things written about the subject of sexual difference, and it is Gayatri Spivak's reflections on Derrida's *Spurs*.[1] The context is the figure of woman standing in for the figure of truth, a figure who is always veiled, as Derrida, like Nietzsche, describes her. Spivak first takes up Derrida's remark that Heidegger's critique of Nietzsche on metaphysics has been "idling offshore" ever since it ignored Nietzsche's figure of the woman as truth (I am quoting very approximately). Spivak went on to look at how far Derrida himself actually interrogated the significance of the tie between the figure of woman and the figure of truth.

It is always difficult to represent someone else's position with any degree of accuracy, but as I understand it, in that paper and subsequent papers, Spivak is giving equal weight to two issues. On the one hand she is saying: "Look, unless we interrogate the actual specificity, and it is in some sense always an historical specificity, of the tie between woman and truth, of that which is behind the veil, we are not going to move." And on the other hand, "Because this tie keeps being made it is probably standing in for something. Whatever it is standing in for is something that needs to be addressed, something that we have not begun to properly formulate."

This two-sided approach has returned many times in the course of the last decade. The most recent instance I am aware of is Kelly Oliver's outstanding treatment of Derrida in her book, *Womanizing Nietzsche*.[2] This two-sidedness seems to recur especially in relation to various concepts which are meant to be prior, "behind the veil," but which partake of the "unsaid" history of sexual difference insofar as they ally the prior with the feminine. This is true of the founding of metaphysics; we find it in Plato's idea of the *chora*. I think it is true of the Lacanian idea of the Real. I think it is presupposed yet again in the Derridean concept of the "beyond." All of these concepts attempt to think that which is beyond representation, that which is not speakable. All of them align the unrepresentable with the feminine to some degree. The question of whether this alignment with the feminine is right is the question that keeps coming up. As Thomas More said, "I hope I make myself obscure."

I do not want to pretend that these concepts can be collapsed, nor do I wish to get into a dogmatic dispute about the differences between them. I am not saying they are all one and the same, nor that they are all allied with the feminine. Indeed, it is precisely this that differentiates the concept of *Dasein* from the other concepts just mentioned. *Dasein* does not identify itself in any way with the feminine. As we have seen, Heidegger expressly consigns sexual difference to the secondary mode, the ontic. From the perspective of a new and necessary concept of the neutral, this consignment might seem a positive move. I am not so sure. But more of that later.

For now let us concentrate on the other concepts mentioned: the *chora,* the Beyond, the Real. The important thing is that despite the differences between them, they all in some way attempt to formulate that which is beyond signification or even beyond formulation. They all address that which is behind the veil in one way or another. Let us take the idea of the *chora,* something Derrida has discussed at length, as has Luce Irigaray—the woman who has probably done the most to say that sexual difference is always philosophical, as a question, or, rather, that philosophy is imbued with the idea of sexual difference.[3]

Actually, I have real problems with Irigaray. But regardless, Irigaray has said a great deal about how philosophy is built on the repression of the feminine, on the repression of the maternal, and that without this repression there could be no philosophy. This idea seems both to be like, yet not like, Derrida's formulation of the founding violence of any truth system: that there is always some necessary repression, always some necessary exclusion. Irigaray would insist that it is always the maternal or the feminine that takes the excluded place here. In doing so she neglects many other contemporary realities, chief among them the way exclusion works in relation to racism and various forms of neocolonialism. Whether these can come to stand in for the feminine in certain contexts is another question.

But at this point I will stay with the concept that both Irigaray and Derrida attend to: the first of these behind-the-veil concepts, Plato's *chora.* This thing that is unspeakable, unrepresentable, is it or is it not always feminine? For Derrida, the *chora* and the feminine are not necessarily the same thing. The *chora,* for Plato, is that receptacle into which all forms enter in order to take their shape and come to being—in a sense, the *chora* is the way through which they become representable.

Now, there are a lot of metaphors scattered throughout the *Timaeus* and other parts of Plato's oeuvre, where you get the impression that the *chora* is this great big maternal receptacle: something like a fierce vagina in the sky. Additionally, it is clear that the *chora,* and this is a point which Derrida dwells on, is not something that can be defined. The minute that it is defined, it is within the categories of that which is given form, that which is in some way already represented. In fact, I think Derrida asks: "Is this not the virgin spot in the territory of metaphysics?"—this concept, or thing, which even Plato cannot begin to interpret. Because once we are engaged in the process of interpreting, we are already losing the distinction that Plato found so necessary between that which holds the possibility of naming, speaking, representing, coming-to-mind, coming-to-consciousness, and doing these same things as acts in themselves.

Irigaray, on the other hand, would insist on the tie between the *chora* and the feminine, but she wants (and she is famous for this) to say at the same time that, nonetheless, the feminine remains that which cannot be defined. The feminine as that which cannot be defined is pure Lacan, as distinct from that which cannot be defined but which is, possibly, a neutral space—neutral in the new sense Derrida has foreshadowed.

How do we move from here? I think we can continue by taking the idea of the Lacanian Real, and looking at the debates that are going on around it at the moment. It is the area where that which cannot be spoken, the unspeakable as it were, in some way resides. I apologize for using these metaphors of habitation, but at the moment there is no other language for the unspeakable. For a Lacanian, that which is unspeakable, or unrepresentable, that which cannot come into the symbolic order is in the territory of the Real, and it will always return in the Real. This is one of Lacan's most interesting formulations. You cannot put something away forever. It will always return, and it may do so in a way that maybe you (or Lacan, when it is a question of feminine) wished it hadn't.

That which returns in the Real is the territory of psychosis. The Real, then, is the territory of the disruptive, in both the bad and also the good sense. The feminine is clearly not psychotic, but because it is excluded from representation it is placed alongside and intertwined with what constitutes psychosis. In other words, in addition to psychosis, the territory of the Real contains that which is the feminine unspeakable: it contains the experience of the woman who, in the classic Lacanian configuration, "knows it but cannot say anything about it." Lacan makes this remark when he is speaking of the great mystics.

On this point, I find Lacan patronizing. To know something and to choose not to say anything about it, or to know it and know that the experience itself cannot be communicated, is very different from knowing something and not being *able* to say anything about it. In fact, Teresa of Avila said a great deal about it, and about the disappearance of time in the mystic state, a very useful discussion for those of us who are interested in temporalization. Her writings are an instance where we have, on record if you like, an idea of the complete absence of time, the suspension of time altogether. This suspension has indeed had "something said about it," and it may be very relevant to how we think about the real, and moreover, the beyond. That is to say, it points to "that about which one can say nothing" as that which is beyond time. I am suggesting that it is here that the Real is tied very much, Professor Derrida, to your idea of the Beyond, particularly in Drucilla Cornell's reading of the concept.

But first there is more to be said about the Real. The Real is historically imbued with what is presently, but not inevitably, unspeakable in that the feminine has been assigned to it, and thus denied representation. The Real as we know it and have experienced it, perhaps even for millennia, is certainly equivalent, historically, with the feminine in some aspects. That does not mean that it is necessarily always so. And that is where I come back to what both of you, I think, were putting forward—particularly you [to Derrida], on rethinking the idea of the neutral in relation to the idea that sexual difference has a history. That is the sense in which I have understood you here.

The question of the historical specificity of the feminine confronts us when considering any of those concepts which present themselves as somehow unchangeable, while somehow imbued with the feminine: the *chora*, the Lacanian real, the Derridean beyond. The fact that we keep coming up against the same problems reveals that there is a cycle in thinking: It illustrates the way we come to a boundary past which it seems we will not go. We get to those questions, they come up, we push at them and yet stay somehow behind the veil of these "Beyonds," "Reals," "*choras.*"

When Derrida said earlier that we need courage to think these questions through, the courage that I think of immediately is that which is needed when one risks social disapproval, especially the kind which makes itself felt in academic, theoretical contexts. Contexts in which what is acceptable and what is not acceptable are already shaped according to fairly strict lines of debate. These lines are policed by the fear, always, of somehow conceptually getting it wrong, being inaccurate, or using the concept inappropriately—those things which get in the way of being able to think past the fixed points we already occupy. I have talked about this idea of "fixed points" elsewhere and here will elaborate on how the idea of fixed points bears on these behind-the-veil areas we cannot think: the Real, the Beyond, the *chora*.

To do this I will return to something that I have already hinted at in this talk: the notion that the *chora*, the Beyond, the Real, are attempts at conceptualizing something that is outside time. This might seem a long way away from the psychical theory of fixed points. After all, I have just been alluding to the fixed points that embody identifications. That is to say, by my argument, the social identifications we make or (not quite the same thing) identifications with the social order constitute fixed points in the psyche, points we have to think past before we can admit a new idea to consciousness. However, in *History After Lacan*[4] I extended this argument and tried to show that the fixed points of the psyche parallel those of the socioeconomic order, overlaying that which is, effectively, "behind the veil." To amplify, I will discuss the psychical, then the social.

Before we can identify with anything at all, we have to have a position to identify from, an apparatus that enables identifications to be made. The formation of this apparatus, known to us as the ego, involves identifications, but it also involves energy. The beginnings of the ego, I have argued, lie in the repression of the first hallucinations. These hallucinations have to be repressed, because the psyche responds to them as if they were real. You are hungry, you want the breast, you hallucinate the breast. You then, in Freud's terms, amass energy in expectation of satisfaction, gearing yourself up. But then you are disappointed, and your amassed energy results in feelings of displeasure. To deal with these feelings, you learn next time round to repress the hallucination.

The repression of a hallucination constitutes, I suggest, the first fixed point in the psyche, the first point which enables us to get our bearings as something separate, a separate self. This repression, whether it is the breast or the mother that is hallucinated, simultaneously involves an identification. If you repress an image of something, you embody that thing in your psyche: At the most literal level, you identify with it. But the identification would be insufficient as a starting point for the psyche unless that identification also effected the sense of separateness that is the basis of subsequent identifications. It is precisely here that concepts of energy are relevant.

Energy is bound when we repress; maintaining a repression involves a persistent expenditure of energy. The energy involved in repression gives us a sense of separateness because the repressed energy contrasts with the "freely mobile energy" (another term of Freud's) into which we are born. You cannot perceive yourself as separate unless there is a contrast between you and your environment. What I am proposing is that such a contrast is provided by the distinction between freely mobile energy and the energy bound in the repression of, and the identification with, a hallucination.

Another way of seeing this contrast is to consider it in terms of a contrast between a more rapid and a slower time. After all, it is the experience of *delay* that prompts hallucination, the preeminent mechanism of *instant* gratification, in the first place. But how is it that we can experience delay unless we have experienced a state in which delay was not a factor? I have argued elsewhere that the requirements for such a state are provided by the fact that there is an intrauterine existence before birth. They are provided by it if we hypothesize that in utero, there is no delay between the experience of a need and its fulfillment. Hunger, elimination, and so on are dealt with without the delay that is an inevitable accompaniment of being born.

By this account, "delay" correlates with repression, both as its cause and its consequence, as repressed energy is slower than freely mobile energy. Freely mobile energy, in other words, is energy without communication blocks, in which a call and its response take place without delay. I hypothesize that it is the experience of communication without delay that prompts hallucination; hallucination, in other words, is an attempt to recapture a mode of communication and satisfaction that has been lost.

I will say more about the temporal contrast between repressed and freely mobile energy after turning briefly to the social equivalent of the psychical fixed points. The social equivalent of the psychical fixed point is nothing less than the commodity, in the broadest sense of that term. The commodity binds natural energy; it binds the energy produced by nature and labor. Energy bound in this way cannot as a rule reenter the reproduction cycles of natural time. It is to a greater or lesser extent outside of the generational time of nature. In sum, what is at issue in both the psychical and the social case is a contrast between freely mobile and bound energy, or to say the same thing, between a faster and a slower time. The faster time is associated with the natural order, although this natural order cannot be known in an unmediated way. The slower time is profoundly social.

But what would it mean if there were no contrast between faster and slower time? In the social case, it would mean that technology would look very different, and that commodities would not be produced out of synch with the generational time of nature. In the psychical instance, it would mean that there would be no ego, no separate sense of self. Needless to say, I am not advocating here and now (or at least not yet) that we dispense with the ego altogether. The point rather is that without these psychical and social constructions there would not be a contrast between a faster and slower time. And without this contrast, I do not see how we can talk about time at all.

But it is enough for here to suggest that if we want to approximate what it is that underpins all these key concepts—the *chora*, the Real, the Beyond—it would be the faster time of unmediated communication. As a rule this cannot be known directly; hence it is unspeakable, beyond representation. Moreover it is a time that is "faster" only by virtue of the contrast with slower time. And I suggest that in fact, it is not experienced as faster time, but as the absence of time, given that the experience of time as we know it (slow time) is dependent on the experience of delay. "Faster time," in short, is experienced as timelessness. The unconscious memory of this timeless state in human experience is tied to the intrauterine state, which means it is tied to the maternal, and in this sense, to the feminine.

This returns us to where I began: This was the two-sided response to the question of the feminine and its tie to "behind the veil" concepts: the *chora,* the Real, the Beyond. On the one hand, Derrida has insisted on the historical specificity of this tie, and Derrida has argued for a rethinking of the concept of neutrality. On the other, the fact is that the tie between the feminine and that which is outside the symbolic and social order has been remarkably persistent; and Derrida, in *Spurs,* was reluctant to divorce the figure of woman from that which is behind the veil.[5] We might reconcile these different takes on the question of whether "behind-the-veil" concepts are feminine by differentiating between: (1) the feminine-as-maternal and (2) the feminine as one side of sexual difference. The feminine in this second sense is that which is opposed to the masculine, femininity as the other of, or to, masculinity.

By the argument outlined here, the feminine-as-maternal is tied to the *chora,* the Real, and the Beyond. But there is nothing implying that sexual difference, femininity and masculinity, are also outside time. What buttresses the privilege accorded masculinity, by Lacan among others, is a negative concept of the feminine, the woman who is not all. This is not the same thing as the maternal. So we might say both that Heidegger was right to assign sexual difference to the secondary mode of experience, the ontic; and also that he was profoundly wrong to remove, in effect, the maternal from the ontological. We can also say that Derrida is right to propose that sexual difference and the question of neutrality be rethought in relation to the Beyond. But from the perspective outlined in this talk, Derrida was also right in his earlier reluctance to divorce the woman from the question of what lies beyond the veil. For the woman is also, although of course not only, the maternal. Finally, by this argument, the experience of the maternal is the keystone of ontology. Irigaray's insistence that philosophy is built on the repression of the maternal is true in more senses than she intended.

If I had more time, I would explore why the feminine, as part of sexual difference, belongs in the slow time of lived experience. Or perhaps, if I had more time, I would talk about fixed points here in terms of how psychoanalysis is useful in the experience of doing feminist philosophy. It is most useful in unpacking the personal politics of fixity and the socially constituted fear of offending, in myriad ways, the numerous little superegos who sit on one's shoulders when one is writing an essay on sexual difference in philosophy, superegos saying "No, you cannot say that," or "No, you've got that wrong." You can spend years of a precious life working out whether you have this or that concept down accurately. I did a great deal of this with Lacan. Perhaps I gave him more than I should have, which is not in any sense to say I gave him more than my time. But time is time. In fact the chair is passing me notes saying my time is up. [To Derrida] Not for nothing did you write *Donner le temps*.

Notes

1. Gayatri Chakravorty Spivak, "Feminism and Deconstruction, Again: Negotiating with Unacknowledged Masculinism," in *Between Feminism and Psychoanalysis,* Teresa Brennan, ed. (London: Routledge, 1989).

2. Kelly Oliver, *Womanizing Nietzsche: Philosophy's Relation to the "Feminine"* (New York: Routledge, 1995).

3. Luce Irigaray, *Speculum of the Other Woman,* Gillian C. Gill, trans. (Ithaca: Cornell University Press, 1985); *This Sex Which Is Not One,* Catherine Porter, trans., with Carolyn Burke (Ithaca: Cornell University Press, 1985).

4. Teresa Brennan, *History After Lacan* (New York: Routledge, 1994).

5. Jacques Derrida, *Eperons: Les Styles de Nietzsche (Spurs: Nietzsche's Styles),* Barbara Harlow, trans. (Chicago: University of Chicago Press, 1979).

4

Discussion

Teresa Brennan, Drucilla Cornell, Jacques Derrida,
and Emanuela Bianchi (Chair)

BIANCHI: Would any of you like to respond to one another?
DERRIDA: Just two brief points [to Teresa Brennan]: Thank you for
what you said. By the end of your remarks, I understood that you
felt you had given too much of yourself to a reading of Lacan. And you
regretted having done so. Perhaps, I don't know, but generally speaking
that is precisely what a gift does. The essence, the essenceless essence of
a gift is that you cannot and you should not try to take it back. First of
all, it's impossible to do so. Gifts challenge the very idea of restitution.
To take back what you have given, even symbolically, may make sense.
I won't deny that. It makes sense to think you should not have paid so
much or given so much. That certainly makes sense, but a gift doesn't
make sense. It should not make sense. You waste your time, we waste our
time, by assuming that it should.

BRENNAN: I have to. . . .

DERRIDA: I'm not sure you did, but if you think you did. . . .

BRENNAN: Okay, no, no. I never conceived of my work on Lacan as
a gift to Lacan; it would have been the kind of gift he would have had to
refuse. I'm far too obsessed with other ideas. I saw Lacan as a gift to my
working through those ideas. What I was really saying was that I should
have just got on with it.

But I agree with this very Nietzschean point you are making, that
"you can only will to have been what has been." Otherwise you end up in
the rancorous situation which is the very opposite of giving, in the sense

26

I think you are intending it. In other words, you end up in the states of regret and rancor (I feel a little bit that I am using this word "rancor" because my friend Wendy Brown influenced me here very much, in the reading of Nietzsche): of the rancorous, the *ressentiment,* the envy, the enormous pettiness, which is opposed to the gift. The contrast is very well drawn by Melanie Klein in her work on envy and gratitude. It is true that you can give your creative energy to explicating another thinker's thought, which can be a gift. But this "gift" is not necessarily courageous. There is a negative side to it, which I mentioned earlier, where you feel that you cannot say what you want or have to say, unless it has been exegetically approved in the form of a "fixed point." In this context, the thinking of gratitude becomes very hard.

DERRIDA: It's impossible, yes. Now I want to raise two brief points with you [to Drucilla Cornell]. One has to do with the question of courage again. I agree that sometimes courage means the courage to face social resistance, to confront objections; to take an opposing position in a social situation dominated by a hegemonic discourse. This requires one kind of courage. Another kind [and that's what you spoke about] has to do with reading, thinking, doing justice to a concept, and so on, doing the work, the homework, with concepts: an infinite, endless task. This too requires courage. But I was thinking of yet another kind of courage and it is needed here. It has nothing to do with social hegemony or resistance, nor with concepts in their philosophical, theoretical, or speculative form. It has to do with our own psychological, phantasmatic, archaic structures.

To ask such questions, such difficult questions, requires that we change the most resistant, protected, archaic structures of our desire. If I say I am no longer a "phallogocentric" thinker or writer and make this claim publicly in verbal statements and published texts, while I remain, on another level, under the speculative layer, caught up in the phallogocentric structures of my own desire, of my own relationship with others, then nothing has changed. But in order to ask the question, to have the motivation, the energy, the clarity to read texts differently and to resist hegemony in society, you have to work from the inside out. I won't refer to the unconscious, but that is what is at stake. If you don't do this kind of homework in life, day and night, with every member of the family and with those outside the family, if you don't work in order to change your phantasmatic or psychological, unconscious approach to these problems, you won't change anything and probably won't find the necessary social courage and theoretico-philosophical courage to address these questions. So that's where psychoanalysis is needed, and here I have to be very careful. Without some form of psychoanalysis of your own approach to the problem, nothing will change. This doesn't mean that you have to go into analysis, to be on the couch—not necessarily. You can do this, or try to do this, by yourself, but not necessarily alone by yourself. You do it through everything you experience: through reading, and so on, which is always very difficult and dangerous.

As if the process were not difficult enough, what we call "psychoanalysis" itself makes a number of phallogocentric assumptions, not only in the discourse, be it Freud's or Lacan's, but in the institution itself, and in the way analysis is practiced: the scenario, the couch. Psychoanalysis, in all its institutionalized forms, is marked and limited by these phallogocentric presuppositions. So it is not enough to say that you have to psychoanalyze yourself, to change yourself. You have to deconstruct— let me use this word to save time—to deconstruct what needs deconstructing in psychoanalytic theory and in the social institution of psychoanalysis itself. This is not only a matter of deconstructing the discourse as it is published in books and presented in lectures in the academy, it's something you have to do by yourself and with others, constantly. And this requires courage, another kind of courage: to contest yourself, to transform your own desire. This is of course the most difficult task of all and it never ends, but if you don't face it, if you don't try, you will be left with only the lectures and published texts—some of which will be interesting, some less interesting, some stereotypic, some not, but nothing will have changed.

My second point concerns the Beyond. I won't go back to the issue of neutralization, but I will focus on the question of "beyond time." I agree with what you say [to Teresa Brennan], but I don't want to end the discussion by simply acknowledging that "beyond time" is beyond time. I would like to add that it's not beyond any time, that is time in general; it's beyond a time that has been dominated by the present. This is the way time has been interpreted, experienced. The past is a present past, the future is a present future, and the now is a present present. So beyond time, in the case of a gift, in particular of gifts that involve sexual difference, beyond time wouldn't mean to me beyond time in general, but beyond a certain determination of time as present. And it is not coincidental that "present" means, at the same time, both a modality of time and a gift. The interpretation of the gift, the gift as "present," the gift, as we consider it here and now, is something that goes beyond restitution, beyond economy, and even beyond any possible presence. A gift should not be present to the other, not even present to the donor or the donee. We have to think of a gift as something that could not be a "present." So this gift beyond "presence" (or presents) is not simply beyond time, it is perhaps the condition for having access to another dimension, another sort of time. The same is true for history; it is historical. The gift is historical at the very moment it transcends what we usually understand as "history," as "time." I don't know whether you would agree with this.

BRENNAN: Yes, with the gift as history, absolutely, and with exchange as marking the always-double tie to the present. It not only marks the positions of givers and receivers in general terms; it is also crucial to sexual difference specifically. But the gift can only mark history and time in this way when there is a simultaneous consciousness, a consciousness of the present and of the past. A small question here: It's something that I am really unsure of, and it concerns the idea of the experience of "timelessness." I wonder whether there can be any experience of time which is not an experience of the present. That doesn't mean that there is not "another time." I just doubt that it could be experienced that way, that one could *experience* "another time" as such. The alternative to the personal *experience* of present time, which is necessarily passing time, is the experience of timelessness. Perhaps what is at stake here is a difference between the concept of "another time" and the direct experience of it. Certainly in the mystics' writing on meditation, and this is something that intrigued me, what are recorded again and again are expressions such as "time ceased," "time did not pass," "the time was one o'clock and then it was four o'clock; there was no difference in this passage of time." This is very interesting in terms of the "experience" marker of time. It is precisely not "another time," outside of present time, which is at issue for the mystics. It is a sense of no time, of time suspended.

DERRIDA: It is difficult. But briefly, let me say that of course you are right. It is difficult to think of an experience of time which is not an experience of the present, the presence of the present. But then there is more than one way of experiencing the presence of the present. Perhaps the mystic experiences another experience. Perhaps he or she experiences presence as something that cannot be, or as something that can only be on the condition of nonsimultaneity with itself, as a nonidentity with itself. A nonpresence structures it. That is what I call "out of jointness" ("The time is out of joint," Hamlet says)—the present as something which is not present. In other words, the concept is enigmatic and very difficult to identify. But every experience of time is an experience of the presence of the present. Still, the possibility of this experience is also something that makes possible the impossible, or something that requires a nonpresence within the present, and this is an experience of time which is not reduced to the experience of presence. That is difficult. . . .

CORNELL: Can I suggest that it may be, at least for me, analytically incorrect to say that the only experience of time is the experience of presence? I think that what Kant really struggled to show was that the only way we can experience "presence" is, in a sense, by having "time" as a backdrop which cannot be brought into the experience. So that in fact our experience of "presence"—and though Kant would never have used these words, Reiner Schürmann certainly did—is through a sort of phantasmatic dimension that spatializes. Time, then, is the backdrop which itself can never in fact be experienced. The entire problem in Western philosophy, insofar as it turns on an analytic of experience, is that time as a transcendental condition of experience cannot itself be experienced. Since Kant, then, time has persistently dropped out in accounts of the concept and constitution of objectivity.

I understand you, Jacques, in your work on time and the giving of time, to be not only insisting on the limit of experience—as I just described it—but also to be saying that the experience of time that can't be experienced, such as in mysticism, itself disintegrates the very concept of experience. What Meister Eckhart experienced in writing, and this is conveyed in Reiner's extraordinary book, was exactly that: the complete end of experience as we know it and thus the end of presence. He experienced this in his writing as the making present of the time that disintegrated the present itself. So that when time becomes present as the limit of experience, it is, paradoxically, that which disintegrates the present.

Now I've come back to Reiner once again, in the context of the experience of the limit of history, of the limit of the present. And it is in this absolute limit of finitude that we are, of course, returned to the absent friend, the absent other. At certain moments, it is only the absent other that can be present. And that is, perhaps, the most profound experience of time conveyed in Heidegger's *Being and Time*. Jacques's work has problematized that analytic of finitude by putting us into confrontation with the death of the other, and by understanding absence as the most profound experience of finitude, which cannot be an "experience" in the analytic sense.

BRENNAN: Drucilla, I think you are absolutely right to remind us that a concept of the end of experience has to be simultaneously a concept of the end of the present. I just want to put in a footnote here, for anyone who is wondering why we have engaged so much with the mystics, a footnote concerning Lacan's idea that the mystic is the person who is closer to the Big Other (God) or the Real but can say nothing about it, or rather who knows the Real, like the "woman," the woman mystic, who can still say nothing about it; that was the point of departure for this exchange.

What underlies this notion of an inability "to say anything about it" is the idea of that which is beyond the speakable, beyond the representable, beyond the nameable. But in fact the mystics have said a great deal about it, and one of the things they have said, as I have stressed, concerns the experience of the "suspension" of time. There is a related point about Meister Eckhart which shows that the experience of time is bound inextricably to the experience of the self. [To Drucilla Cornell] It's terrific that you brought this in. Meister Eckhart is clear that the end of experience means the end of the experience of one's self, of you as a contained ego, which is an exchanging individual, an *individual* precisely, and one in relationships of reciprocity, of exchange, and of presence, in which the experience of the ego is central. Now when one is out of that experience of the self as the focus of everything, then one is out of present time. In other words, when you are out of your ego, in the (psychoanalytic) narcissistic sense of ego, you are quite literally beyond yourself.

BIANCHI: I am afraid I must impose time . . . as we have run out of it. Thank you.

PART 2

ESSENCE, IDENTITY, AND FEMINIST PHILOSOPHY

5

Women, Identity, and Philosophy

Marjorie C. Miller

A widely debated and provocative issue in feminist theory concerns questions of identity and difference: Given differences between and among women, given historically and culturally located differences in the meaning of the category "women," and given that the differentiating characteristics which have historically defined women have been generated in phallocentric cultures, how can "women" be identified at all? Further, given the multiple locations within which women have been identified, and according to which women have identified themselves, is the project of identifying women *as* women a valid or valuable one? Finally, given the widely shared conclusion that definition occurs in the process of political praxis, and given the dangers of the essentialism which is often carried in the folds of abstract theories, is there a role for philosophy in carrying forward this central problem for feminist theory?

I shall argue that there is such a role, that it is the "space designated by philosophy" that most adequately accommodates the clarification of these issues, and that it is through doing such philosophical work in clarifying feminist projects that feminist philosophy reveals itself *as* philosophy.

I

Women of color, lesbians, working class, and so-called third-world women have articulated their frustration with the practices of erasure practiced by white, upper- and middle-class, and heterosexual feminists as well as by the patriarchal male culture. These articulations have appeared in theories developed in a number of academic disciplines and in a variety of political practices. The reiterated insistence that race, gender, class, and sexuality are intersecting categories which cannot be discussed in abstraction from one another, while crucially important in every theoretical context, may nevertheless benefit from further theoretic clarification. I will argue that such clarification is aided by the development of an adequate ontology of identity and difference. Such an ontology should be one which reveals both connection and difference, which is neither fixed nor prescriptive, which takes account of the many ways we *are*. Such an ontology is indeed a project which takes place in the space designated by philosophy. I will argue that its development is an example of philosophy which is feminist by virtue of impetus, content, and project.

So, I think an understanding of identity can be of some value. I think such an understanding can be of value in providing not the immediate vocabularies to be used in articulating new identities and identifications, but rather in enriching the vocabularies to which the developers of new vocabularies may appeal. Working at generating such general vocabularies, at framing sets of categories of high generality, is what I would call doing metaphysics. But to theorize a metaphysics of identity in a feminist context is to enter two intersecting contested domains. As Butler and Scott note, "'[t]heory' is a highly contested term within feminist discourse."[1] Clearly, metaphysics is an equally contested term within contemporary philosophic discourse. I have argued elsewhere[2] that feminist theory is possible. Here I should like to argue that it can be enriched by a metaphysics of identity and that a feminist metaphysics of identity can be a powerful tool for philosophic analysis. In this paper, I want to focus on the identity of the category "women:"

I am using metaphysics, here, in a way which I think follows the direction begun by William James's theorizing and by John Dewey's use of the term.[3] I draw here, also, on the work of Justus Buchler,[4] a later significant naturalist in the pragmatic tradition. I refer not to foundations or to eternal truths, but to fallible claims about useful, highly general terms. Such terms are validated by their usefulness in developing other vocabularies and pursuing many purposes and by the sense of order they provide to current confusions. That is, they are validated by their quality of being compelling in helping to clarify theoretically difficult problems. I do not see such terms as transhistorical or transcultural, but I see them as capable of being shared between cultures, with the aid of thoughtful and creative "dictionaries" and inspired teachers. We can, in this sense, learn *about* one another's metaphysics and learn from each other and

continue to refine what we have developed in light of what others have—
we can recognize areas of overlap and strengthen them, knit together
edges of contact, work at areas of difference. We are different, not the
same—but our very differences can be better addressed if we compare
understandings of difference.

There are two dimensions of the problem to be addressed: (1) in
attempting to identify *women,* am I not eliding the many ways women *are*
women, the many contrasting—even contradictory—meanings "women"
as category identifies in diverse historical, social, cultural, sexual, racial,
and economic contexts? (2) in attempting to identify *women,* am I not
reducing the identification of any individual woman (myself, for example)
to the pervasive but *not* exclusive being of that self *as* woman?

That is, I am a philosopher and a woman, white, middle-aged, an
American, a person who resided in China for two years, a middle-class
person, an academic, and a woman. It is clear to me that while my integrity
as woman is extraordinarily pervasive, relevant to everything that I do, it
is not, I think, *determinative* of everything that I am or do. I have other integrities, and sometimes (under some circumstances), it is my integrity as
teacher or professor, say, or as American which is the order most strongly
relevant to the active, exhibitive, or assertive judgments I produce.[5] But
if being a woman is so pervasive, what is it to be a woman? How can the
differences in social and historical conditions produce any single group
or category relevant to me and to Madame Song and to Winnie Mandela
and to Maxine Hong Kingston? Audre Lorde has used the locution "my-
selves" when referring to the objective form of the first person.[6] Judith
Butler, in *Gender Trouble,*[7] wishes to subvert gender identity altogether.
Each wishes to preserve the sense in which, as individuals, we exist in
multiple locations; as women we *are* in an enormous variety of ways. The
problem here is that in spite of the fact that, traditionally, the self has
been inappropriately identified as somehow supporting or transcending
its multiple locations, and although gender categories have indeed been
stultifying and oppressive to women—nevertheless, personally I do *want*
to identify myself as having uniquely related multiple locations, and I do
want to recognize the category of women as meaningful and potentially
valuable—because it is so pervasive in the orders in which my many
integrities are located.

Further, as activist and as scholar, as American in New York and as
foreigner in Shanghai, as sister, mother, and wife, I *need* to be able to clarify
theoretically the centrifugal forces and communal pressures which pull
and tear and create puzzles for both thought and action. That is, I want
and need to understand a sense in which difference does not preclude
sameness, nor sameness obliterate difference. I want and need to know

how the Chinese understanding of my womanhood genuinely affects me, and how my dean's understanding of womanhood may disempower me—without my knowledge. I want and need to know how I can understand my self *as* woman without reducing my identity to my sex or my gender. I want to know how to understand the possibilities for common cause with my friends and students and the strangers who are women in so many different ways.

In order to satisfy both desires and needs, however, I want to be enabled, by an adequate metaphysics of identity, to appreciate the identity of anything, category or self, in a way that is nontotalizing while remaining open to change and transformation; that maintains identity while neither precluding nor erasing the differences—even the contradictions—between traits characterizing my various "selves," or those characterizing various women. The search for the identity (of category *or* self) cannot focus on some foundationalist or essentialist grand Self, nor rest in some list of stable, consistent, common, or "essential" traits said to constitute that identity. Nor can I make use of a metaphysics of identity which ignores the distinctions between the possibilities and limitations implicit in my self-identifications, my identifications of others, and those imposed by others' versions of the categories which identify me.

II

In developing a feminist metaphysics of identity and difference, I am drawing on the work of Justus Buchler, who formulated a definition of identity which provides a useful framework for analyzing the complex "women." His definition of identity reads: "The identity of a complex is the continuous relation that obtains between the contour of a complex and any of its integrities."[8]

Integrity, here, is simply a way of naming a location of a complex—of specifying a complex *as located* in a particular order.[9]

Indeed, there are real differences between the various integrities of "women," profound differences in the traits possessed by each integrity in its particular ordinal location. But these are different integrities of a complex recursively recognized as *the same* complex, a complex with many and profoundly different ordinal locations. In theorizing the identity of "women" I am struggling both to distinguish between integrities and to recognize the continuity of the relations between the integrities of the complex.

"Women" is identifiable as a complex.[10] A "complex," as I am using the term here, is just a very general word for "thing," or item, or whatever. But I use complex to focus on the fact that categories, as well as individuals, are "things" in the sense I want to talk about. As complex, it is an order, a sphere of or for relatedness, and it is located in other more comprehensive orders. As term, it is located in a linguistic order and is related to other terms, to grammatical rules, and to pervasive linguistic structures. As set, it embraces an enormous number of beings—historically, geographically, existentially diverse. Sets overlap, and members of the set "women" may also be members of other sets: literary figures, for example, or mythological figures, or senior citizens, Muslims, African Americans, or Chinese. As category, it is among the most pervasive of those used to interpret human existence, though its pervasiveness has often been masked by the false universalism of the category "men." Much contemporary attention has been focused on the fact that "women" is *different* as term, set, or category—and as category in various historical, cultural, and linguistic communities. Each location of the category "women" (in the order of languages—as term, in the order of the many different cultures or groups within which "women" are located, or in the order categories with which we order and organize our experiences, for examples) is an integrity of the category.

Understood in this way, it is clear that the identity of "women" is already a matter of relations. Specifically, it entails the continuous (ongoing, perhaps changing and evolving, certainly flexible) relation between the contour of the complex "women" and any of its integrities. The contour of a complex, in Buchler's terms, is "the continuity and totality of its locations, the interrelation of its integrities. . . . A contour is the integrity of a complex not insofar as the complex transcends all orders but insofar as it belongs to many orders."[11]

The contour of the complex "women," then, is the continuity *and* totality of its locations—not the totality alone, since that would imply a mere aggregate of integrities, a fixed and finished "thing." And the category, like other complexes still living or in use, is neither fixed nor finished—it grows and changes, and its "contour" is always dependent on the particular historicity of its locations. And it is also the interrelation of its integrities—the conditions under which the various integrities of the complex "women" mutually condition one another's scope.

Finally, the continuous relation which determines identity is between the contour of the complex and *any* of its integrities. Thus, in these terms, one begins where one finds oneself, in the integrity of "women" as located in the shifting and contested discourses of one's own time and place, sex, race, age, and class. But one recognizes that the identity of the complex "women" is not determined by this limited discourse, this single integrity. Without having to grasp *every* integrity, without needing to possess an exhaustive grasp of what women are, have been, and will be in all places and under all circumstances, one recognizes that the identity of the complex is thick, shifting, and constantly contested. The identity is a continuous relation obtaining between the integrity whose location is most narrowly available and the contour of the complex "women"—the continuity and totality of its locations, the interrelation of its integrities.

In this vocabulary, for any complex, for categories as for persons or things, to be located in an order, to have an integrity, is to have the particular traits (the actual and potential traits, which certainly include relations) that location in that order provides. In Maria Lugones's sense, each order is "a world."[12] Using this vocabulary, it is clear that the traits possessed in one order may differ from, even contradict, those a complex possesses in another order, another integrity, another "world." Thus "women" in the representations of *upper-class* Victorian England may have been delicate, sickly, modest creatures, uncomfortable with embodiment and ill-at-ease in nature, whereas representations of *lower-class* Victorian "women" may have characterized them as earthy, robust embodiments of nature, mired in an uncontrollable sexuality. Whereas "women" in middle-class, 1950s America may have been constituted by family roles, confinement to the "private" or "domestic" sphere, and so on, "women" of the same era and citizenship but in the orders of non-middle-class experience may have been constituted as supporters of the community, sustainers of the church, or wage-earners and laborers with added responsibilities for children and the elderly. "Women" may be located in orders of female persons' self-identification at some particular period and under some particular cultural circumstances; or "women" may be located in orders generated by male persons' perceptions of themselves and "the other."[13] Such different orders are likely to locate integrities of "women" bearing very different traits of actuality and possibility.

Some of the traits attributed to given integrities of women may have been falsely attributed. As in the Victorian example above, a historian may validate the claim that such traits belonged to women in an order of patriarchal stereotypes, but the historian would also note that such traits were falsely applied to most of the women located in orders of spatio-temporal existence. Nevertheless, the location in an order of patriarchal stereotypes affected what *women* located in that order *could be*.

As the category "women" is located in many orders, among the orders in which "women" are located are the many orders of individual selves. That is, the category "women" is a trait of the integrity which is me—Marjorie. I am a trait (located in the order) of "women" and "women" is a trait (located in the order) of "me." The language of ordinality is not the language of hierarchy: Whereas some orders are more pervasive than others, or of wider scope than others, none is an order without also being a trait, and none is a trait without also being an order. But each trait is an integrity of a complex, and every complex is multiordinally located. So, while my identity influences "women," the identity of "women" influences me. And what "women" *means* as a trait of me is only one integrity of what "women" *is*. Further, what "women" means in my various integrities may be quite different: In the order of my biological being, or in the order of myself as married woman, or in the order of myself as professor, or scholar, or American, or upper middle class—in all these what my identification with "women" means will be quite different.

What is quite crucial here is to note that the oft-reiterated notion of identity as something negotiated in the context of conflicting and divergent power structures is clarified theoretically only if the structure of identity is recognized to entail diverse and conflicting integrities, some of which may be intentionally inhabited, and some of which may be unwillingly, even unconsciously, inhabited. Integrities locate actual and possible traits—so an integrity which is part of my contour, part of the totality and continuity of my locations, will entail some of the traits which identify *me,* even if that integrity is determined by a set of widely believed stereotypes and not at all true of the integrities in which I would choose to be known or to discover myself. I may actively reject identifying myself by false, stereotypical traits associated with categories with which I otherwise identify myself (shallowness among Americans, passivity or incompetence among women, for example), but the fact that these traits are traits of some integrities of the complexes which are integrities of my own identity makes it obvious that outright rejection cannot be straightforwardly carried out. Denying the truth or validity of such characterizations does not vitiate their power in the determination of the category. This is not to say that others' false and stereotypical assumptions are necessarily *determinative* of what and who I am, only that they have *a role* in determining the integrities which are part of my contour. I ignore these integrities at my peril—for to do so involves a failure to recognize the power such categorical integrities *may* wield in the determination of my identity. To respond with awareness is to struggle to attain the power to minimize the role of such integrities. It is quite the opposite of the denial that they have existed, do exist, and are real and powerful threats.

The traits of women in imaginative and in spatiotemporal orders may differ from, even contradict one another, as may those of different historical, cultural, and class locations. These contradictions do not mean that there is "no such thing as women."[14] Nor are they resolvable by reference to a single Reality underlying these different attributes, nor by a list of essential traits which all these integrities have in common. It is not as foundational or as transcendent that identity has nonhegemonic meaning—it is as the continuous relation among multiordinal locations and any *given* location of a complex, viewed as *a* complex.

To insist that "women" is an identifiable complex is not to maintain that its identity can be captured in a linguistic, performative, or visual formula. Even more, it is not to maintain that our identity *as* women could be given in such a formula. But it is to argue that we are related, and to argue that what it is that relates us can be encompassed in our systems of meanings without submerging us in a fixed, totalizing, or restrictive discourse.

III

Although it has often been suggested that the alternative to dangerous and false essentialisms is a form of shifting political solidarity, a declaration of "we-ness" emerging in the common commitment to particular political goals, I would argue that this view fails to recognize at least one significant dimension of the difficulty of creating effective political coalition. That is, in the process of forging such a coalition, such an *identification,* one often needs to persuade others that there *are* links of relatedness which cross lines of difference. One often needs to clarify the ways in which oppressive relations in one order are linked to, controverted in, or differently relevant in another order, another integrity, of the same complex. It is precisely with reference to contested identifications that clarifications of difference are significant—and such clarification is enhanced if we are able to theorize a nonrepressive, nontotalizing sense of the same.

An example of occasions in which such discourse may be of value is to look at the difficulties which emerge in the attempt of Asian and Western feminists to make common cause. With such issues as reproductive rights, for example, the construction of the issues varies quite profoundly among different feminist groups. Some Asian groups (the All China Women's Federation, for example—a group closely linked with the government but also representing some 500 million Chinese women) have argued that Western feminists understand "women" and "women's problems" as well as "women's rights" in contexts which provide no common ground with Asian experience, Asian values, and Asian needs. Sometimes, indeed, they have been quite right! But suppose we use this language of integrities, recognize that there are different integrities of the category "women" in different cultural, national, and political contexts, and look to see what integrities of the category we may frame as including common traits and hence common problems and at least the possibility of a common agenda for action. The matters of maternal and child health, for example, do involve a common integrity of women as child-bearers—and in this order, we have some common concerns and experiences. But where we are not located in the same order, for example, where we find ourselves under very different pressures regarding abortion choices, we need to be clear about the differences in traits this entails, what possibilities obtain or fail to obtain in each order, and what consequences such differences have. More profoundly, however, I think we need to interrogate the forces which locate these different integrities of women and attempt to determine the orders which determine the locations.

Butler and Scott raise a question about the possibility of critiquing the category "women," arguing that use of the category appears to require us to forego interrogating the "political construction and regulation of this category," by relying on "a fixed or ready-made subject, usually conceived through the category 'women.' "[15] I want to argue that critiquing the category may most effectively consist of analyses of the orders in which it has been or is being located, with integrities established in given orders indeed being integrities that serve (or subserve) specific political purposes. I want to argue that the interrogation of the specific purposes served is not only *not* foreclosed by an adequate understanding of the category, it is in fact made possible by the recognition that it is *women* who are multiordinally located, and whose multiple locations entail different integrities—oppressive and liberating in very different terms.

But if our system of meanings is laden, as we know it is, with phallocentric traits, how do we identify *women* without falling prey to phallocentrically determined limitation? If we understand *women* as natural complex with multiple integrities, multiple ordinal locations, then we can understand that some integrities are located in orders of feminist consciousness and feminist practice, and some are located in orders pervaded by masculinist or other oppressive practices. We can recognize some of our "selves," some of our integrities, as framed within orders whose character and relations limit and oppress us; and we can recognize other integrities as located in orders whose traits include possibilities for growth and solidarity.

It is crucial to recognize that orders may be locations in which I am located voluntarily or involuntarily, aware or unaware, critically or uncritically. The integrities of categories which figure in identities are determined by the power relations which structure orders: "spheres of or for relatedness." Clearly, traditional identifications of women have been oppressively mired in phallocentric categorizations. But to deny the identity of women is to lose the capacity to recognize the continuous relation which obtains between our integrities in liberating orders and those shaped by historical and cultural oppression. To nurture and encourage liberatory integrities I must be able to understand their relation to those repressive integrities which enter into my identity and into the identity of the category, *women.*

This is not to argue that the categorial term "women" obtains its power or significance because it refers to some fixed subject called *women.* Rather, it is to argue that the discursive category itself is a complex with an identity, a complex whose identity entails its multiordinal locations.

It has been argued[16] that all theory and theory building are necessarily directed toward singleness, requiring assumptions of sameness among those who are to subscribe to, or be described by, the theory in question. Many contemporary feminists want to focus on difference and diversity, undermining every attempt to theorize the category "women." But an adequate theory must be one which holds in tension identity and difference. To dissolve the tension in favor of anarchic devotion to difference—in a gesture which intends to keep open the site of identity for continuous political contestation—is to fail to provide the framework for analyzing, understanding, celebrating, and using difference in the service of common and related political projects. To fragment and isolate are as destructive to women as to overwhelm and submerge. The theoretical appreciation of the identity of a complex, in this case the category "women," is crucial for the appreciation of the power and plasticity of the category, its enormous range, its destructive and constructive history, and the differences and contradictions between the traits of its various integrities.

A vocabulary of general identity categories can thus help to frame the questions within which common identities are forged and liberatory actions undertaken. The questions of what order we are inhabiting, what traits of actuality and possibility are entailed by our integrities in this order, and how our integrities in this order differ from those we can recognize in other orders—such questions focus on what we have in common and what needs to be changed without denying that there is much we do not have in common, and without denying that who "we" are (as well, and just as much, as who "I" am) is a complex, shifting, contested affair which begins with the integrity of ourselves we are framing, but which acknowledges the whole contour of the ordinal locations which constitute us.

An adequate metaphysics of identity is one which enables me to recognize the identity of anything, category or self, in a way which remains open to change and transformation; which maintains identity while neither precluding nor erasing the differences encountered and experienced—even the contradictions—between traits characterizing my various "selves," or those characterizing various women. I cannot soothe my need to get "a handle" on "women," or on myself *as* woman, by accepting a view of identity which requires me to freeze or entify or isolate that which is moving, enmeshed in shifting and changing relations.

IV

I have not offered a universal condition of validity for any first-order discourse referring to identity, nor have I offered a foundation or grounding in the Real for true identity claims. I have not offered a transhistorical or God's eye view, but I have offered a view obtainable by climbing up on a hill—right here where we are. This is a very general account of a categorial term, useful in *many* first-order discourses—it is highly general, situated, not universal. It surely begins in the discourses common to my experiences and cultures. (Again, I am unhappy with the singular use of "culture" or discourse—as the identity account shows, I have integrities in many orders, and many orders are determinative of the complex I call "myself.") But it needn't ethnocentrically end there—for many of the orders in which I am located are orders in which you are located as well. There are constant and shifting and intersecting and overlapping integrities which allow us to locate the limits of our common orders—to establish a "we" from which we can continue our discussions. Women, as a categorial term, is not univocal—I cannot find usable "we"-ness with everyone located by the term. We may be located in integrities which are in real, difficult, even intractable conflict with one another. The task before us is to find out whether an integrity can be framed within which we can recognize common location and common interests.

My version of metaphysics does not directly do this crucial task. It cannot. It is too general. It is in the service of political engagement, but it is philosophy, not politics. It gives us categories which direct attention to the work to be done, it does not complete the project.

The sort of metaphysical analysis of the identity of the category just undertaken is clearly a project which takes place in the space designated by philosophy. The general ontology on which it is based has been reread to address problems of the conceptualization of identity emerging in feminist practices as diverse as the active pursuit of specific political change, feminist publishing, campus women's unions, academic women's studies programs, critical legal studies, and various disciplinary and interdisciplinary investigations.

It is feminist in project in that such an analysis provides theoretical tools for assisting women (and men) to confront ourselves and each other in ways which focus on the location of given integrities in particular orders and which remain aware of the contour of the relationship of various integrities to one another in an indefinitely large number of orders. Such an analysis provides interrelated categories which clarify the crucial relations between the various integrities of women—characterized by different actual and possible traits, different actual and possible relations— as integrities are located in different orders: racial, ethnic, religious, age group, sexual, national, class, temporal, among others. The analysis provides categories which make clear the lack of priority or hierarchy of orders in the determination of identity, and supports the necessity of a "thick" appreciation of claims made on the basis of identity.

The problematic dimension is my assertion that this analysis is feminist in content. Although it clearly serves feminist projects, in what sense is the content itself feminist? Feminism itself is a natural complex with multiple ordinal locations, multiple integrities, and an identity which consists of the relation obtaining between the contour of the complex, the continuity and totality of its locations, and any of its integrities. It has different traits in the order of political activity from those it has in the order of academic discourse—though the integrities are related to each other through the contour—the gross integrity. In the order of philosophy, feminist theorizing seems to be characterized by an aversion to hierarchical structures, a commitment to the recognition of plurality, a concern to broaden or revise the conception of experience, and a demand that women's experiences and projects be fully integrated into the resources and prospects of any philosophic analysis. Further, contemporary feminism has come to insist that any philosophical analysis, to be considered feminist, must take account of the many ways in which women are women, and must not privilege any race, class, sexual, age, or ability grouping in its attempt to identify what women's experiences and projects *are*.

By all these measures, the analysis undertaken is indeed feminist philosophy, significant for both feminist and theoretical projects.

Notes

An earlier version of this paper was read at the New School for Social Research, October 9, 1993, as part of the conference "Is Feminist Philosophy Philosophy?" arranged by the Graduate Faculty Women in Philosophy at the New School. Since that time, versions of the paper have been read at Purchase Women's Studies Faculty Colloquium, Purchase College SUNY, 1994; as part of a series of lectures given at Peking University in 1995; and at a conference on Feminist Philosophy organized by the Philosophy Institute of the Chinese Academy of the Social Sciences in Beijing, PRC, in 1996. I have benefited from the thoughtful comments, criticisms, and discussions offered on each of these occasions.

1. Judith Butler and Joan C. Scott, *Feminists Theorize the Political* (New York and London: Routledge, 1992), xiii.

2. See Marjorie C. Miller, "Practice, Feminism, and Theory," *Journal of Humanism and Ethical Religion* 5, no. 1 (Winter 1992).

3. Cf. Marjorie C. Miller, "Rorty and the Postmodern Turn in American Philosophy," *Fudan Xuebao: She Hui Ke Xue Ban* (*Fudan Journal:* Social Sciences Edition) (in Chinese, Mo Wei Ming, trans.), no. 2 (1996).

4. Justus Buchler, *Toward a General Theory of Human Judgment,* 2nd rev. ed. (New York: Dover, 1979).

5. For an examination of these categories of judgment, see Buchler, *General Theory.*

6. Audre Lorde, "Breast Cancer: Power vs. Prosthesis," originally in *The Cancer Journals,* Spinsters Ink, 1980. Reprinted in *Women's Voices: Visions and Perspectives,* Pat C. Hoy II, Esther H. Schor, Robert DiYanni, eds. (New York: McGraw Hill Publishing Company, 1990).

7. Judith Butler, *Gender Trouble: Feminism and the Subversion of Identity* (New York and London: Routledge, 1990), 22.

8. Justus Buchler, *Metaphysics of Natural Complexes,* K. Wallace, A. Marsoobian, and R. Corrington, eds. (Albany: State University of New York Press, 1965. Second, expanded ed., 1990).

9. "Integrity" is another formal term in Buchler's system. Although, like most of Buchler's categories, its meaning is refined throughout the system, the most direct statement of definition is:

> Whatever the boundaries or limits of complexes may happen to be, whatever may be the conditions under which these limits obtain, wherever these limits may lie, any complex has just the status, just the relations, just the constitution that it has. This is its integrity, that in which its being "a" complex and "that"

complex consists. Integrity entails both uniqueness and commonness. . . . The integrity of a complex is always conditional, in the sense that it is minimally determined by the location of the complex in this or that order of complexes. A complex has an *integrity* for each of its ordinal locations. (21–22)

10. This term is taken from Buchler's general ontology. See Buchler, *Metaphysics*.

11. Ibid.

12. Maria Lugones, "Playfulness, 'World'-Traveling, and Loving Perception," in *Women, Knowledge and Reality,* Ann Garry and Marilyn Pearsall, eds. (Boston: Unwin Hyman, 1989).

13. In addition to the obvious reference to de Beauvoir, see also Sandra Lipsitz Bem, *The Lenses of Gender* (New Haven and London: Yale University Press, 1993); Judith Lorber, *Paradoxes of Gender* (New Haven and London: Yale University Press, 1994); and Hilde Hein, "Liberating Philosophy: An End to the Dichotomy of Spirit and Matter," in *Women, Knowledge and Reality,* Garry and Pearsall, eds.

14. Cf. Denise Riley, *"Am I That Name?" Feminism and the Category of "Women" in History* (Minneapolis: University of Minnesota Press, 1990 [1988]); and also cf. Teresa Brennan, "Essence against Identity," in *Metaphilosophy* [special issue: *Contributions and Controversy in Feminist Philosophy*] 27, nos. 1 and 2 (January/April 1996), reprinted in this volume.

15. Judith Butler and Joan C. Scott, eds., *Feminists Theorize the Political* (New York and London: Routledge, 1992), xiv.

16. For example, by Gail Stenstad, "Anarchic Thinking: Breaking the Hold of Monotheistic Ideology on Feminist Philosophy," in *Women, Knowledge and Reality,* Garry and Pearsall, eds.; and by Sandra Harding in many of her works, in particular, "Feminist Justificatory Strategies," in *Women, Knowledge and Reality,* Garry and Pearsall, eds. This view also characterizes Judith Butler's position in her "Contingent Foundations" essay in *Feminist Contentions,* Benhabib et al.

Bibliography

Bem, Sandra Lipsitz. *The Lenses of Gender.* New Haven and London: Yale University Press, 1993.

Benhabib, Seyla, Judith Butler, Drucilla Cornell, and Nancy Fraser. *Feminist Contentions: A Philosophical Exchange.* New York and London: Routledge, 1995.

Brennan, Teresa. "Essence against Identity." *Metaphilosophy* [special issue: *Contributions and Controversy in Feminist Philosophy*] 27, nos. 1 and 2 (January/April 1996). Reprinted in this volume.

Buchler, Justus. *Toward a General Theory of Human Judgment.* New York: Dover, 1951. 2nd rev. ed., 1979.

————. *Metaphysics of Natural Complexes*. K. Wallace, A. Marsoobian, and R. Corrington, eds. Albany: State University of New York Press, 1965. Second, expanded ed., 1990.

Butler, Judith. *Gender Trouble: Feminism and the Subversion of Identity*. New York and London: Routledge, 1990.

————. "Contingent Foundations." In *Feminist Contentions: A Philosophical Exchange*, ed. Seyla Benhabib et al. New York and London: Routledge, 1995.

Butler, Judith, and Joan C. Scott, eds. *Feminists Theorize the Political*. New York and London: Routledge, 1992.

Garry, Ann, and Marilyn Pearsall, eds. *Women, Knowledge and Reality*. Boston: Unwin Hyman, 1989.

Harding, Sandra. "Feminist Justificatory Strategies." In *Women, Knowledge and Reality*, Garry and Pearsall, eds.

Hein, Hilde. "Liberating Philosophy: An End to the Dichotomy of Spirit and Matter." In *Women, Knowledge and Reality*, Garry and Pearsall, eds.

Lorber, Judith. *Paradoxes of Gender*. New Haven and London: Yale University Press, 1994.

Lorde, Audre. "Breast Cancer: Power vs. Prosthesis." Originally in *The Cancer Journals*. Spinsters Ink, 1980. Reprinted in *Women's Voices: Visions and Perspectives*, Pat C. Hoy II, Esther H. Schor, Robert DiYanni, eds. New York: McGraw Hill Publishing Company, 1990.

Lugones, Maria. 1989. "Playfulness, 'World'-Traveling, and Loving Perception." In *Women, Knowledge and Reality*, Garry and Pearsall, eds.

Miller, Marjorie C. "Practice, Feminism, and Theory." *Journal of Humanism and Ethical Religion* 5, no. 1 (Winter 1992): 50–66.

————. "Rorty and the Postmodern Turn in American Philosophy." *Fudan Xuebao: She Hui Ke Xue Ban (Fudan Journal: Social Sciences Edition)* (in Chinese, Mo Wei Ming, trans.), no. 2 (1996).

Miller, Marjorie C. Guest Editor, with Kathleen Wallace. *Metaphilosophy* [special issue: *Contributions and Controversy in Feminist Philosophy*] 27, nos. 1 and 2 (January/April 1996).

Riley, Denise. *"Am I That Name?" Feminism and the Category of "Women" in History*. Minneapolis: University of Minnesota Press, 1990 (1988).

Stenstad, Gail. "Anarchic Thinking: Breaking the Hold of Monotheistic Ideology on Feminist Philosophy." In *Women, Knowledge and Reality*, Garry and Pearsall, eds.

6

The Personal Is Philosophical, or Teaching a Life and Living the Truth: Philosophical Pedagogy at the Boundaries of Self

Ruth Ginzberg

> Surely in view of these questions and pictures you must consider very carefully before you begin to rebuild your college what is the aim of education, what kind of society, what kind of human being it should seek to produce.
>
> —*Virginia Woolf*[1]

One of the difficulties of so-called cultural feminism is that it comes dangerously close to associating women with nature and men with culture. Of course this association is not new; it is as old as the European Enlightenment. Unfortunately, in reinforcing the apparent dichotomy between nature and culture, and in assigning "nature" to women, by default that gives men a putative claim on "culture" as male. Elsewhere I have suggested that theorizing a sharp dichotomy between nature and culture is itself a mistake. Now, of course, the more robust versions of cultural feminism argue that there is a different kind of culture: a female lifeworld, which, among other things, values intersubjectivity, nurturing, connectedness, responsibility, and the "natural" or unmolested state of things more highly than it values individualism, accumulation, rights claims, and the production of artifacts.

This version of cultural feminism is often supported by two some-what different claims: One is that, by virtue of biological connections between women's menstrual cycles and the phases of the moon, pheromones which create menstrual synchrony among us, and our phys-ical connections to the next generation via umbilical cords and lactation, women are more "in tune" with ourselves as part of, rather than distinct from, "nature." A somewhat different claim is that, because of culturally produced gender-role assignments (which may or may not have a basis in reproductive biology), women historically have been assigned to handle the births, the deaths, the warm, moist and sticky, the generation and the decay, the feeding and the nurturing, the consolation of those who are grieving, and the tending of the dying. These activities, the argument goes, give women a better perspective on our fundamental embeddedness in, and our inability to transcend, the physical world. A common, and somewhat Hegelian, feminist claim is that this perspective offers a more accurate rendition of the human condition than that given by privileged European men, who have had the luxury of being able to maintain the fantasy that *contemplation* was the essence of human existence.

However problematic or appealing these views may be, by far their most deleterious effect is that of infusing the act of *learning* itself with gendered significance. The problem is this: What is "natural" (translation: "gendered female") supposedly need not be *learned;* indeed, it is some-what of an embarrassment if one needs actually to learn what is supposed to come naturally. Needing to learn those things which are supposed to come naturally hints at some kind of congenital deficiency, a defect, a lack of Darwinian "fitness." So when women are understood as being those who are more "natural" we are also construed as those who do not need to learn or who have no stake in knowledge production. We are imagined already to know (innately?) whatever we need to know. In such a schema, to whatever extent we seek to learn that which we do not already know or to engage in practices of knowledge production, we appear to be doing so either (1) in order to extend ourselves outside of our gendered roles as women, and thus we are assumed to be seeking access to "nonnatural" (that is, male) spheres, to which we are not entitled; or (2) because we are defective *qua* women in the first place, and we seek to learn that which women are already supposed to know; in other words, we are suspected of seeking remedial measures to compensate for our "natural" defects.

On the other hand, that which is "culture" (translation: "gendered male") must be learned or produced, for it is exactly this which distin-guishes it from Nature within a Nature-Culture dichotomy. What is more, the passing of culture from one generation to the next is more than just a tradition; it is what allows the civilizations of Man (*sic*) to progress.

Thus, men are construed as those for whom learning or knowledge production is a noble calling, a fulfillment of one's telos. In this light, to whatever extent men seek to learn things they do not already know or to produce knowledge with their life activities, they appear to be doing so in ultimate fulfillment of their social and biological roles within the human community.

Small wonder, then, that pedagogy, education, and other practices of knowledge production should be experienced as gender-laden.

In an essay titled "Shame and Gender,"[2] Sandra Bartky examines the phenomenon of shame—women's shame—which, she argues, is not the same sort of shame as the allegedly generic but actually male-gendered shame which is currently a hot topic in contemporary moral psychology.[3] She argues that the shame which is the subject of recent and, she argues, distinctively androcentric moral psychology is eventlike, with more or less discrete beginning and ending points. For privileged white men this might be an accurate description: Feeling shame is an experienced event, distinguished from an otherwise differently experienced moral milieu. A man experiences himself-in-the-world as ordinary; then he might temporarily experience shame; but afterward his feelings are expected to return to "normal." On the other hand, Bartky argues, women's shame is a "pervasive affective attunement to the social environment, . . . a profound mode of disclosure both of self and situation" (85). Women's shame doesn't stand, eventlike, in relief, against a general background of nonshame; woman's shame *is* the background against which other experiences stand. This, she claims, is phenomenologically different from men's shame; enough so that recent theories from moral psychology about "shame" don't manage to account for the phenomenon of women's shame. Bartky illustrates her point with an extended example involving adult women's behavior in her philosophy classrooms. As students, she says, many women bear the characteristic marks of shame: mumbled apologies for the inadequacies of their submitted work, hesitant use of speech, questioning intonation attached to simple declarative sentences, excessive use of qualifiers, and so on.

I want to suggest that it is no accident that Sandra Bartky found a paradigmatic illustration of gendered women's shame in a philosophy classroom. The scenario she describes has a familiar ring. I've seen it all too often, not only in my students but in myself as well. Sandra Bartky is on to something important here; indeed, it is something even further-reaching than her original point. In the process of constructing her argument, she has highlighted, perhaps inadvertently, the gendered differences between learning as an honorable "public" event of constructing one's culture (male) and learning as a "private" event which we pretend oughtn't be happening at all, let alone where others might see it (female).

Adrienne Rich first unearthed this problem more than 15 years ago, in her collection of essays, *On Lies, Secrets, and Silence.*[4] Included in that collection were four essays explicitly focusing on feminist pedagogy and one very sobering essay on Hannah Arendt's failure to see the separation of the "public" and "private" spheres as a gendered separation. Perhaps more tellingly, in the essay entitled "Women and Honor: Some Notes on Lying" she writes, almost as a puzzle, the following syllogism:

> "Women have always lied to each other."
> "Women have always whispered the truth to each other."
> "Both of these axioms are true."

leaving it as an exercise for the reader to discover that the only coherent solution to the puzzle is:

> "Women have always lied to each other." (publicly)
> "Women have always whispered the truth to each other." (privately)
> (Private Woman and Public Woman are different entities, which is how it is possible that) "Both of these axioms are true."

One might well ask what it is that gendered women need to learn, that gendered men don't. Indeed, gendered women, on Sandra Bartky's account, need to learn the internalization of discipline necessary to produce our Foucauldian "docile bodies," bodies which, she points out, must turn out to be *more* docile than men's bodies, when all is said and done. All this is supposed to remain hidden—hidden enough, indeed, to make the power differences between women and men appear to be innate.

I agree with Sandra Bartky but think that her explanation does not go far enough toward explaining the troubled philosophy and psychology of feminist pedagogy. First, the gendered public/private split extends to the domain of learning and the institutions in which learning is to take place. There is a cultural norm in force which does not have the same impact on women and on men: Men's learning may be public and is publicly acknowledged as culturally important and valuable; women's learning must be private (if it occurs at all). We are not supposed to be "caught" learning, because learning is an act of cultural (re)production. Culture, in turn, is alleged to be none of our business. So we are supposed to learn outside of the public gaze, if we do it at all.

Now, this is one of the little lies, secrets, and silences of which Adrienne Rich speaks: that women must learn. The sharing of practices of knowledge production, for both "approved" and "unapproved" sorts of knowledge, is the content of those lies which Adrienne Rich noticed that we utter publicly, but whisper privately, to one another.

Publicly, the phenomenology of women's learning is that we disappear from the public gaze; later we return knowing whatever we need to know. Or not. But if not, we are alleged to be defective, not in need of education. "Polite company" doesn't discuss what happened in the meanwhile. Women's learning paradigmatically resembles the process of changing a tampon: that is, intellectually, most men and women probably could describe the details of what goes on behind closed doors (if pressed), perhaps without even blushing, but in actual lived practice, any particular woman at any particular time is supposed to accomplish whatever needs to be done without having the fact that she did anything at all intrude on the public sphere. And certainly a woman is supposed to be embarrassed at least, if not seriously shamed, if someone (from the public sphere) actually "catches her" doing it. Unruffled Woman Quietly Leaves Room; Unruffled Woman Quietly Returns. Nobody ever mentions her absence, what she did while she was gone, or anything slippery, moist, warm, intimate, or penetrating. A polite little fiction is maintained that "nothing" really happened.

This is the archetype for women's learning, connected to the notion that the most important things women learn (that is, our gender roles and practices; our position of submission) are supposed to be "natural," that is, unlearned. If we "get caught" learning, what is at stake is a real danger that the Big Secret of the social construction of gender will be revealed. Like the famous "writers' blocks" that so often haunt women's writing, paralyzing us with unconscious fears that we might publicly expose things that aren't supposed to be told, I suspect that women also suffer from "learners' blocks." We unconsciously fear that if we ever "get caught" learning, we might (accidentally) publicly be seen learning things that aren't supposed to be learned; things that are supposed to be Natural, or things that aren't supposed to be known at all. Thus, women in classrooms being "caught learning" are ashamed—for much deeper reasons that the "behavior-shaping" theory of inattention (or mal-attention) to women in classrooms would have it. Sandra Bartky's claim that women's shame is a form of "being-in-the-world" whereas men's shame is a form of belief comes closer to describing this—but doesn't offer a political phenomenology of knowledge production sufficient to illuminate a gendered theory of pedagogy.

Unfortunately, I am *not* able to present a feminist political phenomenology of knowledge production here in the space that I have, but suffice it to say—and this is to address the title question of this conference—there ought to be no question that this is a *philosophical* task.

Instead let me outline what that task ought to address.

If we wish to develop a nonoppressing philosophy, if we wish to practice, philosophize, write, and teach in ways that are not simply unreflective reiterations—and, more problematical, reproductions—of past gender, class, race, and other power inequities, it is not enough merely to alter the content of our curricula. It is a step in the right direction, but it is not enough, merely to search the literature for women and non-European men to include in our syllabi. Nor is it enough to point to the racist, sexist, or heterosexist remarks of the canonical Western texts in order to note that such remarks are "unfortunate products of their times." Nor is it sufficient to tack a parenthetical "or she" (quickly) onto every reference to "he" in the texts we read. In believing these measures to be enough, we are committing the error of believing that the history and practice of knowledge production are themselves timeless, genderless, classless, raceless, and culture-independent; we are trying to proceed as though our embeddedness within—not outside of—a culture, whose history has been dominated by the interests of European, moneyed, adult (but not "old"), heterosexual, and largely Christian males, is irrelevant to the philosophy produced by that culture. This certainly cannot be the case.

I am not interested here in tabulating or arguing for the existence of some alleged sins of alleged oppressors against some others who are allegedly oppressed. Nor am I interested in arguing whether academic institutions are tools of oppression or not, though I personally believe that they are. I am certainly not interested in rousing either guilt or resentment among those who discover, much to their dismay, that they may, perhaps unwillingly, share class membership with some historically or currently notorious oppressor class(es). This is not about what they, or their predecessors or compatriots with similar demographics may or may not have done "wrong"; it is not about guilt or blame. This is about how it matters who (in particular) you and I are, right now, within this very relationship, when we come together to engage in practices of knowledge-production with one another. It is about the ways in which who we are and what we do when we enter into a knowledge-producing relationship with one another, matter: epistemically, pedagogically, socially, politically, and philosophically. It is about how the production of knowledge is not distinct from the production of Selves, and about the social and political importance of those activities, as well as their necessary intimacy.

I want to urge, as a necessary step toward the production of a feminist philosophy, a shift in perspective from the "banking" concept of knowledge, in which knowledge is viewed as a commodity with no production history of its own, to what I have called elsewhere an "erotic" concept of knowledge. This erotic conception of knowledge has quite a bit of kinship with both relatively Marxist conceptions of knowledge (Paulo Freire, Habermas et al.) and with relatively feminist conceptions of knowledge (Mary Kay Belenky, Lorraine Code, Susan Bordo, et al.). We need to reject the notion that knowledge is a commodity-like thing-in-the-world which can be possessed, transmitted, bought, sold, accumulated, shared, or otherwise "banked" in repositories of any sort, which purport to be independent of the knowledge itself. Among the implications of this rejection is the need to free ourselves from the long-standing belief that such things as books, vaults, computer storage devices, films, or people's memories are structurally independent of whatever knowledge is supposedly contained "in" them. This most emphatically need *not* imply an entirely unconstrained epistemic relativism, nor need it imply that knowledge is the same thing as belief, nor need it (necessarily) presuppose a consensus theory of truth. Nor need it hold that all means of knowledge production are equally credible; that if, for example, Holocaust revisionists ever become the majority then it will become "true" that there were no gas chambers. It need not claim that all perspectives are equally acceptable, *nor* that they are equally explanatory, nor that the world to which they refer is entirely "constructed" by the sum of all such references.

It seems that there are two models present against which one might assess what does, or ought to, go on in the practice of knowledge manipulation. One, by far the dominant model in post-Enlightenment Western philosophy at least, is the military model of the "defense" of knowledge "claims." Philosophers may recognize their own terminology easily in this model: They "take" a "position" and attempt to "defend" it against the "attacks" of other scholars; they "argue" for their "claims"; and others—perhaps even their best friends—may attempt to "shoot down" or to "shoot holes in" those "claims." Indeed, the very induction ceremony into the credentialed community of academic scholars nearly universally involves the "defense" of one's dissertation. Adrienne Rich points out that these sorts of terms suggest the connections—actual and metaphoric—between the style of the university and the style of a society invested in military and economic aggression.

Not incidentally, philosophy professors also construct stories about this sort of terminology for ourselves and for the students who find it offensive that we use such militaristic and violent imagery: We say that "argument" doesn't really mean "argument-as-in-dispute," that to be "critical" doesn't really mean that one is being "critical-as-in-derogatory," that when one "attacks" and "defends" "positions" one isn't really engaging in war games—that all these are just words-that-don't-really-mean-what-they-sound-like. Many students remain skeptical, as well they should.

In the model just presented, the reason for engaging in philosophy *at all* is to become a participant in a military game, to fight for a position on the philosophical battleground (that one can call one's own), or to weaken the position of another scholar who is fighting for the same philosophical territory. Students are trained and rewarded for successfully "attacking" or "defending" some logistically important "argument" on the philosophical battlefield. Tenure and job promotions are awarded to those who stake out and win the most intellectual turf, those who literally "capture" the greatest number of column inches in the "toughest" professional journals, largely through their "attacks" on previously published ideas. In this military model of scholarship, departmental requirements for written publication amount to "marching orders" from generals in competing armies; scholars "capturing" column inches in professional journals, square footage in scientific laboratories, or postdocs and graduate assistants who will carry out the details of their competing research plans are merely the foot soldiers in a much larger battle.

One of the important steps toward a feminist political phenomenology of knowledge production is that of reclaiming *gendered* processes of knowledge production, indeed (re)claiming the (re)production of culture itself, as the legitimate provinces of gendered women. We must not have to choose between our gender identities and our agency as participants in the production of knowledge. We can learn to philosophize for the purpose of connecting with others rather than for the purposes of pleasing an authority or of "winning" a philosophical "war," or engaging in other knowledge-producing activities which have been paradigmatically, historically, "male." We must conceive philosophy as other than a verbal form of men's wars, as other than the (re)creation of male-gendered, political battles over "public" space.

This leads to a final consideration that I will mention here today: that of the fundamental tension between producing a feminist philosophy within a university and the fact that American universities are not feminist institutions. If, as I would argue, all knowledge production is political, then it is unlikely that practices of feminist knowledge production can take place within nonfeminist institutions. At the bottom, we are left with two choices: change the university into a feminist institution or create separate feminist institutions for the purpose of feminist knowledge production. I don't know which of these would be "better," or even which is more likely to succeed. This is a future direction for research and action. But it seems important to take the lessons of the history of philosophy seriously. Scholasticism wasn't challenged within the universities of the times. Scholastic philosophy was still being taught in European universities up until the time of Kant. Modern philosophers had to work outside of universities to develop their paradigm before it became accepted as "legitimate" within the official institutions of knowledge production of those times, more than a century after it emerged. Serious feminist philosophers should take note of this history in considering how we ought to proceed.

Notes

Parts of this paper were originally written for presentation on a panel, "Integrating Feminism in the Philosophy Curriculum" at the American Association of Philosophy Teachers International Summer Workshop in Toledo, Ohio (Summer, 1984) and at their meeting in conjunction with the Western (now Central) Division American Philosophical Association meeting in Chicago, April 1985. Other portions of it have appeared in the APA Newsletter on Feminism and Philosophy, Spring 1989, as "Teaching Feminist Logic."

    1. Virginia Woolf, *Three Guineas* (New York: Harcourt Brace Jovanovich, 1938), 33.

    2. Sandra Lee Bartky, "Shame and Gender" in her *Femininity and Domination: Studies in the Phenomenology of Oppression* (New York: Routledge, 1990).

    3. Cf. Bernard Williams's book, *Shame and Necessity* (Berkeley: University of California Press, 1993).

    4. Adrienne Rich, *On Lies, Secrets, and Silence* (New York: Norton, 1979), 189.

7

Musing as a Feminist and as a Philosopher on a Postfeminist Era

Patricia S. Mann

originally planned to call my first book *A Micro-Politics for the Twenty-First Century*. My press said that it was inadvisable to put numbers in the title, explaining that to do so was to date it, to limit its ultimate relevance. Actually, I wondered at the publisher's expectations for my book. I, myself, felt quite willing to settle for one hundred years of relevance. But when the publisher suggested the alternate title, *Micro-Politics: Agency in a Postfeminist Era,* it seemed like a good idea, in that it highlights three concepts that are important to my analysis.[1] I even hoped that the term "postfeminism" would prove controversial. In the year since I chose the title, however, Katie Roiphe and Naomi Wolf have published works that have saddled postfeminism with truly noxious connotations.[2] Yet I am as committed as I ever was to the concept of a postfeminist era.

Basically, I believe that we feminists have to have the hubris to claim the contemporary social relevance of our gendered perspective *directly*— not qua feminist, but rather qua social philosophy and truth. That was not possible 25 years ago when the Second Wave of feminism began. And it was certainly not true when the First Wave of feminism began in the nineteenth century. But I think it is possible today. That is why I maintain, with gladness in my feminist heart, that this is a postfeminist era.

I

Let me explain more fully. I am a feminist. In my writing, in my teaching, in friendship and in love, in sickness and in health, in my dreams and my nightmares, I am a feminist. And I will always be a feminist. But I think of it as a wonderful, highly contingent historical identity shared by those of us who found ourselves swept up or shaken up by the women's movement during the seventies when the Second Wave of feminism was at its height. And shared, as well, by some younger feminists who identify with issues articulated by the Second Wave of feminism. A feminist identity today, however, says more about such shared historical references than about specific contemporary beliefs. (How much do you have in common with Christina Hoff Sommers, Wendy Kaminer, Naomi Wolf, and Katie Roiphe, all of whom call themselves feminists?)

It is as a feminist that I herald a new postfeminist era today. In fact, I hope to persuade you that we should embrace the concept of a postfeminist era as the basis for achieving feminist goals in this last decade of the twentieth century.

Why, you may well query, should we take kindly to a concept of "postfeminism"? It's a term flung at us, as likely as not, antagonistically.[3] The answer, I will suggest, is both simple and complicated. The simple answer is that a lot has changed in the 25 years since the Second Wave of feminism began: Gender is everybody's problem in the 1990s. It is in the back pages and often on the front pages of newspapers on a daily basis. Not stories about feminists, for the most part. Rather, we read stories about female agents filing sex discrimination charges against the FBI, about officers and enlisted women pursuing sexual harassment cases against the military, about battered women acquitted of murdering their batterers by juries who have somehow been persuaded to recognize the relevance of prior patterns of gendered injustice. We also read about burgeoning reproductive technologies, impoverished single mothers, corporate child-care anxieties, and increasingly varied parent-child arrangements.

These stories reflect several things. In the first place, they bespeak major changes within kinship relationships over the past several decades, and the dramatic effects these have had on people's lives. As masses of women leave their homes every morning to go into the public workplace, workplaces are changing, if not very fast or in readily theorizable ways. The homes people return to at night are changing, as well. Everybody is now involved, willingly and unwillingly, in small and large ways, in the transformation of male and female roles. Many of the issues identified with feminism 20 years ago—reproductive rights, employment rights, violence against women—have become pressing mainstream concerns. And that is a big deal, both for those who are newly experiencing these issues and for feminists who have been living with them for a long time now.

There is a second and more subtle phenomenon to be inferred from these ubiquitous stories of gender confusion and conflict: a loss of faith in the righteous dominance of male humanity. The automatic respect and authority that went with being male—in familial and workplace relationships with women, anyway—is being dramatically eroded. (On this issue, I feel impelled to respond directly to Marilyn Frye's powerful Second Wave essay on sexism that I still teach regularly: I would say that of course it is still an advantage to announce oneself as a man. But many white men perceive themselves as having lost the advantage they grew up expecting to have. Many experience themselves as disempowered in relative terms, even though this is not the case in absolute terms, whereas for some young women the opposite phenomenon may be true: They feel relatively empowered, even though in absolute terms they are still operating with a gendered disadvantage.[4]

Women of all ages and political orientations are beginning to recognize and take umbrage against sexual harassment; women like Desiree Washington and Patricia Bowman are questioning traditional forms of male sexual entitlement, and women like Lorena Bobbitt are striking back against men who abuse them. These women are not feminists by any stretch of the imagination. They are postfeminist victims/political agents, enabled to some degree by the feminist movement and to some further degree by changing social institutions to question particular forms of oppressive male behavior—without necessarily buying into the larger picture of social change that empowers feminists.

It is a very strange moment for us as feminists. Insofar as feminist issues have permeated a nonfeminist culture, we have to start thinking of these issues and of our relationship to these issues/our issues rather differently. For many years during the seventies and early eighties we had a secure and proprietary sense of who we were as feminists and of where we stood as social radicals in relation to the larger culture. In the last few years, that sense of security has been challenged from within, as it were, by the angry voices of women from different cultural backgrounds questioning the universalizing tendencies of white middle class feminists.[5] In response, we white, middle class feminists have become more cautious and even defensive about the moral and political claims we make on behalf of the potentially problematic category of "women" within feminism.

The challenges of a postfeminist era are, however, different; they come from the larger dominant culture to which we have considered ourselves marginal. Insofar as gendered conflicts have seeped into all the cracks of this culture, we feminists can no longer be viewed as radical outsiders. Is there a category for radical insiders? Some feminists have surely compromised their radical principles in order to gain an inside position and various sorts of institutional power. But we currently have a situation in which feminists who have not changed their principles fundamentally may yet feel themselves embraced by institutions that perceive such feminists as potential sources of necessary information and ideas. How shall we operate constructively as radical insiders?

Indeed we have expertise in relation to a set of problems that have begun to baffle male heads of large universities, corporations, and government agencies, as well as judges and politicians. Not that they will necessarily want to implement feminist solutions. But the nonfeminist women who are struggling with these problems, in workplaces and homes and at the interface between the two—these women are our natural constituency. Men struggling with new gendered issues, of sexual harassment, for example, may also receive our advice gratefully. Such persons may often put our suggestions to good use, perhaps recruited to feminism along the way; most likely not.

Many people associate the notion of postfeminism with the idea that the struggle is over insofar as we have either won or lost, as feminists. I am suggesting the term to signal that, in a sense, we have won as feminists, but not by achieving our ultimate goal of defeating patriarchy. Rather, we have won by seeing feminist struggles transformed into a hegemonic set of contemporary social problems. It has become apparent that late-capitalist patriarchy is rife with internal conflicts, diseased as it were, yet hardly terminal at this point. It is equally apparent that struggles involving issues of gender, sexuality, ethnicity, and economics are multiplying, not just in the United States, but globally.

In a postfeminist era we feminists are justified in thinking big. Not big as in universalizing on a particular notion of women's morality, not big as in essentializing a particular vision of womanhood. By "thinking big" I mean that it is appropriate to assert the relevance of gendered conflicts and struggles in most arenas of life in this country and globally. The multitude of situations in which a gendered analysis is appropriate makes it obvious that there can be no essential or universal conception of either the quality of the problems or the solutions. But I think we can venture to assert that if gendered problems are not properly addressed there will be no solutions at all.

In *Micro-Politics: Agency in a Postfeminist Era* I analyze a number of contemporary gendered problems in the United States, from housework inequities to pornography to abortion and sexual harassment and date rape. My first goal is to demonstrate that as gendered problems, all of them force us to reach beyond previous theoretical frameworks to find any sort of adequate analysis. My second goal is to offer an alternative theoretical rubric; I suggest a "micropolitical" analysis of social conflict and change, emphasizing the need for a more dynamic and complex understanding of social and political agency.

A macropolitical perspective analyzes political relationships in terms of the political institutions of society. A micropolitical perspective assesses the actions and potential actions of individuals in terms of relationships between individuals. Michel Foucault's notion of micropolitics emphasizes the fact that all individual relationships occur within a network of power relations. I am interested in understanding the qualitative dimensions of individual actions which Foucault did not address. I maintain that social power relations affect even our ability to recognize the agency of individual actors. In our modern Hobbesian/Cartesian tradition, philosophers have assumed a reductive, one-dimensional account of individual agency emphasizing that individuals act out of individual desires. As an idealized, abstracted account of individual agency, encouraging individual equality and autonomy of action in the public sphere of economic and political action, this vision of individual agency has played an important role in modern development. But, as an everyday explanation of individual actions, it is a highly misleading account.

I began to question its adequacy when I noticed that traditional women appeared to lack a sense of individual agency, according to this account. Women's social inferiority in modern society became associated with what was deemed a "selfless" devotion to family, a feminine lack of precisely the desiring agency that was presumed basic to male selves within a liberal, capitalist society. My efforts to rethink our notion of individual agency were based on my frustration with these implications of a Hobbesian, one-dimensional theory of agency in relation to women. I did not buy the idea that women lacked agency, and I also did not buy feminist maternalist claims that women's altruism was a special, improved sort of nonindividualistic agency. Women's qualitatively different kind of agency was linked to the subordination of women in modern society, I believed.

Indeed, over the last 25 years, beliefs about women's capacity for agency have been transformed as large numbers of women have entered the workplace, and a great many women have demonstrated a remarkable capacity to acquire, practically overnight, male-identified forms of social and economic desiring agency. To me, this indicated a need to reassess the activities of women within the patriarchal family. I maintain that women exhibited alternative dimensions of individual agency rather than selflessness in their traditional familial roles. I argue that by reconceptualizing women's caring and nurturing activities in the family as neglected dimensions of agency, it becomes possible to envision a richer theory of individual agency in general.

In my book *Micro-Politics,* I suggested that we require a multidimensional account of individual agency in order to adequately understand the agency not merely of women, but of every one of us, particularly in our current moment of social transformation. According to my three-dimensional theory of agency, a full understanding of actions involves understanding not only one's desires, but also one's sense of responsibility, as well as one's expectations of recognition and reward in taking a particular action. The three dimensions of desire, responsibility, and recognition and reward have always, in fact, been important grounds for understanding the actions of individual men and women alike. When we are interested in fully comprehending why someone acted in a particular way, or why they came to a particular decision, we tend to inquire into all these aspects of their decision. Nevertheless, a one-dimensional paradigm of Hobbesian desiring agency was the gendered foundation upon which dominant institutions and values of modern Western society developed. Women's apparent lack of desiring agency was the grounds for excluding them from the developing public sphere of modern society.[6]

I originally formulated this theory of agency in *Micro-Politics* in order to represent the changing relationships of women and men in the context of the U.S. women's movement. A three-dimensional theory of agency relations reveals social hierarchies between individuals insofar as societies distribute the dimensions of agency among individuals according to particular social patterns. In modern society, the agency of various subordinate groups—not just women, but also servants, slaves, and workers—is seen primarily in terms of the dimensions of responsibility. Correspondingly, modern societies have emphasized the desires and given the most important forms of recognition and reward to a privileged group of men.

It is thus possible to identify and track diverse forms of social hierarchy—of gender, but also of race, sexuality, and age—as revealed by the distribution of desire, responsibility, and expectations of recognition and reward. These hierarchies are obscured by a Hobbesian theory of desiring agency. And we can chart changing power relations in terms of changing distribution of the three dimensions of agency. The empowerment of women today is reflected in greater concern for their desires, as well as by their growing expectations of recognition and reward.

One of the salient features of my micropolitics is its highlighting of the intersectionality of gender with issues of race, class, and sexual preference in most situations. Solutions to social problems today have to be gendered, but they will typically address these other social hierarchies as well. They will thus not be feminist solutions in any pure sense.[7]

So the simple answer to why we should call this a postfeminist era is that we want to mark the conclusion of a lengthy historical period during which feminism was a separate, marginal ideological discourse. We feminists now possess knowledge and perspectives on gender that will prove increasingly relevant to a mainstream culture beset by gendered conflicts and change. And so we may think in terms of articulating our position as a central, if still highly inflammatory, ideological discourse.

II

The more complicated answer involves several further layers of analysis as to why this is a postfeminist era. One of these layers is a theory of historical periodization. I argue that gender relations have replaced economic relations as the primary site of social conflict and change in our lives today. I make this judgment as part of an attempt to extend and rework, from a gendered perspective, the familiar historical/theoretical narrative explaining the birth and development of our modern era. Insofar as this argument succeeds, gender relations will be acknowledged as a fundamental component of our contemporary social and political fabric, no longer relegated to sidebar discussions of personal, psychological, or ideological issues. (As a theoretician, this is what I want more than anything else.)

According to the familiar narrative, modernity begins when the serfs are evicted from the ancestral lands and communities of feudalism. This massive unmooring of peasants from communal feudal relations of production made it necessary to comprehend more individuated efforts to satisfy the basic forms of material neediness. Thus, peasants recently unmoored from feudal communities become desiring beings engaged in an anarchic premarket frenzy of material redistribution in Thomas Hobbes's *Leviathan*. Each man became equal insofar as he could imagine having and getting whatever anyone else had. Hobbes's vision is not about scarcity but about equality. Fifty years later, John Locke had a more pastoral vision of individual efforts to satisfy material neediness, envisioning men producing private property by mixing their labor with nature. Liberal society was thus gradually organized in terms of these desiring and productive forms of public male agency.[8]

Of course, society was also organized in terms of various unarticulated forms of private familial agency. This economic man of liberalism was also an "incorporated male family self," his public agency only fully comprehensible in terms of his familial relationships with women and children. Marxism and feminism were both born as reactive, critical modes within a modern society of supposedly autonomous liberal men, who were also patriarchally incorporated familial selves.

The modern era begins to wane, as I see it, with the economic unmooring of women from the patriarchal family of liberalism. I believe that we are experiencing a second period of social unmooring today, as women's new economic and reproductive agency brings to an end the prescribed and hierarchical relationships of patriarchal families. Traditional kinship practices organized around and giving primacy to women's maternal role are rapidly vanishing as countries struggle against overpopulation and promote women's use of contraception. And, as their kinship roles decline, women are a growing presence within the global workforce. Women now have not merely the right, but the responsibility to participate within the public workforce and to choose when and if they will have children according to their ability to support them.

With these recent transformations in women's economic and repro-ductive agency, patriarchal institutions of reproduction have lost their structural viability. Lifetime commitments between men and women become unnecessary, families come to be headed by women as well as by men, and increasing numbers of people live alone or in nonfamilial groupings. We make and unmake family units in response to a logic of individual choice that has long structured public interactions. There is a radical sense in which individualism now goes all the way down, into the most personal aspects of our lives. Metaphorically, but also quite literally, women and children, and men as well, are unmoored today from the lifetime family unit that has historically provided individuals with their most basic interpersonal foundations.

As at the end of feudalism, it is clear that a great many basic hu-man needs which were previously satisfied in the context of prescribed, hierarchical communities must now be satisfied in new ways. In the early modern period, philosophers provided new notions of individual self-hood and agency corresponding to demands for individual participation in new social forms of production and distribution. It is not yet evident how society will be reorganized in our postmodern era, but insofar as intimate and familial connections are no longer a function of patriarchal forms of social coercion, we require new conceptions of selfhood and individual agency to provide the social logic for new sorts of interpersonal connections. I believe that such new conceptions of selfhood and agency will also create the theoretical basis for developing new forms of economic and political connections.

In *Micro-Politics,* I demonstrate that liberal individualism cannot maintain itself in the face of these changes in gender roles. As the relationships anchored by patriarchal kinship structures break down and are renegotiated, liberal individualism will gradually evolve into what I call forms of Engaged Individualism.

So my theoretical argument for calling this a postfeminist era links the new centrality of gendered conflicts with the waning of liberal individualism and the relationships of a patriarchal modernity. Economic relations cease to provide a sufficient explanation for social transformations. A postfeminist era articulates a distinctly gendered trajectory of postmodern development.

III

In another layer of my argument for designating this a postfeminist era I address feminist theorists specifically. As modernism and the normative identification of humanity as masculine and male demonstrably begin to wane, our position as feminist philosophers changes. I propose that we distinguish between two sorts of feminist philosophical agency. On the one hand, there is the intellectual commitment to doing philosophy as a feminist, that is, to insisting on a thoroughly gendered philosophical analysis. I take this to be a necessary foundation of important theorizing today, regardless of who is doing the theorizing. On the other hand, there is the decision about whether to designate the products of what we do as something called "feminist philosophy." Whereas it has become a meaningful category of philosophical production, I submit that it is no longer in our best interests as feminist philosophers to so label our work.

I will suggest four reasons why we should consider weaning ourselves from a notion of feminist philosophy. The first involves our relationship with ourselves as feminist theorists and activists committed to social change. The second refers to our relationship with the discipline of philosophy. The third is about our relationship with the world at large. And the fourth is about our relationship with the next generation, our students.

Our feminist commitment to social change and to a micropolitics in which dimensions of race, sexual preference, and class intersect with gender in a variety of ways provides the first reason for weaning ourselves from a notion of feminist philosophy. Gender identities and relationships are now up for grabs, radically destabilized in globally diverse situations. A feminist politics based upon identifying with the interests/concerns

PATRICIA S. MANN

of women is no longer workable. As Judith Butler has demonstrated, once we interrogate our consciousness "as women," we find that we are many women; collectively and even intrapersonally, we women are all over the place.[9] This does not mean, however, that we cannot cogently refer to ourselves and others as "women" or even to particular political projects as dealing with "women's issues." Wittgensteinian "family resemblances" are quite sufficient to explain a uniting of women within particular micropolitical contexts. This fragmentation, pluralization, and differentiation within our concept of womanhood mean, however, that we cannot infer or derive a politics or a political philosophy from the fact of our womanhood—or even from the fact of our feminism. Christina Hoff Sommers calls herself a feminist! And I don't think there is much point in disputing her claim.

In labeling our work feminist philosophy, we presume or imply linkages with a feminist identity politics. Yet if Butler is right, and I think she is right about this, political positions can no longer be grounded in unstable gender identities or in the forms of consciousness that were long assumed to accompany gender identities. This is also the problem with trying to use race, class, or sexual preferences as the basis for identity politics. It is *not* that we cannot finally label a particular politics as a gay politics, or as a black or Asian or feminist politics. It is that we cannot *come to or develop* a politics via Womanhood, or Blackness, or a Lesbian identity. (This problem of identity politics is quite recalcitrant. Important theorists like Donna Haraway and Judith Butler are still struggling to get free of it, formulating notions of anti-identity identity politics without fully breaking out of this framework of political consciousness.)[10]

I develop a notion of intersectional micropolitics in my book, emphasizing the concrete institutional locations of political struggle today. The political dimensions of race, sexual preference, and class potentially intersect with gendered issues *at every point of such institutional conflict today*. Whereas a gendered analysis is theoretically primary for me, it cannot be *politically* primary. For this reason, I do not think we should label our work in a manner which privileges gender over these other dimensions of struggle.

The second reason for weaning ourselves from a notion of feminist philosophy involves our relationship with the discipline of philosophy. In the past, we were always trying to play ball with one of the boys' bats: We were liberal feminists, we were Marxist or socialist feminists, we were psychoanalytic feminists. Or as radical feminists, we had to be willing to wait until the boys went home at night so we could play by ourselves.

In a postmodern, postfeminist era, feminists do not have to accept such compromising terms of play. Liberalism, Marxism, psychoanalysis, along with utilitarianism, Kantianism, and all the other old patriarchal bats, are still in play, of course. And people are still using them to get on base. But sluggers and theoretical home runs are a thing of the past with these old wooden theoretical bats.

Feminist philosophers, with their recognition of the significance of gendered social changes, have the inside track in ethical and political philosophy (and probably in epistemology and metaphysics as well, although those are not areas I can speak about with confidence).[11] Gendered conflicts provide a cardinal impetus for reworking ethical and political categories and frameworks today.

Of course, few male philosophers (or other theorists) recognize the centrality of gender as yet, even when their own theories transparently reflect gendered social changes. As is the case with ethical theorists newly worried about problems of pluralism and the evaluation of personal relationships. As is also the case with poststructuralist philosophers analyzing the decline of the rational subject who also happens to be a patriarchal subject. In fact, Jacques Derrida, a philosopher who does assume the significance of the category of Woman, also assumes that philosophy comes to an end with the critique of phallocentrism. This is not what a feminist envisions.[12]

The question is how to improve the status of feminists within the discipline and the world. I would suggest that one step toward changing our status is to stop labeling our work "feminist philosophy."

Why should we continue to give metaphysical lip service to the old assumption that women, or women's actions or women's interests or women's theories should be signified as a *marked* philosophical term, over against the regally *unmarked* concept of (male) philosophy? Feminist philosophers have more than enough grounds today to contest the notion that philosophy, with a capital "P," continues to be about men and their actions and interests. We are feminist philosophers, and we are doing Philosophy, with a capital "P," period, even (or especially) when we focus on women or on gender.

The third reason for weaning ourselves from a notion of feminist philosophy has to do with our relationship to the world at large. I fear that a notion of doing feminist philosophy or feminist theory has begun to cut us off or distance us from the problems of a postfeminist world. Don't get me wrong. I believe feminist theory is on the cutting edge of poststructuralist theory. It is the most interesting, wide-ranging social theory being written. Yet it is terribly "meta." We are criticizing a long tradition of patriarchal discourses, and we have developed highly specialized orientations toward these previous discourses. As a consequence, we tend to address fewer and fewer readers capable of understanding our positions.

I am not sure we can remedy the problem. And yet, we have become comfortable with particular concepts and regulative ideals that are increasingly difficult to make sense of in an antiessentialist, fragmented social moment. In chapter 3 of *Micro-Politics*, for example, I maintain that we cannot give a moral argument for abortion without giving up an Ur-feminist commitment to celebrating the maternal capacities of women. I think Mary O'Brien is correct in saying that after the contraceptive revolution, women cease to be part of an organic biological continuum.[13] In fact, we are cyborgean maternal agents, our biological capacities inextricably intertwined with the technologies of contraception and conception. Reproduction is now only morally justifiable as a social decision rather than as a natural consequence of female bodily capacities. In a postfeminist era, Shulamith Firestone reemerges out of a repressed Second Wave political unconscious to take her rightful place beside all those of us struggling to make sense of gendered social transformation.[14]

The fourth and final reason for weaning ourselves from a notion of feminist philosophy involves our relationship with the next generation. I agree very strongly with Susan Bordo about the significance of this next generation. That is why we need to confront their different historical situation today honestly.

I teach a feminist-texts course in which we have read Roiphe, MacKinnon, Wittig, Butler, Cornell, Haraway, Tronto, Patricia Williams, and now my book, *Micro-Politics*.[15] The other night I had an intense and fascinating conversation with one of my graduate students. Jodi, a very political, articulate, as well as intellectually engaged young woman, called to say that she was in turmoil over my notion of postfeminism. In the conversation that followed, I mostly just listened, in an encouraging mode. What emerged in the course of the conversation was a complicated layering of responses to feminism. I think it is worth briefly recounting the conversation and what Jodi said:

> Your notion of postfeminism makes a lot of sense. But I am upset by it. I feel very protective of feminism. My mother who died many years ago was a strong feminist, and I have always been strongly committed to feminist goals. But although my friends are very political, they see feminism as outdated, and I find myself having to defend it.
>
> In fact, I often find it easy to sympathize with my friends' impatience with feminism, even though it makes me feel guilty. After all, calling oneself a feminist is almost like drawing a caricature of oneself. The word "feminist" becomes a pigeon-hole, it makes you seem less relevant. Feminism is a theory removed from everyday reality; a feminist sets herself apart.

At such points, I evince sympathy for what Jodi is saying. Certainly academic feminists do frequently write in a mode that sets them at quite a distance from reality—from even their own reality.

Jodi continued apologetically:

> I really don't like to talk about this, but I do have my own private antagonism for the word "feminism." My generation is concerned with the effects of words and images on everyday life. But "feminism" today can be reduced to cartoon notions of equality. It is identified with Camille Paglia and Christina Hoff Sommers. I don't know what the word "feminism" *really* means anymore. It almost seems as if it no longer means anything at all.

She hastens to assure me that, nevertheless, her male friends are sympathetic to gendered politics. Recently diagnosed with endometriosis, a serious gynecological disorder, and angry at the quality of medical attention she has received, she is encouraged by a male friend fully supportive of her feminist critique of the medical establishment. "Women and men of my generation accept the reality of micropolitical forms of change. But the idea of defeating patriarchy is such a limited goal. We want to construct something new," Jodi concludes, somewhat exasperated, but hopeful.

In this discussion I have suggested that for reasons of generational generosity, we feminists consider the timeliness of a notion of postfeminism. With a notion of postfeminism, we can put a bit of closure on a historical period of feminist struggle we are proud of. We can let our most politically committed students off the hook. They and we can stop engaging in what has become an interminable metadiscussion of "What it means to be a feminist." And we can all, together, get on with the business of social transformation.

Notes

1. Patricia S. Mann, *Micro-Politics: Agency in a Postfeminist Era* (Minneapolis: University of Minnesota Press, 1994).

2. Katie Roiphe, *The Morning After* (New York: Little, Brown and Co., 1993). Naomi Wolf, *Fire with Fire* (New York: Random House, 1994).

3. See Mann, *Micro-Politics,* 118, for a more extensive discussion of why I reject conservative claims for this term and seek to appropriate it for a progressive contemporary agenda.

4. See Marilyn Frye, "Sexism," in *The Politics of Reality* (Freedom, Calif.: Crossing Press, 1983). See also Wolf, *Fire with Fire*.

5. See Chandra Talpede Mohanty, "Under Western Eyes: Feminist Scholarship and Colonial Discourses," *Colonial and Post-Colonial Theory*, Patrick Williams and Laura Chrisman, eds. (New York: Columbia University Press, 1994): 196–220. See also Gloria Anzaldúa, *Borderlands/La Frontera* (San Francisco: Spinsters/Aunt Lute Book Co., 1987).

6. See Mann, *Micro-Politics*, chapter 4.

7. Ibid., chapter 5. See also Kimberle Crenshaw, "Mapping the Margins: Identity Politics, Intersectionality, and Violence Against Women," *Stanford Law Review* 43 (July 1991); Patricia Williams, *The Alchemy of Race and Rights* (Cambridge: Harvard University Press, 1991), for race and gender intersections. See Arlie Hochschild, *The Time Bind: When Work Becomes Home and Home Becomes Work* (New York: Metropolitan Books, 1997), for a gendered analysis of recent workplace change.

8. Thomas Hobbes, *Leviathan*, C. B. MacPherson, ed. (New York: Penguin, 1981), chapter 13; John Locke, *The Second Treatise of Government* (New York: Liberal Arts Press, 1952). See also Mann, *Micro-Politics*, chapter 4.

9. Judith Butler, *Gender Trouble* (New York: Routledge, 1989).

10. Donna Haraway, *Simians, Cyborgs and Women* (New York: Routledge, 1990).

11. See Linda Alcoff, *Real Knowing: New Versions of the Coherence Theory* (Ithaca: Cornell University Press, 1996) for a recent feminist take on epistemology.

12. See Rosi Braidotti, *Patterns of Dissonance* (New York: Routledge, 1991).

13. Mary O'Brien, *The Politics of Reproduction* (Boston: Beacon, 1983).

14. Shulamith Firestone, *The Dialectic of Sex* (New York: Bantom, 1970).

15. Katie Roiphe, *The Morning After;* Catharine MacKinnon, *Feminism Unmodified* (Cambridge: Harvard University Press, 1988); Monique Wittig, *The Straight Mind* (Boston: Beacon, 1992); Drucilla Cornell, *Transformations* (New York: Routledge, 1993); Joan Tronto, *Moral Boundaries* (New York: Routledge, 1993); Patricia Williams, *The Alchemy of Race and Rights*.

8

Essence against Identity

Teresa Brennan

f the analysis of identity as a construction is the strongest contemporary argument against essentialism (so well developed in Butler),[1] the best arguments for reconsidering essentialism stress the importance of a sense of identity, or subjective power, in political agency.[2] They also stress the need for a shared foundation for identity in political action[3] for something essential that unites as women, women of color, gays, lesbians, people of color. This is the main point made by Schor and Weed, *The Essential Difference.*

Paradoxically, concern with political transformation was also at the heart of early criticisms of essentialism. But part of the problem with the essentialism debate today is that much of the history of the concept in seventies' feminism is forgotten. Critics forget that the main reason for opposing essentialist reasoning was that, to the extent that such reasoning imputed an immutable essence, it assumed the existence of something that could not be transformed. This means that if we accord women even the nicest of essences, we accord it permanently. We also deprive ourselves of intellectual grounds for disputing arguments that impute essential characteristics with which one would rather dispense, and thereby restrict the potential range of social transformation.[4]

The 1992 U.S. presidential election campaign provided a neat illustration of how essentialism can be used to the potential detriment of change. At the Republican convention, Marilyn Quayle said "Most women do not want to be liberated from their essential natures." Subsequently, in an opinion piece in *The New York Times,* Ms. Quayle invoked the names of Betty Friedan and Carol Gilligan, author of the feminist psychology classic *In a Different Voice:*

> One statement of mine has been subject to particularly wild and hostile misinterpretation. I said that I sometimes think liberals are angry, because it turns out that most women do not wish to be liberated from their essential natures as women.

The people who have objected most vehemently to this sought to construe this phrase as an argument for keeping women tied to the home. This is puzzling because central tenets of feminist thought spring from writings by Carol Gilligan and Betty Friedan. They have, Quayle notes, made the case that women and men are different, especially in their approach to relations with others, and that liberation wouldn't be worthwhile if it simply turned women into clones of men.[5]

Gilligan indeed had allied herself with that strand of feminist thought which seeks to revalue the traditional feminine virtues: compassion, nurturance, care, and attention to the concrete exigencies of sustaining life. But she was appalled at the appropriation of her work by Quayle. In a prompt reply, which *The New York Times* did not publish, Gilligan argued that the "different voice" women and girls were trying to make heard in the campaign was a voice for movement and change.

These brief notes consider how essentialism is or can be allied with movement and change. But they do so by an unorthodox route which involves a different idea of essence, one that is opposed to identity and fixity. An alliance of sorts among movement, change, and essence has already been established in practice, although it needs to be theorized. It has been established in that some of those arguing for a reconsideration of essentialism are not only saying that we need the concept for identity politics. They are also opposed to the dogmatic fixity that marked the later stages of the debate about essentialism. Thus, Russo: "Antiessentialism may well be the greatest inhibition to work in cultural theory and politics at the moment, and must be displaced."[6]

Whereas some early arguments against and subsequent arguments for essentialism share a commitment to transformation, critiques of essentialism lost their political moorings and replaced them with academic, institutional ones. Writing critiques of essentialism became less a matter of political principle than an academic identification with postmodernism, deconstruction, and/or (usually or) Lacanian psychoanalysis. Lacan's antiessentialism has little to do with changing the relation between the sexes, because it maintains that woman must occupy an immutable place in order that the subject gets its fixed bearings. Whereas Juliet MacCannell has put the ahistoricity of Lacanian thinking in question,[7] Lacan's own assumptions about immutability remain. The extent of their necessity is another story.

The thing here is that the word "essentialism" enabled some feminists to reconcile at least two of their psychical identifications, parts of their identity which might otherwise come into conflict. The first is their identification with an apparently political standpoint: being antiessentialist signified commitment to change. The second is their identification with an academic, institutional standpoint: the "critique of essentialism" now signifies familiarity with, knowledge of, a certain psychoanalytic and deconstructive theoretical currency with spending power in the academy. This currency does not rest primarily or even practically on a critique of assumptions about gender immutability.

A terminological note before proceeding: I am using the term "identification" in Freud's sense.[8] Identifications are the stuff out of which the ego is composed. In turn, one meaning of the word "ego" is the identity the subject experiences as belonging to it. Identity, which I will use interchangeably with ego, is composed out of different, usually unconscious, identifications (with groups, parents, lovers, significant living and dead others, nations, institutions, and of course ideas. These identifications can be deep or transitory. This is one of the most interesting things about identification; once one has a concept of it, some of one's unconscious identifications can become conscious, although they are unlikely to reveal themselves to consciousness in all their intricacy (few things do).

Two things about the procedure of identification concern me here. The first is that an identification depends on a received view or a given image. One has to identify with something that already exists and, in that it conveys part of one's self-image, depend on it for one's identity. The second is that the diverse identifications out of which identity is composed have to be made to cohere, in order for identity to be experienced as coherent. Whereas identifications are similar to the "I-slots" discussed by Spivak[9] and Fuss,[10] Freud's emphasis is not only on their diversity but on their synthesis also. Whatever the theoretical arguments against identity as a coherent notion, experiencing an incoherent identity is not pleasant.

But this coherence has its price. It means that the often contradictory implications of different identifications have to be papered over, and the result is often a refusal to think through certain ideas, dependent on certain identifications, past the point where their logical incompatibilities become apparent. So that whereas this refusal results in a stability of identity, it also results in fixed points, ideas we refuse to entertain because of the fixity they threaten. Nor is fixity limited to incompatible ideas.

Fixity, in fact, is the price extracted by an identity that depends on an identification with another (person, institution, ideas). This means it is the price extracted by any identity at all. This is not to say one can dispense with identity; it is just that one can be aware, at least in theory, of the costs of maintaining the illusion of coherence.

My argument that the concept of essentialism has been used to enable conflicting identifications to cohere is a two-edged argument. On the one hand, it is an argument that assumes identity is constructed; in that sense, it is antiessentialist. On the other hand, it is an argument that the concept of essentialism has been used to block movement in feminist debates. Other concepts have been used in similar ways. "History," "metanarrative," and so on, have all produced their moments of self-conscious inhibition. In my terms, they produce fixed points which, although they serve as reference points for identity, also restrict movement.

But then, how do we move at all? In other words, if one depends on identification with received ideas, and other personal and social reference points, if the stability of identity depends on an artificial coherence that creates fixed reference points in thought (and action), how do we know, do, or write anything at odds with a received view? How do we explain those moments or movements which escape from the compound of existing identifications?

As I indicated, I want to begin answering this question by divorcing two key ingredients in proessentialist argumentation: commonality and identity. I want to propose that what enables us to move is also what we have in common. I am also proposing that what restricts this movement is the other factor called upon in some essentialist reasoning: identity and its maintenance. In other words, I want to suggest that something held in common disrupts identity and existing identifications. In suggesting this, I am not pretending that either the idea or its implications have been fully thought through, but it might help move the sclerotica in the present debate.

The something-held-in-common is unconscious more than conscious, and present in (and I think among) human beings. I want to give a brief illustration of how this "something" disrupts subjective conscious intention and thereby disrupts the intention that stems from conscious identity. I will then turn to Freud for some support for the idea of this unconscious moving force and suggest why it has to be a common one.

In the experience of writing, it is sometimes the case that what ends up on the page has nothing to do with the paper that was planned. Now I am told that there are people who know what they are going to say when they start writing and say exactly that. But these people are what we might term perfect subjects—perfect in that their identity and its accompanying preconceptions are never disrupted. They will have difficulty crediting the existence of something that disrupts subjective conscious intention.

Those who have felt taken over and have been disconcerted as their argument unfolded in another direction altogether from the one they anticipated will give me more license. Of course, once an unplanned idea or argument unfolds it is conscious. It is also new, at least to the one writing it. It need not, however, be new to others writing at the same time, which raises an interesting point. Ideas often occur to more than one person simultaneously, even though there is no connection or communication between the people involved, but where do they come from? The ego, one's conscious identity, is generally unimpressed with this question, especially if it has done the writing. But it remains a question. Let us look at whether the theory of the unconscious has anything to tell us about it.

Throughout his *Papers on Technique,* Freud discusses the relationship between unconscious processes and the resistances and censorship imposed by the ego as a "struggle,"[11] or a battle in which "The patient brings out of the armory of the past the weapons with which he defends himself against the progress of the treatment. . . ."[12]

This struggle metaphor poses a problem. It is partly a trick of the English translation that one tends to think of "the unconscious" as a delimited identity, consisting of the contents of what is repressed and, moreover, to think of the unconscious as the obstacle to the realization of ideas and perceptions which would otherwise be available to consciousness. Freud's main metapsychological statement on the unconscious is titled "*Das Unbewusste.*"[13] The German word *Unbewusste* has the grammatical form of a passive participle. It has more the sense of that which is "not consciously known."[14] The German puts the emphasis on consciousness as the agency which fails to know, rather than on "the unconscious" as the force which withholds information. This suggests that one meaning of Freud's notion of the "struggle" is that unconscious processes and information desire to make themselves known to consciousness.

Yet Freud's main and most familiar sense of the unconscious is that it is contingent on repression. Repression, as Lacan and Klein have shown us, is the condition of maintaining a distinct and moderately functional identity. Certain ideas and perceptions have to be excluded, and those which are excluded are those which are incompatible with the subject's identity. The most famous of these ideas and perceptions are the repressed sexual wishes, which seek to make themselves known to consciousness and lead to a battle of their own in the form of symptoms.

But Freud lists other, more timely factors on the side of the struggle for consciousness. On the side of health, the desire to consciously know, he places the patient's wish to be free of suffering, the "love of truth,"[15] the capacity to consider new information thoughtfully, and the belief that the future can be better.[16] Whether these forces, like the repressed wish, are unconscious is not addressed.

But if one thinks about it, the wish to be free of suffering, optimism about the future, openness to new ideas, even the "love of truth," if the lie is literally mortifying, are all on the side of living. I think they embody the unconscious "life-drive," a concept Freud never explained much but adduced; something had to counter the death-drive.[17] If one drive drove us toward death, the other opposed it. Freud thought death was on the side of fixity and repetition. He stopped short of saying it was on the side of the ego, although his reasoning implied that the life-drive was unfriendly to the ego or distinct identity in other ways.[18] The poet Rilke reasoned similarly. Reflecting on a moving force in the form of the terrible Angel of Inspiration, an exhausted Rilke still begged to point out that humans are finite, they need to be loved, they get tired, too much of life can kill them, and other things that are incomprehensible to Angels.

However they are experienced—in writing, active loving, or the battle of the treatment—the lively factors or forces Freud identified disturb current identity. They have to; they are on the side which will help disrupt the subject's preordained conscious beliefs. Yet there is nothing about the life-drive itself that means it has a specific content; it is an energetic force that seeks opportunities to keep living. Because it competes with consciousness, with fixed ideas, it has none of the defining properties that mark out fixed identities, which are necessarily composed of fixed points.

What I need to address now is the idea that this life-drive (although I prefer to call it a moving force) is held in common. By this, I do not mean that it is essentially the same in everyone. I also mean that it connects being to being.[19] Freud's work was severely limited by the illusion that subjects were energetically self-contained. He needed some notion of a common life-drive between beings to explain why the health (his term) of some suffered, whereas others benefited, through identifications with the same social constellation: the heterosexual family. He could have explained it if he had allowed that some positions in that family gained energy through the attention of others; it was not only that those who gained had less to repress. By the same token, repression is not only self-imposed; one can be on the receiving end of an image from the other that represses or fixes.[20]

If the "unconscious" is not only an obstacle but also the vehicle for a moving force held in common, it is both the life-drive, as an energetic stream of disruptive perceptions and ideas on the one hand, and a series of repressed blocks or fixed points on the other. As a moving force, the unconscious might make its effects felt most at those moments of political change when distinct identities (with their endless ego politics and paranoias) are submerged in a collective aim.[21] Such submergence, with all its anonymity and generous folly, marked the beginnings of the women's movement. Similarly, apart from figuring in the battle of the treatment, the optimism and wish to be free of suffering that embody the life-drive also characterized that movement.

But precisely because it motivates any movement for living change, the life-drive is not specifically feminine. It is an essence in the sense that essence means being. In other words, whereas it is essential in the substantial energetic sense of the term, it is also precisely common to all beings. But because it is counterposed to fixity, it is more likely to make itself felt in those who need to move in order to survive. These, preeminently, are people of color and women without power. They have more to gain by disrupting fixity, in identity and ideas, to the extent that disruption means redistributing energy in ways that help them move.

I should stress here, for this is vital, that this redistribution is not only a matter of psychic energy; psychical fixity is reinforced massively by socioeconomic forces which can make it close to impossible to escape from a deadening identification, without a corresponding change in socioeconomic position. Psychic and monetary economies are closely connected in energetic experience, as anyone who has been unemployed, let alone unsure how to survive, knows well. Monetary economic anxiety means that even more energetic attention is given to those who already benefit from their psychical positioning. On a lesser scale, the same is true of anxiety over institutional placement. There is good practical reason for identifying with some ideas and their established exponents rather than others.

But institutional pragmatism aside, there is still a psychical problem with how it is that fresh ideas emerge. In one respect, it is not a problem that is easily solved because everything that comes from the unconscious is already circumscribed by the range of available representations. As we learn from Freud, it is, for example, only the *impulse* to dream which comes from the unconscious. The means for *representing* the impulse comes from the preconscious. The thoughts in which this impulse takes shape and the language in which it expresses itself are given to it by the preconscious.[22]

As this example from the dream is illuminating for the fresh ideas problem, I will, at the risk of digression, stay with it for another paragraph or two. Whatever the information or force arising from the impulse to dream, it may only express itself in thoughts which have been constituted by the subject at some point, even if they are later repressed. Hence we can see part of the difficulty in any systematic elaboration of ideas which tell a truth about the subject, especially if they are ideas the subject does not want to know about. In principle then, thinking is restricted by the fact that we are always thinking in established linguistic terms. This, perhaps, is another way of saying what Caverero says when she writes:

> Her language is not *hers*. She therefore speaks and represents herself in a language not her own, that is, through the categories of the language of the other. She thinks herself as thought by the other. . . .[23]

Nonetheless, we do have a notion of an *impulse* from the unconscious which seeks expression. I am tying this impulse to the moving force, the life-drive. This drive plays with the available range of representations to find a way through those of them that are deadening. This means that the common moving force, the life-drive, seeks to express itself despite the obstacles of available language and the censorship imposed upon it. Perhaps the only way it can do this is by shifting the energetic emphasis on different ideas, which brings them into different alignments which open out novel perspectives. Energetic shifts may also be why something we have only half-formulated, been vaguely aware of, or even always known can strike us with a force it lacked hitherto. But this notion of energetic shifts, as with everything else I have written here about a moving force, life-drive, Spinoza's One Substance, Nietzsche's will and necessity, whatever you call it, can only be inferred. But the basis for the inference is strong: Something has to be the source of the energy we move with and of the perceptions that conflict with the subject's constructed view of itself, others, and reality. We can infer too that these perceptive ideas are not readily available to consciousness. They have to be fought for.

In psychoanalytic treatment, fresh thoughts (insights, as we say in the trade) are won when the wishes that were bound to the past are brought into the present. How they are won in everyday life is another question; but I suggest that the extent to which they are won is a measure of how far a given identity is fixed onto ideas which deaden it. For that matter, overcoming the obstacles that stand between fresh ideas and consciousness is what makes acting, thinking, and writing into a labor.[24] In this labor, the ideas that emerge are less the source of personal credit than is the labor of letting them through. This labor, and labor is always an energetic process, is one which involves moving from beneath the weight of imposed ideas, moving from the fixed position in any relational, institutional, or intellectual context.

Thus far, I hope it is clear, or clear enough, why the above account provides material for arguments for and against essentialism. As an argument for it, it is an argument that depends on a notion of a life-drive, an essence of being. Because this essence disrupts constructed identities, it must be available outside the confines of those identities; if only in this sense, it is communal.

Yet of course this communality leaves us with a community as large and vague as humanity (and maybe nature) in general, which means the question becomes: What is the political point in drawing attention to this common moving force? The point is that the various identities that are constructed in relation to that moving force do not all benefit from it equally. How far perceptions and ideas from this common source are permitted expression depends on the construction that is the foundation of a given identity. Obviously, identities vary in what they permit and exclude, but they also vary in terms of how far they benefit or suffer energetically from others through what they give or impose, and what they have to gain through rejecting those impositions. The process of uncoupling and re-making existing identifications may mean that the benefits of movement can make themselves felt to those who carry the weight of stultifying ideas and imposing others, intrapsychically and intersubjectively.

The last points to be made are straightforward but necessary. Because identities are composed of identifications, one can conclude that how far the ideas that disrupt an existing identity are permitted self-expression will depend on whether a new or hitherto repressed or unrecognized identification will give them a way out that had been foreclosed. For instance, in making this argument in a certain way, I am depending on Freud for an identification which will help me situate myself and sustain my identity as I write. But whether what results is useful depends on how far it goes beyond straightforward recapitulation and releases me from a constraining way of thinking and acting.

Of course I can attribute ideas which are not Freud's to Freud and thus go beyond recapitulation while keeping the security of a recognized name. Actually this device is quite common. Felman writes off some of her labor to Lacan, Cornell writes off some of hers to Derrida, Butler to Foucault, and so on. But the intra- and interpsychical politics of this are not the present issue, except for this: Moving beyond an existing identification requires another identification which will effect the shift. It requires it because identifications are also reference points. These are needed to stay relatively sane and remain in communication with others who recognize similar reference points.

This means that people move beyond existing positions through what we may call facilitating identifications. The content of these identifications might be called essentialist, but this misses the point of what they facilitate. If an identification permits ideas and perceptions, which have to be commonly available, entrance to identities which have suppressed or excluded them, or a way of bypassing discourses which tacitly deny their existence, that identification is the vehicle for political and intellectual movement. So political change does not depend on the subjective claim, "that is our/my essence or identity." But it probably does depend on thinking, "I or we identify with that."

If, in thinking this, in making that identification, an essential moving force is released in a productive way, that identification takes us further than we are now. It is most likely to be released in a political movement when one relies on a common point of identification with others (as "women," "women of color," "lesbians"). Such identifications in themselves run counter to the fixed ego's sense of its uniqueness, which is usually imperiled by its likeness to another. A common identification allows otherwise jostling, supposedly self-contained identities that do not want to know about their similarities to come together. But common identifications only release a shared moving force for a time. Such identifications settle too soon into the structures and fixed securities that are so friendly to identity; then likeness turns to dislike, passion to paranoia, and excitement to fear.

By this account, "our essence" is not the exclusive property of women, or any other real or imagined group. At the same time, as I indicated at the outset, those arguing for another look at essentialism were also, often, opposing fixity in debate. In this, they are on the side of life and of a moving force for change. It is possible to be on this side without believing that the essence of women is life-giving and life-fostering, and even have some sympathy for how that rather nauseous idea gathers the support it does. It is a kind of category mistake, a way of saying that deadening ideas and impositions have to be resisted, that what matters in the end is living.

Notes

1. J. Butler, *Gender Trouble: Feminism and the Subversion of Identity* (New York and London: Routledge, 1990).

2. T. de Lauretis, "The Essence of the Triangle or, Taking the Risk of Essentialism Seriously: Feminist Theory in Italy, the U.S., and Britain," in *The Essential Difference*, Naomi Schor and Elizabeth Weed, eds. (Bloomington and

Indianapolis: Indiana University Press, 1994), 1–39; and N. Schor, "This Essentialism Which Is Not One: Coming to Grips with Irigaray," in *The Essential Difference*, 40–62.

3. D. Fuss, "Reading Like a Feminist," in *The Essential Difference*, 98–115; and D. Cornell, *Beyond Accommodation: Ethical Feminism, Deconstruction and the Law* (New York and London: Routledge, 1991).

4. This, and much of the argument in the next few pages, summarize T. Brennan, "Introduction," in *Between Feminism and Psychoanalysis*, Teresa Brennan, ed. (London and New York: Routledge, 1989).

5. M. Quayle, *The New York Times*, Op Ed (September 11, 1992).

6. M. Russo, *The Female Grotesque: Risk, Excess and Modernity* (London and New York: Routledge, 1994), 198 n. 20.

7. J. F. MacCannell, *The Regime of the Brother: After the Patriarchy* (London and New York: Routledge, 1991).

8. S. Freud, *Group Psychology and the Analysis of the Ego, SE*, vol. 19, 1921.

9. G. C. Spivak, *In Other Worlds: Essays in Cultural Politics* (New York and London: Methuen, 1987); and "In a Word" (interview with Ellen Rooney), in *The Essential Difference*, 151–84.

10. Fuss, "Reading Like a Feminist."

11. S. Freud, "On Beginning the Treatment (Further Recommendations on the Technique of Psycho-Analysis, I)," *SE*, vol. 12, 1913: 123–44.

12. S. Freud, "Remembering, Repeating and Working-Through (Further Recommendations on the Technique of Psycho-Analysis, II)," *SE*, vol. 12, 1914: 147–57.

13. S. Freud, "The Unconscious," *SE*, vol. 14, 1915: 166–204.

14. Ibid., 165 n. 1.

15. S. Freud, "Analysis Terminable and Interminable," *SE*, vol. 23, 1937:248.

16. S. Freud, "Remembering, Repeating and Working-Through," 152 and passim.

17. S. Freud, *Beyond the Pleasure Principle, SE*, vol. 18, 1920.

18. Freud claimed that the life-drive was on the side of the species, against the individual ego (Freud, *Beyond the Pleasure Principle*). Thus the life-drive was on the side of sex, which diverted libidinal attention away from oneself and onto the other. But it is unnecessary to follow Freud on this one, with its procreative implications, to keep the opposition between egoic intentionality and the life-drive. Cf. Lacan, "Some Reflections on the Ego," *International Journal of Psycho-Analysis* 34 (1953): 11–17. Lacan, who recognizes the opposition, goes so far as to say that the life-drive is really the death-drive as far as the ego is concerned. Once detailed, Freud's position on the life-drive is thoroughly contradictory. On the one hand he associates it with procreation. On the other, he associates it with all sex. If the life-drive is expressed in all sex (as Eros) and if it is opposed to imposed identities, this should mean that the imposition of a normative sexual identity could block it. This holds preeminently for psychoanalytic treatment.

19. The life-drive's commonality may bring Jung's notion of a collective unconscious to mind. But what Jung had in mind was more a matter of collective content (archetypes). The notion of a common unconscious force, as a life-drive,

is about energetic connections as much as contents. And if this idea is still embarrassing, the embarrassment may owe less to any evocation of the unstylish Jung than to the nature of constructed identity, the conscious ego itself. The ego is the vehicle for the self-consciousness, embarrassment, and consciousness of social and theoretical appropriateness. It also depends on the illusion of self-containment, and this illusion is jeopardized the moment one allows that one's energy, let alone one's feelings and ideas, could be part of a force common to others.

20. See my *Interpretation of the Flesh: Freud and Femininity* (New York: Routledge, 1992) for a theory of how the "individual" comes to be bound; in other words, to experience itself as self-contained through the "fixing" images it receives.

21. Alice Jardine, in kinder language, charts a similar phenomenon in the increasing preoccupation with institutional status that marks feminist scholarship. See A. Jardine, "Notes for an Analysis," in *Between Feminism and Psychoanalysis.* Teresa Brennan, ed. (London and New York: Routledge, 1989), 73–85.

22. S. Freud, *The Interpretation of Dreams, SE,* vols. 4–5, 562. Freud's fluctuations (especially in "The Unconscious") about whether or not a drive was a psychical representation of psychical energy, or a direct manifestation of that energy, could be a reflection of this difficulty: The only language available to the impulse is the language that also censors it.

23. A. Caverero, cited in de Lauretis, "The Essence of the Triangle," 15.

24. Of course this possibility depends on how labor is defined. Marx defined it as the expenditure of the energy in the face of a sensuousness that resists it. See K. Marx, *Economic and Philosophic Manuscripts of 1844,* M. Milligan, trans. (Moscow: Progress Publishers, 1959), 97 and passim. By labor I mean the opposition (drawing on the senses) to what Lacan elliptically refers to as the ego's "inertia" (Lacan, "Some Reflections on the Ego," 12).

Bibliography

Brennan, T. "Introduction," in *Between Feminism and Psychoanalysis.* Teresa Brennan, ed. London and New York: Routledge, 1989.
———. *The Interpretation of the Flesh: Freud and Femininity.* New York: Routledge, 1992.
Butler, J. *Gender Trouble: Feminism and the Subversion of Identity.* New York and London: Routledge, 1990.
———. *Bodies that Matter.* New York and London: Routledge, 1993.
Cornell, D. *Beyond Accommodation: Ethical Feminism, Deconstruction and the Law.* New York and London: Routledge, 1991.
de Lauretis, T. "The Essence of the Triangle or, Taking the Risk of Essentialism Seriously: Feminist Theory in Italy, the U.S., and Britain," in *The Essential Difference.* Naomi Schor and Elizabeth Weed, eds., Bloomington and Indianapolis: Indiana University Press, 1994, 1–39.

Felman, S. *Jacques Lacan and the Adventure of Insight.* Cambridge, Mass.: Harvard University Press, 1987.

Freud, S. *The Standard Edition of the Complete Psychological Works of Sigmund Freud,* translated and edited by James Strachey in collaboration with Anna Freud, assisted by Alix Strachey and Alan Tyson. London: The Hogarth Press and the Institute of Psycho-analysis, 24 vols. (1953–74) (*SE*).

———. *The Interpretation of Dreams. SE.* Vols. 4–5. 1900.

———. "On Beginning the Treatment (Further Recommendations on the Technique of Psycho-Analysis, I)." *SE* Vol. 12. 1913: 123–44.

———. "Remembering, Repeating and Working-Through (Further Recommendations on the Technique of Psycho-Analysis, II)." *SE* Vol. 12. 1914: 147–57.

———. "The Unconscious." *SE* Vol. 14. 1915: 166–204.

———. *Beyond the Pleasure Principle. SE.* Vol 18. 1920.

———. *Group Psychology and the Analysis of the Ego. SE.* Vol. 19. 1921.

———. "Analysis Terminable and Interminable." *SE.* Vol. 23. 1937: 216–53.

Fuss, D. "Reading Like a Feminist," in *The Essential Difference.* Naomi Schor and Elizabeth Weed, eds. Bloomington and Indianapolis: Indiana University Press, 1994: 98–115.

Hampshire, S. *Spinoza.* Harmondsworth, England: Penguin, 1976.

Jardine, A. "Notes for an Analysis," in *Between Feminism and Psychoanalysis.* Teresa Brennan, ed. London and New York: Routledge, 1989: 73–85.

Lacan, J. "Some Reflections on the Ego." *International Journal of Psycho-Analysis* 34 (1953): 11–17.

———. "La direction de la cure et les principes de son pouvoir," in *Écrits.* Paris: Seuil, 1966: 585–645, translated as "The direction of the treatment and the principles of its power," in J. Lacan. *Écrits: A Selection.* A. Sheridan, trans. London: Tavistock, 1977: 226–80.

MacCannell, J. F. *The Regime of the Brother: After the Patriarchy.* London and New York: Routledge, 1991.

Marx, K. *Economic and Philosophic Manuscripts of 1844.* M. Milligan, trans. Moscow: Progress Publishers, 1959.

Quayle, M. Op Ed. *The New York Times,* September 11, 1992.

Rilke, R. M. *Duineser Elegien.* Leipzig, Germany: Insel Verlag, 1923.

Russo, M. *The Female Grotesque: Risk, Excess and Modernity.* London and New York: Routledge, 1994.

Schor, N. "This Essentialism Which Is Not One: Coming to Grips with Irigaray," in *The Essential Difference.* Naomi Schor and Elizabeth Weed, eds. Bloomington and Indianapolis: Indiana University Press, 1994: 40–62.

Spivak, G. C. *In Other Worlds: Essays in Cultural Politics.* New York and London: Methuen, 1987.

———. "In a Word" (interview with Ellen Rooney), in *The Essential Difference.* Naomi Schor and Elizabeth Weed, eds. Bloomington and Indianapolis: Indiana University Press, 1994: 151–84.

PART 3

ENGENDERING THE SOCIOPOLITICAL BODY

9

Feminist Interpretations of Social and Political Thought

Virginia Held

O bviously, traditional social and political thought needs to be examined for gender bias and needs to be revised. But it was not until feminists demanded that it be examined and revised that its gender bias became apparent to us, because, sadly, established thought throughout the Academy had succeeded in causing earlier feminist thinking to become invisible and forgotten. By the early 1970s, women began to be aware of the *degree* to which we had been excluded from the liberal principles of freedom and equality that were said to guide the systems we lived in. There had been almost no explicit discussion of how all women were left out of the picture drawn by the principles of democracy and no discussion of why such omissions had *not* been corrected.[1] As women began to look at all the ways we did not enjoy equality, glaring inequities leapt into view, and feminists addressed them.

By now, some 20 years later, feminist theorists often suggest that instead of seeing the world and society and everything in it from the point of view of men, and then correcting that view for bias, we ought to try seeing the world and society and everything in it from the point of view of women. Perhaps this view will only be a temporary stage to go through, a period in which we can all gain a correction across the board of the misleading views of the past. But we cannot know whether it will be temporary. Perhaps the point of view of women will turn out to be genuinely better for gaining moral insight and social knowledge, and everyone will be able to recognize this.[2] The perspectives of women

⇢ should be considered not only as a corrective but as offering the possibility of an alternative world view that may be better and truer.

Here as elsewhere, feminist transformations are suggesting new avenues for moral and social inquiry. Traditional moral theory is thought to be oriented around an ethic of justice. Formal principles or abstract rules of justice, autonomy, liberty, and equality are adopted, and moral problems are dealt with in terms of reasoning from such abstract principles; notions of social contract and individual rights are prominent. In the alternative approach being developed by a number of feminists, caring relationships among actual human persons are the basis for interpreting what a particular situation calls for in the way of responsible moral behavior; the reasoning involved is more apt to be narrative and contextual. An "ethic of care" is the phrase which is gathering most support as a way of designating an alternative feminist moral outlook. Although no label seems adequate yet, "care" seems to come closest, and to contrast well with traditional approaches based on rationality, rules, and the conceptualization of morality in terms of such public or political concerns as justice, or liberty, or equality.

In the domain of "particular others" central to the approach of many feminists, relationships are salient, whereas the "self" and "all others" of traditional moral and political theories seem artificial and problematic. Feminists are also questioning the contractual view of society so central to the liberal tradition, and underlying that still growing and imperially expanding field of endeavor known as rational choice theory. From a feminist perspective, society as it exists, and certainly as it ought to exist, can be seen as noncontractual if it includes, as a reasonable view of it would, relationships within the family and between friends. At best, society may contain contractual enclaves, but they should probably be embedded in noncontractual relationships of trust and concern.

Most of those trying to clarify the alternative ethic of care question the individualistic assumptions of much moral theory. A relationship of care or trust between a mother and a child, for instance, cannot be understood in terms of the individual states of each taken in isolation.[3] And the values of relationships cannot be broken down into individual benefits and burdens; we need to assess the worth of relationships themselves. As Carol Gilligan sees it, "Care is grounded in the assumption that self and other are interdependent. . . . The self is by definition connected to others."[4] Further, most of those pursuing the nonindividualistic aspects of feminist theory think that persons are not only deeply affected by their relations with others but are also at least partly or largely constituted by these relations, though we may seek to change them.

What are the implications of such developments for our notions of liberty and equality? To begin with, to the extent that liberty and equality have been developed in contractual terms, they may be deficient for representing the moral considerations most fundamental from a feminist perspective. Liberty and equality may be highly important within certain regions of human interaction, but these regions themselves may be less extensive and less important than has been thought. To the extent that liberty and equality have been formulated in strictly individualistic terms, as in the liberal tradition, we can notice, again, how they fail to provide evaluation of our protections for the *relationships* that may be most central to our human well-being and to our abilities to lead our lives as we, together with those with whom we share our lives, choose.

Many feminists have been concerned with extending principles of liberty and equality to women and to what occurs within the household, so that, for instance, the physical safety of women and children would be protected against domestic violence the way the safety of men as they venture forth into public space has been protected by centuries of legal attention. And feminists emphasize the case for equality between women and men in, for instance, the division of labor needed within the household and in the care of children. These are extraordinarily important issues, and to suggest that liberty and equality are more limited concepts than the tradition of liberal political thought can acknowledge does not diminish at all the need to persist with these arguments and their implementation.

We can, however, understand the ways in which these are efforts to rectify certain serious defects in liberal thought and in existing societies, not ways to give adequate expression to the concerns *we* might take to be central to women in a society that had overcome male dominance. In postpatriarchal society, the moral minimums of personal safety against attack and of fairness in the division of labor might be relatively easy to achieve, and our efforts might be largely devoted to all the valued concerns over and above such minimums: to creating conditions that would be conducive to the flourishing of children, not just protection from injury. We would discuss the ways in which children can *best* grow and develop, sustained by loving relationships, not just by adults who respect the rights of a child not to be assaulted or killed. And in relations between women and men, we would seek the joy and laughter and affection and trust that such relationships can bring over and above the respect for each others' claims to equality.

To take an example: Even in patriarchal society, structured as it is to maintain domination and to take conflict as given, there are many pockets of cooperation. When several women, say, cooperate in an endeavor, there may be minimal levels of a fair distribution of expenditures of money and time that will be met. But such cooperation is often characterized to a much greater extent by shared attention to and interest in aims over and above an equal distribution of burdens and benefits. The focus might be on what might make the endeavor one of *shared* satisfaction, of increased *mutual* understanding. It is by no means to be conceded that this sort of perspective on what is important and what is trivial is suitable only for, say, private outings among friends. Many feminists are now considering how a comparable focus may be suitable for social and political concerns at a much wider level.

Outlooks toward birth and life and death may differ between women and men in significant ways. Let's consider some implications of these possible differences for our concepts of equality and liberty.

Birth and death are obviously central events of human experience. They may have been conceptualized, or misconceptualized, I believe, from a male rather than from a gender-neutral point of view. Death has been understood as an obviously human event, an event associated with what distinguishes us as human beings most clearly from animals. Because we can risk death and choose what to die for and be conscious that we will die, our deaths are distinctively human. We represent this consciousness and this choice in our art, literature, music, and theories of all kinds. Birth, in contrast, has been construed as a natural event, something that happens, and women, in giving birth, are thought of as doing something very similar to what nonhuman animals do when they give birth. This contrast results, I think, from seeing birth and death from the point of view of men. From this perspective, one sees birth in terms of getting born (in terms of one's own beginnings), or one sees it from the point of view of the observer.

All this changes if we see birth from the point of view of those who give birth. From the standpoint of conscious human subject, birth becomes as fully a human event as distinct from a natural one as is death. Women, unlike nonhuman animals, can be fully conscious that we may give birth, or that we have done so. We can give birth, or try to avoid doing so, for as may reasons as men can choose to die or to cause death. From the point of view of those who give birth, birth could be associated with imaginative human representation in art, literature, music and all our theories, as fully as death has always been associated with such imaginative representation.

What might the implications be for equality and liberty? Many conceptions of equality are tied to empirical claims regarding death, Hobbes' view is perhaps the most notorious: All men are vulnerable to the swords of their fellows and hence must recognize each other as equals.[5]

Others may argue for equality on the basis of an abstract moral principle rather than of any empirical description, but their justifications of such a principle often rest on such observations as that we are all not so different: We are all born, feel pain, and die. And as moral and political arguments are extended to women, it may be supposed that such characterizations apply equally to women.

But let us pause. From the point of view of those who give birth, all this changes: *We* give birth, and you do not. This *is* a radical difference, and the fact that you lack this capacity may distort your whole view of the social world. From the point of view of those who give birth, the social, political, economic, legal, educational, cultural, and familial realms should be organized to be, *first of all,* hospitable to children. From this perspective, it seems pathetic that, instead, these realms are seen as contracted for by men equally able to kill or harm one another, or arranged to promote the self-interest of agents in a marketplace, or aimed at satisfying the preferences of individuals conceptualized as existing in isolation from one another. Occasionally, for those who give birth, equality will be an important concept as we strive to treat children fairly and have them treat each other with respect. But it is normally greatly overshadowed by such other concerns as that the relationships between ourselves and our children and each other be trusting and considerate.

And liberty? From the point of view of those who give birth, it is absurd to assume that we are born free. We are born helpless infants and will remain unfree for many years. We are only relatively free if those who have cared for us have empowered us to be so. From the point of view of those who give birth, the familial, cultural, educational, legal, economic, political, and social realms should be organized to assist children to develop in such a way that they will flourish, in harmony with others, growing in their capacity for free expression.

It is obvious that a world of militarized states and armed groups, geared to inflict death on each other's and their own people while they progressively despoil the environment, cannot provide such assistance. And to bring about the kind of world that will indeed allow its children to be free will require transformations far more fundamental than anything envisaged in the tradition that has given us the liberal concepts of liberty and equality.

These are dangerous thoughts. As long as the world is structured and thought of from the point of view of those who do not give birth, then to have a fair chance in this world, women may need to emphasize how little difference it should make that women are those who bear rather then beget, as Plato put it. As long as the social world is structured by and for those who think of themselves as equally vulnerable to the sword of their fellows, or equal abstract rational beings, feminists need to keep in view how extraordinarily important rather than peripheral are the concepts of equality and liberty, both as traditionally understood and as reformed by feminist critiques.

When we dare to give voice, on the other hand, to how we think the world ought to be, we can imagine that whether one adopts the point of view of those who create human life or ignores this point of view may radically change one's perspective about what is most important. From a feminist perspective, the best that could be achieved by attending to the requirements of equality and liberty might fall far short of what an even adequate society needs to provide for the future of the world's children.

Democratic theorists influenced by the Marxist tradition characteristically have a fuller understanding of what it means to live as a free person than do theorists squarely in the liberal tradition. They argue, for instance, that a person cannot be free without the means to live and work and act, and feminist views of liberation appreciate these understandings. The experience of most women makes clear how unsatisfactory is a conception of freedom that does not include access to the means to be free. Clearly, freedom from interference with our possession of property and our exercise of our rights cannot provide the liberation women seek if we have no property and are unable to acquire the means to live and act and to feed our children. But Marxist theories often not only ignore but also obscure a wide range of problems that need to be addressed for women to be able to develop *our* capacities.

Consider, for instance, Sandra Bartky's discussion of a kind of disability that, at least under social conditions so far and in given societies, women are more apt to suffer than men: shame. Bartky considers the shame of embodiment attendant on women's sense of being a spectacle, of being continually on display, but she is concerned with a less specific kind of shame. "This shame," she writes, "is manifest in a pervasive sense of personal inadequacy that, like the shame of embodiment, is profoundly disempowering." She examines the "affective taste, the emotional coloration" of the traits that textbooks in the psychology of women report to be characteristic of women: lower self-esteem, less overall confidence, poorer self-concepts, as measured by women's beliefs and dispositions. She cites a variety of empirical observations to confirm that women experience such disempowering feelings more than men do.[6] The self-development of women involves changing the affective tastes, the emotional coloration, with which we experience the world, not only the outer obstacles in that experience discussed by Marxist social and political theorists.

Consider, next, a kind of transfer of power differing from the one examined by many democratic theorists who, influenced by Marxist critiques, enlighten us on how the transfer of power from the nonowners to owners of capital conflicts with the principles of democracy. Consider the transfer of power in what Ann Ferguson and Nancy Folbre call sex-affective production. In exploring the ways in which Marxist views of production and reproduction need to be reconceptualized from a feminist point of view, they focus their attention on the production of all that is required for childbearing, child rearing, and "the fulfillment of human needs for affection, nurturance, and sexual expression." They discuss the ways women have been oppressed by a division of labor that results in most of the requirements and responsibilities of sex-affective production being met by women. Women are socialized into a gender identity such that their sense of identity "keeps them willing to give more than they receive from men in nurturance and sexual satisfaction."[7] The division of labor providing that the burdens of sex-affective production fall more heavily on women than on men is not a neutral division that assigns separate but equal roles. It is a division that is based on inequality, that is upheld by social relations of domination, and that oppresses women. Without the insights of feminism, democratic theory, even when informed by the insights of Marxism, does not contribute to our understanding of how transforming gender relations may be at least as fundamental a project as transforming relations between the owners of capital and those who must sell their labor.

Feminist theory insists on reconsidering the concept of the person who is to enter into the public life of government or economic activity. There are not two or three separate entities here, a public or a working person, and a private person; there is only one person, involved in and affected by both public and private social realities, however they are understood. And if we must rethink the liberal concept of a person to acknowledge how artificial and male-biased is the individual of classical liberal theory, springing full-blown out of nowhere into a self-sufficiency from which he considers entering into social relations, then of course we must rethink the social and political theory built around this concept of person. And if we must rethink the concept of a person selling his labor, recognizing that it too has been constructed without adequate regard for the labor of those who have created and brought up and continue to care for this worker, then again, we must rethink the social and political theory built around this concept of person.

Feminist theory asks why the relationships among persons in what has mistakenly been relegated to a private sphere beyond public concern should not be considered in the construction of broader social arrangements. Certainly we reject arguing from the patriarchal family to the patriarchal, monarch-headed society, or to a paternalistic workplace. But if we look at the postpatriarchal relations of care and concern that we expect to be possible in family relationships or in relationships among friends, it is not unreasonable to suggest that some perhaps weaker but still analogous versions of these should characterize social relations generally. In place of the development of individual powers that at best do not *diminish* the powers of others—the sort of self-development at which many theorists of democracy would aim—we might aspire to the development of social *relations,* such as relations of trust, or relations of care and concern, of mutually appreciated expression, of shared enjoyment.[8] It is not at all utopian to consider the sorts of political and social institutions that can foster such relations. Feminism is bringing about fundamental transformations in moral theory that will require transformations as well in social, political, economic, and legal theory. From a feminist point of view, radical changes are needed in, for instance, our standard conceptions of reason and emotion, of the public and private, and of persons and their relationships.

It may be that it is our historically located and changeable circumstances that have led women to interpret moral problems more in terms of social relationships between actual persons and less in terms of either abstract rules or individual interests. But it may also be that, on reflection, we will insist on seeing feminist concerns as the framework for moral theory within which other approaches must be fitted, among them the fair treatment of persons thought of as individuals in a political system. And then of course with a feminist approach to what morality requires, we may have a view of what it is that social arrangement should facilitate or foster that will be quite different from the views of any of the currently leading social and political theories. There is a long history of communitarian critiques of the isolated liberal individual. Communitarians have recognized the ways in which persons are constituted by their memberships in communities and the ways in which political life is built on traditions and practices as much as, or rather than, rational agreements.[9] Feminists have compelling reasons to be skeptical of communitarian alternatives to individualism because communitarians have so impoverished an account of how women are to break with traditions that have, throughout history, so oppressed us. To suppose that selves-in-relation can be adequately discussed in terms of independent, isolated entities and their states is misguided, but it is equally misguided to supposes that selves-in-relation are *only* what they are because of the communal, class, or historical contexts in which they are embedded. Relational selves are relational, but they are also capable of radical change.

Parallel points can be made about evaluation. It can neither be satisfactory to value selves-in-relation in terms grounded only in values applicable to independent, isolated individuals *nor* in terms of the values grounded only in the social wholes to which communitarians have attended. An adequate view of human beings involved in personal, political, and social lives will neither absorb us completely into traditional and communal groups nor leave us in the artificial isolation of liberal individualism. Democracy should be a way of life for persons understood as inherently relational *and* capable of transformation.

Notes

This paper is based on two chapters of my book *Feminist Morality: Transforming Culture, Society, and Politics* (Chicago: University of Chicago Press, 1993).

1. For an account of the treatment of women in the history of political thought, and how its assumptions persist, see Susan Moller Okin, *Women in Western Political Thought* (Princeton: Princeton University Press, 1979); Lorenne Clark and Lynda Lange, eds., *The Sexism of Social and Political Theory: Women and Reproduction from Plato to Nietzsche* (Toronto: University of Toronto Press, 1979); Carole Pateman and Elizabeth Gross, eds., *Feminist Challenges: Social and Political Theory* (Sydney, Australia: Allen and Unwin, 1986); Jean Bethke Elshtain, *Public Man, Private Woman* (Princeton: Princeton University Press, 1981); and Mary Lyndon Shanley and Carole Pateman, eds., *Feminist Interpretations and Political Theory* (University Park: Pennsylvania State University Press, 1991). For a detailed discussion of theoretical issues concerning women's lack of legal equality in the nineteenth century, see Mary Lyndon Shanley, *Feminism, Marriage, and the Law in Victorian England: 1850–1895* (Princeton: Princeton University Press, 1989).

2. See Nancy C. M. Hartsock, "The Feminist Standpoint: Developing the Ground for a Specifically Feminist Historical Materialism," in *Discovering Reality: Feminist Perspectives on Epistemology, Metaphysics, Methodology and Philosophy of Science*, Sandra Harding and Merrill B. Hintikka, eds. (Dordrecht, Holland: Reidel, 1983).

3. For a relevant discussion see Naomi Scheman, "Individualism and the Objects of Psychology," in *Discovering Reality*, Harding and Hintikka, eds.

4. Carol Gilligan, "Moral Orientation and Moral Development," in *Women and Moral Theory*, Eva Feder Kittay and Diana T. Meyers, eds. (Totowa, N.J.: Rowman and Littlefield, 1987), 24.

5. Thomas Hobbes, *Leviathan*, C. B. Macpherson, ed. (Baltimore, Md.: Penguin Books, 1971).

6. Sandra Lee Bartky, *Femininity and Domination: Studies in the Phenomenology of Oppression* (New York: Routledge, 1991), chapter 6.

7. Ann Ferguson and Nancy Folbre, "The Unhappy Marriage of Patriarchy and Capitalism," in *Women and Revolution*, Lydia Sargent, ed. (Boston: South End

Press, 1981), 317, 319. See also Ann Ferguson, "On Conceiving Motherhood and Sexuality," in *Mothering: Essays in Feminist Theory,* Joyce Trebilcot, ed. (Totowa, N.J.: Rowman and Allenheld, 1984); and Ann Ferguson, *Blood at the Root: Motherhood, Sexuality and Male Domination* (London: Pandora, 1989).

8. Jane Mansbridge examines two types of democracy: "adversary democracy," where interests conflict, and "unitary democracy," where interests are shared. She provides an enlightening critique of the way prevailing democratic theory regularly assumes that interests conflict. Feminist views of democracy would surely give more emphasis to the kind of participatory democracies Mansbridge studied, in which the ultimate concern was what was thought of as solidarity, community, fraternity, or sisterhood. "It was from this concern," Mansbridge writes, "that their commitment to equality, face-to-face assembly, and consensus are primarily derived." Jane Mansbridge, *Beyond Adversary Democracy* (Chicago: University of Chicago Press, 1983), viii.

9. See Alasdair MacIntyre, *After Virtue: A Study in Moral Theory* (Notre Dame, Ind.: University of Notre Dame Press, 1981); and Michael J. Sandel, *Liberalism and the Limits of Justice* (Cambridge, England: Cambridge University Press, 1982).

10

Mothers, Citizenship, and Independence: A Critique of Pure Family Values

Iris Marion Young

n recent years in the United States, many liberals have joined conservatives in espousing "family values" as the moral foundation of peace and prosperity. This philosophy says that the "intact," two-parent, heterosexual family is the preferred family form. Although this is not good news for gay men and lesbians, it also devalues all single mothers, and by implication all mothers. In this essay I assess the implications of the family values discourse for the citizenship status of mothers by means of an examination of the writing of one its most articulate and liberal proponents, William Galston.

In his book, *Liberal Purposes*, Galston argues that law and public policy cannot and should not be neutral among ends and legitimately ought to encourage in its citizens the virtues consistent with the social good.[1] He infers from this general position that the liberal state ought to privilege the "intact, two-parent" family. This particular family structure, he argues, best promotes the welfare of children and enables them to become good citizens. The state is therefore justified in implementing policies that encourage marriage and discourage divorce and single motherhood. Galston's argument for the moral preeminence of the intact, two-parent family has both empirical and normative aspects. I first examine some of his empirical claims that divorce and single motherhood have bad social consequences and show that the evidence is much more ambiguous than he allows. I concentrate on the normative dimensions of Galston's argument, which hinge on the citizen virtue of independence.

Review of the role of the norm of independence in modern political theory reveals it as male biased and operative in relegating dependent people and their usually female caretakers to an inferior status. Contrary to Galston, promoting equal citizenship requires abandoning the idea that those who are not self-sufficient are of lesser worth. On the contrary, public policy should provide social support to promote the autonomy of the people who need help from others. Only such an abandonment of the norm of independence understood as self-sufficiency can grant equal citizenship to at-home caretakers and people who, for whatever reason, are unable completely to support or take care of themselves. Liberals must affirm a plurality of family forms as valid ways of life. By virtue of its structure, no one family form is inherently better at realizing the values of family life. I conclude by discussing some general implications of this argument for public policy.

I

In arguing for the moral superiority of stable marriage, Galston distinguishes what he calls intrinsic traditionalism from functional traditionalism. Intrinsic traditionalism promotes particular institutional forms and individual behavior simply because they conform with past practice, the precepts of religion, or the commands of some other authority adhered to without reason or criticism. Functional traditionalism, on the other hand,

> rests its case on asserted links between certain moral principles and public virtues or institutions needed for the successful functioning of a liberal community. So, for example, an intrinsic traditionalist might deplore divorce as a violation of divine law, whereas a functional traditionalist might object to it on the grounds (for which considerable empirical evidence can be adduced) that children in divorced families tend to suffer the kinds of economic and psychological damage that reduce their capability to become independent and contributing members of the community. (280)

If a plausible link can be established between a particular family form and the ability of children to take their place as good citizens—independent and contributing members of the community, Galston asserts—this justifies the state's preference for that family form and perhaps even limits the liberty of adults to raise children under other conditions.

Just as parental freedom does not include the right to beat or starve your child, or to treat your child in a manner that will impede normal development, so "you are not free to act in ways that will lead your child to impose significant and avoidable burdens on the community" (252). Consequently, the freedom of parents should be subordinate to the state aim of raising good citizens:

> My focus is on what must be a key objective of our society: raising children who are prepared—intellectually, physically, morally, and emotionally—to take their place as law-abiding and independent citizens. Available evidence supports the conclusion that on balance, the intact, two-parent family is best suited to this task. (285)

The divorce rate in the United States jumped very significantly between 1970 and 1975, peaked in 1981, and since then has been declining back to the 1975 level of 4.7 divorces per 1,000 married couples per year.[2]

The number of children affected by divorce has remained roughly constant since 1975 at approximately 1 million each year. Galston claims that there is strong evidence to support the claim that divorce causes lasting emotional distress in children. He cites a study by Wallerstein and Blakeslee for this evidence. They followed about 60 children of divorce for 10 years and claimed to find that the experience of divorce in adolescence causes a lack of confidence and an inability to sustain relationships in adulthood.[3] This study has been criticized for its small sample, the fact that all the subjects were in therapy at the start of the study, and the fact that there are no comparisons with children from intact families.[4]

A wider look at the literature reveals a much more ambiguous picture of the effects (or lack of effects) of divorce on the capacities and character of children. Some demographic studies show greater risk of school dropout, career and income disadvantage, and greater rates of teen pregnancy for children of divorce than for children of stable marriage, but others find few differences on a range of academic, developmental, emotional, and health measures. Some longitudinal studies find poorer adjustment for adolescent children of divorce, but others find no relationships.[5] Where differences between children of divorce and those from intact families on measures of well-being are found, they are usually rather small. One metanalysis of 92 mostly American studies finds children of divorce to have only slightly lower levels of well-being than those from intact families.[6]

When children of divorce do suffer emotional damage, moreover, it may be that family conflict, rather that divorce itself, is the cause. A 10-year-long study recently released in Australia found no significant differences between children of divorce and children of continuing marriage in level of academic achievement, career success, or ability to enter and maintain intimate relationships. It found that emotional distress tended to be associated with family conflict, whether it resulted in divorce or not, and that even the effects of conflict are offset by a strong relationship between the child and at least one of the parents.[7]

One of the policy recommendations that Galston makes for regulating family life for the sake of raising good citizens is to make divorce more difficult to obtain. Given the very mixed record on the effects of divorce on children, surely it is questionable that the state has a legitimate right to limit the liberty of unhappily married adults to sever their relationship. If family conflict, instead of divorce itself, is a likelier cause of emotional distress in children, moreover, encouraging parents to stay together when they don't want to may cause more harm in children than allowing them to divorce in as simple and peaceful a manner as possible.[8]

Galston argues that not only divorce but also single parenthood, whether the parent has been married or not, is bad for children. In 1992, 26 percent of families with children in the United States were headed by single parents; only 4 percent of all families were headed by unmarried men, whereas 22 percent were headed by unmarried women.[9] Many single-parent families are created by divorce; in 1992, 14 percent of American children lived with a divorced or separated mother only. Because so much of family values discourse is laced with race, I will note that 22 percent of black children were living with a divorced or separated mother, and 13 percent of white children.[10]

Recent discussions of family values, however, focus more on single-mother families created by births to unmarried women. Galston is not alone in suggesting that this "illegitimacy" is on the rise and is destroying the moral fabric of society. So let us dwell for a moment on the facts about births to unmarried women. In 1990, 26 percent of all births in the United States were to unmarried women. Contrary to the image that "illegitimacy" is a black people's phenomenon, 56 percent of these women were white and 41 percent were African American.[11] Again contrary to popular image, the rate of births to unmarried black mothers has been falling in the last 20 years and rising very significantly among white mothers. The proportion of births to unmarried African American mothers is still far higher than to unmarried white mothers, but the gap has been steadily narrowing. The proportion of births to unmarried mothers in relation to all births has been rising significantly in the last decade, largely because married couples are having significantly fewer children.[12]

Popular imagery also assumes that most unwed mothers are black teenagers. There was a significant decline in births to unmarried black teenagers from 1970 to 1986, however, and births to unmarried white teenagers more than doubled during the same period. The proportion of teens among unwed mothers has been declining steadily, moreover; in 1990 more than two-thirds of births to unwed mothers were women 20 years and older. Birth rates among unmarried white women between the ages of 30 and 34 have doubled between 1980 and 1987; among all other races there was only a modest increase in this age bracket.[13]

Thus, unwed motherhood has become a mainstream American phenomenon, not confined to any particular age, race, or educational attainment. Divorce when children are present increased significantly in the 1970s but leveled off in the 1980s and occurs among all races, ages, regions, and income groups. As a result of all these trends, some people estimate that, among children born in the late 1970s, 42 percent of whites and 86 percent of blacks will spend some time in a single-parent family.[14] The single-parent family form, primarily of single mothers, is common in American society, and increasingly common in many other societies in the world today.

Galston claims that the single-parent family is bad for children. He and others suggest that children of single parents have less emotional and intellectual support, and receive less supervision, than do children in two-parent families.[15] It is certainly plausible to claim that parenting is easier and more effective if two of more adults discuss the children's needs and provide different kinds of interactions for children. It does not follow that the second adult must be a live-in husband, however, and some studies have found that the addition of any adult to a single-parent household, whether a relative, lover, or friend, tends to offset single-parent tendencies to relinquish parental decision making too early.[16]

Whereas Galston claims that the evidence is clear that single-parent families are worse for children than intact, two-parent families, many others find the evidence to be more ambiguous. It seems more likely that single-parent families are better for children in some respects and not better in others. For example, although adults in single-parent families tend to spend less time supervising homework, at the same time single parents are less likely to pressure their children into social conformity and are more likely to praise good grades.[17] Children in single-mother households may suffer disadvantages associated with stress on that one parent, but there may also be advantages to single-parent families, such as a greater closeness between parent and child or greater emotional maturity than children have in two-parent families.[18] Growing up in a single-parent family may be a handicap, but having numerous siblings in a two-parent family is also a handicap. Because single parents have fewer children, these two family forms may be comparable in their consequences for children.[19]

Galston's main reason for claiming that single parenthood is bad for children, however, is less contestable. Children in single-mother families are much more likely to be poor than families headed by men. In 1990, 44.7 percent of women-maintained households with children were in poverty, compared with about 7.7 percent of male-headed households. Black single mothers are more likely to be poor, but white single mothers are also at high risk; in 1990, 48 percent of black female-headed households were poor, compared with 27 percent of white female-headed families.[20] More than half of single mothers with a high school education or less are poor, regardless of their race or age.[21]

The primary income for most of these children comes from their mothers. Court-ordered child support awards averaged only $2,100 per family in 1985, and many fathers failed to pay.[22] The primary cause of the poverty of children in single-parent households is women's lack of earning power. In 1990, the median weekly pay for women 25 years and older was $400, compared with $539 for men.[23] About 40 percent of women maintaining households alone are full-time, year-round workers, and another 27 percent work seasonally or part-time. But more than 21 percent of families headed by employed women have incomes below the poverty threshold, compared with 4 percent of families headed by an employed man.[24] Jenks estimates that, if we wanted to ensure that every full-time, employed single mother could live a life of minimum subsistence for herself and two children on her earnings alone, we would have needed a minimum wage of $9 per hour in 1988. Unless the woman has a college degree, she is likely to earn more like $6.50 per hour, and if she does not have a high school diploma she earns an average of $4.10 per hour.[25]

One-third of all single mothers do not participate in the official labor force. (There is no way of telling how many of these women earn income in informal markets, and many of them do.) Some cannot get jobs because jobs are not available to match their skills or because they lack skills. Some believe that they will be better mothers if they can nurture and supervise their children at home, even though they will be poor. Many lack access to decent child care or cannot afford to pay for it at the low wage they can earn. Some reason that living on a state subsidy will be better for their children than accepting employment at or near minimum wage with no benefits, especially because as workers they must pay for clothes, transportation, child care, and other expenses they would not have if they did not have paid employment. Even so, less than 60 percent of poor children were subsidized by welfare in 1986, down from nearly

86 percent of poor children in 1973.[26] Despite racist myths, only about 31 percent of welfare recipients are African American, a proportion that has remained constant during the last 20 years.[27]

Because of the undeniable fact that children of single-mother families are economically disadvantaged, many of them severely, Galston argues that the single-parent family form is itself a bad family form. He recommends marriage as the cure for childhood poverty. "It is no exaggeration to say that the best antipoverty program for children is a stable, intact family" (285). Given that more than 40 percent of poor families are married couple families, this certainly is an exaggeration.

Still, on average adult men of all races earn more than women, and white men earn on average about one and one-third times what white women earn.[28] Galston is right, moreover, to claim that most families today need two wage earners "to maintain even a modestly middle class way of life" (285). Most children who are economically well-off, therefore, depend on two adult incomes. Because couples usually choose to allocate household and child-rearing responsibilities to women, however, many married women work only part-time. This fact, in combination with the fact that men are usually able to earn significantly more than women, means that most economically well-off women and children depend on a male's wage to keep them out of poverty.

II

Now let us proceed to examine Galston's normative argument for the superiority of the intact, two-parent family. Single-parent families are a less desirable family form, according to Galston, and public policy ought to take action to discourage their existence. Galston takes pains to deny that his position is an attack on single parents. Such a proposition would be "insulting to the millions of single parents who are struggling successfully against the odds to provide good homes for their children" (285). Nor does he believe that mothers ought to have primary responsibility for child welfare. Indeed, he rightly believes that fathers who leave mothers alone with children and pay little or no child support are a major social problem. In evaluating Galston's arguments about desirable family structure, however, I will focus on single mothers, because the vast majority of single-parent households are headed by women. I will assume that the only empirical case to be made for the claim that single-parent families are undesirable is that they are more likely to be poor than two-parent families.

Many women parent alone because they have inadequate access to contraception and abortion or because their husbands have chosen to leave the household. Many women of all ages, however, choose to bear children without husbands. Women initiate an increasing proportion of divorces, moreover, and increasing numbers of divorced mothers are not seeking remarriage. Galston's position on the moral superiority of the two-parent family implies that the choices of these mothers are morally wrong, not for reasons of intrinsic traditionalism, but for the functional traditionalist reasons concerning the duty of parents to maximize the welfare of children. Here is how I reconstruct Galston's argument to that conclusion.

Society through the state has a direct and fundamental interest in the raising of good citizens. A good citizen possesses liberal virtues, which are courage, law-abidingness, loyalty, independence, tolerance, willingness to work and delay gratification, adaptability, and the ability to discern the rights of others (221–24). Two-parent families are best able to inculcate these virtues, whereas single-mother families are less likely to do so. Therefore women should refrain from having children out of wedlock; mothers should put the interests of their children above their own and not divorce their husbands in order to pursue greater happiness for themselves, and in circumstances where they have not chosen single motherhood, mothers should try to get husbands. Thus public policy should regulate family behavior, providing disincentives for less worthy lifestyles and actions, and incentives for the more worthy. In what follows I shall show that this argument entails continuing the patriarchal tradition which denies women, and in particular mothers, full citizenship.

Galston identifies independence as one of the primary liberal virtues, because the liberal society is characterized by individualism. Public policy should prefer intact two-parent families because these best nurture such independence.

> To individualism corresponds the liberal virtue of independence—the disposition to care for, and take responsibility for, oneself and to avoid becoming needlessly dependent on others. Human beings are not born independent, nor do they attain independence through biological maturation alone. A growing body of evidence suggests that in a liberal society, the family is the critical arena in which independence and a host of other virtues must be engendered. The weakening of families is thus fraught with danger for liberal societies. In turn, strong families rest on specific virtues. Without fidelity, stable families cannot be maintained. Without a concern for children that extends well beyond the boundaries of adult self-regard, parents cannot effectively discharge

their responsibility to form secure, self-reliant young people. In short, the independence required for liberal social life rests on self-restraint and self-transcendence—the virtues of family solidarity. (222)

This is a rather thin and vague description of independence, but from this and other passages I infer that independence here means primarily having a well-paid, secure job sufficient to support oneself and one's children at a level that can enable them to develop the capacities and acquire the skills to achieve such jobs themselves, and can also provide enough savings so that one does not become dependent on those children or others when one is too old to work.

The major problem with single motherhood, as I construe Galston's argument, is that single mothers tend often not to be independent in this sense; that is, they are poor or close to poor and often depend on government subsidy to meet some or all of their needs and those of their children. I noted earlier that the primary reason for this is that women's wages frequently are far lower than men's and that affordable child care is often unavailable.

I have no doubt of Galston's commitment to sexual equality, including pay equity. Nor do I doubt that he deplores men who dominate women in the household. An argument for the superiority of intact, two-parent families, he says, does not entail a return of women to the status of barefoot in the kitchen; sound families today need mothers as well as fathers in the workforce. He does not note that in most families with two wage earners there is a great disparity between the male and the female wage, either because the mother's full-time work is less well paid than the father's, or because the mother works part-time so that she can also take primary responsibility for caring for the children and doing household work. Most economically well-off women and children are economically dependent on a man.

In the absence of explicit attention to the facts of gender inequality and male domination, and their implications, Galston's argument for the moral superiority of stable marriage comes to this: Mothers should subordinate themselves to and be dependent on men, even if they would rather parent on their own, for the sake of nurturing the independence of their children. Independence is a paragon virtue of liberal citizenship, but a mother's virtue entails dependence on a man. The independence they nurture, moreover, is primarily in their male children because their female children are likely to grow up to be mothers. This argument implies that mothers are less than full citizens in the liberal society.

Now Galston would surely deny that he intends that mothers should subordinate themselves to men. But in the absence of explicit consideration of gender inequalities in earning power and household division of labor, preferring stable marriage over divorce and single motherhood amounts to calling for mothers to depend on men to keep them out of poverty, and this entails subordination in many cases. As Susan Okin powerfully argues, men and women tend not to have equal power in families, and the unequal power derives to a significant extent from the unequal wages that men typically bring into the household.[29] Men fail to take equal responsibility for housework and child care, often doing little of either, because they have the power not to. Women therefore often work many more hours than their husbands at tasks that are undervalued. More often than not men are primary decision makers in a household, not because the women are passive and traditional, but because they depend on their husband's income. Women's lives are disrupted and friendships torn by following the male wage earner to another job. Finally, their subordination and dependence puts women at risk of battery and rape, which far too many suffer at the hands of their husbands. Many women nevertheless stay in battering relationships for a long time because they economically depend on their batterers and believe that it is best for their children to keep the family "intact."

A gender-neutral theory of family values ignores the fact that, in the current gender structure, stable marriage means that women are often dependent on men and often suffer power inequality and various degrees of domination by men both in and outside of the home. It ignores the fact that, for many mothers, leaving their marriage and choosing not to enter marriage are not undertaken in frivolous and selfish pursuit of pleasure, but as a matter of escaping unjust subordination. In the absence of attention to this unjust gender structure, Galston's argument replicates the male centeredness of modern political theory's conception of citizenship.

Liberal and republican political theorists in the early modern period more explicitly recommended the subordinate and dependent status of wives and mothers.[30] The actual unit of liberal or republican society is the household, not the individual person. The male head of household exhibits the virtue of independence, supporting dependent mothers and children. The citizen virtue of mothers does not entail independence but, rather, the virtues of caring and sacrifice necessary for nurturing children to be good citizens.

III

In the tradition of modern political theory, independence is the citizen virtue of the male head of household and property owner. The bourgeois citizen meets his own needs and desires, and those of his dependents, by means of self-sufficient production on his property and by means of independent contracts to buy and sell goods. This social organization depends on a distinction between private and public. Productive activity of meeting needs and desires is organized privately, with dependent wives overseeing their day-to-day provision and the raising of children. This frees the male head of household to conduct the contract business that will enlarge his property and to meet with other independent citizens to discuss affairs of state.[31]

Independence is an important citizen virtue in the modern democratic republic, because it enables citizens to come together in public on relatively free and equal terms. If every citizen meets the needs of himself and his dependents through his own property, then citizens are immune to threats or particularist influence by others on whom they depend for their livelihoods. With independence in this sense they may deliberate on equal terms and consider the merits of issues in terms of the general good.[32]

Thus, the citizen virtue of independence also entails personal autonomy, a sense of self-confidence, and inner direction, as well as the ability to be reflective, not swayed by immediate impulse or blind emotion in the making of political argument. Paradoxically, such autonomy and personal independence is thought to require the loving attention of particularist mothers who devote themselves to fostering this sense of self in their children. Attentive love disqualifies the nurturers of the individuality and autonomy of citizens from the exercise of citizenship, however, because the character of mothers tends to be emotional and oriented to particular needs and interests instead of to the general good. A sexual division of labor is thus appropriate and fitting between noncitizen women who are emotionally attached to men and children whose autonomy they foster by nurturing their particular individuality, and citizen men who have became autonomous and independent thinkers thanks to the loving care of mothers, who exercise autonomous political judgment for the general good.[33]

Galston's statement of the virtue of independence departs from this modern understanding of the importance of independence as a virtue. As I quoted earlier, he defines independence as "the disposition to care for, and to take responsibility for, oneself and avoid becoming needlessly dependent on others" (222). Unlike the dominant modern tradition, Galston does not construct independence as a means to the end of promoting rational political judgment by free and equal citizens. His picture of the polity distinguishes between leaders and citizens, and it seems that only leaders will make public policy decisions. The primary virtue of citizens in this division is that they be moderate in their demands on leaders; they should demand no more from their government than they are willing to pay for in taxes and be self-disciplined enough to accept painful measures when their leaders judge that they are necessary (see 224–25).

Instead of serving as a means to the end of political autonomy, in Galston's account it seems that the primary purpose of independence is to minimize public spending. Divorce and single parenthood, he suggests, cause the poverty, crime, and disability that make people depend on public spending to meet their needs:

> The consequences of family failure affect society at large. We all pay for systems of welfare, criminal justice, and incarceration, as well as for physical and mental disability; we are all made poorer by the inability or unwillingness of young adults to become contributing members of society; we all suffer if our society is unsafe and divided. (286)

Although it is a far cry from the old property-based meaning of economic independence, as I noted earlier, Galston appears to follow contemporary liberal common sense in identifying independence with having a well-paid secure job. On his scheme of liberal virtues, persons who are independent in this sense are more virtuous than those who are not. I wish now to question this commonsense valuation of independence, however, as a measure of the value or virtue of citizens.

Normatively privileging independence in this sense (making it a primary virtue of citizenship) implies judging a huge number of people in liberal societies as less than full citizens. First, there are those unable to care for themselves alone, who thus depend on others to meet some or all of their needs: children, elderly people, many people with physical and mental disabilities, and sick and injured people. Most of us are dependents of this sort at some time of our lives, and many of us are for a good part of our lives. Second, there are those people, usually women dependency workers, who care for dependents of this sort. Most dependency work takes place outside paid employment, in the home. Thus, those who do this work must be supported by others to have their material needs met. Though they do vital, often difficult and time-consuming work, dependency workers are often not independent in Galston's sense. Privileging independence as a citizen virtue thus amounts to defining dependency workers as second-class citizens.[34]

Holding independence as a norm not only renders dependent people and their caretakers second-class citizens, but it also tends to make them invisible. Dependent people and their caretakers come to be defined outside public social relations, marginalized to a private realm beyond the interaction of free and full citizens with one another. Such marginalization renders dependent people and their caretakers more abjectly dependent than they would be if they were acknowledged as equal citizens and received the kind of social support that would enable them to be as independent as possible and to participate in civic and political life.

As women have joined the labor force in large numbers, the expectation that every person should be an independent worker has become more general. Thus, the stigma attached to dependency has increased.[35] Ironically, during this same period it has become increasingly difficult for many people to have well-paid, secure jobs, because employers have closed down basic manufacturing enterprises and have come to rely increasingly on part-time and seasonal workers.

Independence, I suggest, should not be thought of as a basic citizen virtue. But this contradicts many people's stated values. If you ask children, or people in wheelchairs, or old people, or women on welfare what they want for their lives, they will all say that they wish to be independent. In order to respect their experience and at the same time recognize people's needs for support, I suggest that we must distinguish two meanings of independence.

The first is autonomy: within the bounds of justice, to be able to make choices about one's life and to act on those choices without having to obey others, meet their conditions, or fear their threats and punishments. The second is self-sufficiency: not needing help or support from anyone in meeting one's needs and carrying out one's life plans. The modern republican linkage of citizenship with independence tied these two. If you were not a self-sufficient property holder, you were subordinate to a property holder in order to have your needs met and thus could not be a full citizen. But egalitarian social movements claimed equal citizenship for servants, wage workers, and wives. The extension of citizenship to formerly subordinate people meant that the link between self-sufficiency and autonomy had to be broken. The ability of workers and wives to think for themselves in politics and make their own decisions about their lives and actions, however, had to be guaranteed by laws that protected them from the power of employers and husbands on whom they were dependent for their livelihoods.

Autonomy should be considered an important moral value in the liberal society. Respecting individuals as full citizens means granting and fostering in them liberties and capacities to be autonomous—to choose their own ends and develop their own opinions. It also means protecting them from the tyranny of those who might try to determine those choices and opinions because they control resources on which citizens depend for their living.[36]

In contemporary society, however, most people experience this kind of dependence. Most people depend directly or indirectly on the owners of capital for their living. Whole communities depend on employment in a local manufacturing plant and the retail markets that employment generates. When the owner shuts down the plant, furthermore, he says that he is dependent on the world market, on the relation of the dollar to the yen, and must compete with cheaper goods make in Korea. The ideal of independence as self-sufficiency, perhaps a worthy ideal in Thomas Jefferson's America, has become inoperative in today's world of intricate economic interdependence.

Independence as self-sufficiency has come to mean in most people's minds what I have suggested that it means for Galston—having a well-paid, secure job—even though this is not self-sufficiency in Jefferson's sense. I have suggested that privileging independence in the newer sense has the consequence of marginalizing many people—women who take care of children or old people at home, sick people, people who for whatever reason cannot find work, or those whose wages are too low to provide subsistence.

Wealthier liberal societies usually do not allow these people to starve or die of exposure. But they usually limit the autonomy of those to whom they provide aid and support. People who depend on public subsidy or private charity to meet some or all of their needs must often submit to other people's judgments about their lives and actions—where they will live, how they will live, how they will spend money, what they will do with their time. Thus, citizens judged self-sufficient have a right to autonomy, but those who are not independent in this sense often have their autonomy limited in many ways. I submit that this makes them second-class citizens. Too many single mothers fall in this category, and contemporary rhetoric and policy proposals seem determined to deprive them further of their autonomy.

In a liberal polity, independence as being able to make choices about one's life without coercion or threat should be thought of as a liberal right, respected equally in all citizens. Independence in the sense of thinking for oneself and making rational judgments about the public good should be thought of as a liberal virtue; the society is likely to be better governed and more democratic if its citizens think critically and express themselves honestly. Contemporary liberal welfare societies still often tend to recognize a right of autonomy only for those who can meet their needs entirely through private employment. But a humane liberal society should affirm that, in order to be autonomous in both the sense of deciding what to do with one's life and formulating one's own opinions, most people require material and social support, and that some people require more support than others.[37]

IV

Galston would be likely to criticize my claim that independence of choice and thought requires social support for focusing too much on citizen rights and not enough on citizen responsibilities. He thinks that a client, demand-oriented view of citizenship has weakened the expectation that citizens will attend to the public good as well as their own. Although citizens have rights to basic liberty, respect, and tolerance from their fellow citizens and from the state, they have the reciprocal responsibility to contribute meaningfully to the social fabric. The state can rightfully expect such contributions from healthy adult citizens and can rightfully punish and stigmatize noncontributors.

Galston is quite right to expect that citizens should contribute to the social good and should be given equal opportunity to contribute. He is wrong, however, to identify making a social contribution with being independent in the sense of having a job. The following passages suggest this identification of making a contribution with having a job:

> This conception of contribution opportunity applies not only to the availability of jobs for adults but also to the availability of adequate opportunities for children and youth to develop their capacities to contribute. . . .
>
> Contribution has both quantitative and qualitative dimensions. Key quantitative variables include sacrifice, effort, duration, and productivity. The key qualitative variable is the importance of different functions as defined either by the community as a whole or (more typically) by some socioeconomic entity within the community. (185–86)

In other words, the worth of a person's social contribution is usually measured by how much wage or salary that person earns at a job. Galston is hardly alone in identifying making a significant social contribution with having a good job. This is the stuff of popular common sense. It is, however, an incorrect and unjust identification.

Although they do overlap, having a good job and being a contributing member of society are not equivalent concepts. Most of us can think of lucrative jobs and businesses that we judge contribute little to society, except perhaps notches in the gross national product, and that may be positively harmful. Two of my candidates are designing sugary cereal ads to be aired on Saturday morning cartoons and working as a lobbyist for the tobacco industry. Just what sorts of activities count as "contributing" is of course contestable, but most people would agree that some jobs do not contribute to the social good, even though they may contribute to some particular ends.

More important, perhaps, most of us would agree that people can make important social contributions that either do not get paid or receive a token payment disconnected from their social worth. Good art, literature, and philosophy, for example, are notoriously poor sellers in the market. Every society must publicly subsidize its cultural production.

Most relevant to the citizen status of mothers, dependency work makes a vast and vital social contribution. As already mentioned, most caring for children, sick people, old people, and people with disabilities is performed unpaid by women in the home. In American society, as in many others, when these usually female dependency workers are paid in social services agencies, the wages often keep the workers below the poverty line. A just society would recognize dependency work as the significant social contribution it is by giving those who do it decent material comfort.[38]

Community organizing and service provision represent a final category of social contribution outside the labor market. Much of the infrastructure of civic life in American society today, which keeps the society minimally democratic, participatory, and critical, and also does much to preserve what social bonds there are, is done by volunteers or low-paid and dedicated workers: neighborhood crime watches, rape crisis centers, environmental cleanup crews, AIDS prevention and support groups, consumer information lobbies, political issue and advocacy groups, and so on. Poor people, especially poor single mothers, participate in such service providing and organizing activity to an extent that seriously belies the stereotype of the welfare loafer.[39] Many people believe that having the state directly organize political participation and social service provision is both inefficient and tends wrongly to infringe on civil and political freedom. Thus people who do these things—and a healthy liberal democratic society needs a great many more people doing them than we have in the United States today—must depend on public resources for their ability to make these social contributions.

I agree with Galston that society ought to encourage all its citizens to engage in useful social contributions to the extent that they are able. Many children, old people, people with little training, and people with physical and mental disabilities would be able to contribute more to social life than their circumstances allow them today if the norm of the self-sufficient, hale-and-hearty, male adult worker did not hold sway. A more just society would provide the home help, child care, transportation, workplace accommodation, and flexible work hours that would enable more of these people to make meaningful contributions. Many people should contribute through private paid employment. But many of the activities that are basic to a healthy liberal democratic society—cultural production, caretaking, civic and political organizing, the building and maintenance of decent affordable housing—are not and never will be profitable in the private market. Many of these activities, moreover, are not best performed in state bureaucratic jobs. They are best performed privately and autonomously, but the people who do them must be socially supported in a decent life.

V

I have agreed with Galston that the idea of liberal neutrality is a fiction and that it is appropriate for public policy to promote particular ends and goods. Among such ends and goods, some belong to family life: privacy, intimacy, responsibility, caring for particular others, and leisure time play. In addition to these, there are particular family values important for children's welfare: attentive love; nurturance to emotional, intellectual, and moral maturity; relative stability; and orderly change.

There are family values, the ends and purposes of family life, and individual virtues that enact them. There is no doubt that some families better instantiate them than others. Along with many others today using family values rhetoric, however, Galston is wrong to assert that a particular *kind* of family best embodies these values for children—the intact, two-parent, by implication heterosexual, family. These family values can and often are realized in a plurality of family forms: gay and lesbian families,[40] single-parent families, blended families, nuclear families, extended families.

Public policy should promote and encourage the ends and purposes of families. Contrary to what Galston argues, however, public policy should not *prefer* particular means of realizing these ends. It is wrong, that is, for public policy to encourage particular family forms and discourage others. For the sake of protecting children and other household members, the state can properly intervene in or punish particular actions or inactions within families, especially violence and serious willful neglect, but this is quite different from punishing or favoring families based on their composition alone. Such preference is simply discrimination, inconsistent with liberal pluralist principles of giving citizens equal respect whatever their culture or way of life.

Attitudes and institutional assumptions that are unfairly biased toward heterosexual, two-parent families put burdens and stresses on many families that others do not face, which sometimes make it more difficult for them to raise children well. Injustices in the economic system and workplace structures prevent many families, including many single-parent families, from giving their children material comfort and the resources they need to develop their capacities. In light of such prejudices and unjust inequalities, the primary way that public policy should promote family values is by facilitating material and social supports to enable all families to be as excellent as possible. I will conclude by briefly discussing several policy areas affected by this argument.

1. Reproductive Freedom

Many people respond to calls for appreciation and support for single-mother families with the stance that women simply should not have babies that they cannot raise in material comfort on their own. Many single women who do have babies, of course, have inadequate access to contraception and abortion. Policies that truly enabled women to be heterosexually active without having to bear unwanted children would thus probably reduce the need for publicly supporting children.

Reproductive freedom goes both ways, however. People should be free to have children as well as not to have them. In a crowded world each additional child makes for social costs; thus, everyone has a moral obligation to ask whether they should bring another child into the world. The decision of an upper-income, married couple to have their third child may be morally questionable from this point of view. A liberal society that claims to respect the autonomy all its citizens equally should affirm the freedom of all citizens to bear and rear children, whether they are married or not, whether they have high incomes or not.

2. Father Obligations

Many argue that it is unfair for mothers to bear responsibility for financial support of children alone and that fathers ought to be made to pay. In principle I agree. Court-ordered child support obligations of divorced fathers should be much more vigorously enforced, and children-first divorce policies should make these awards larger than they usually are now, when the father earns a good income. Forcing unwed mothers to name fathers of their children is problematic under liberal principles, however, because it may subject the women to harassment or threat of violence from the man she names or force her into a long-term relation with a man she wishes not to see. Trying to force low-income fathers to pay child support they do not have, moreover, will not raise the standard of living of children.

3. Welfare Reform

In 1996 the U.S. Congress passed the most sweeping changes in public assistance programs since the 1930s: the Personal Responsibility and Work Opportunity Reconciliation Act. For the first time in its history, Aid to Families with Dependent Children (AFDC) is no longer guaranteed as an entitlement for parents who meet eligibility criteria. The legislation allows states to limit welfare receipt to 24 consecutive months, and five years during one's lifetime. Most relevant for the purposes of this essay, the law requires most AFDC recipients to work at jobs as a condition of the receipt of benefits.

Already many questions have arisen about whether states are capable of implementing this law as intended, given their politics and budgetary constraints. When issues of child care, transportation, job creation, and viable training programs are included, it turns out to be far more complex and costly to expect welfare mothers to work for their check than most had thought. I do not have the space to address these questions here. The philosophy behind this legislation clearly expresses the fictional value of independence through a job and inattention to the contribution of child raising that I have criticized in this essay. I think that the effect of the reform is to encourage policies that punish women and children for not attaining a norm of independence. At the same time, it does little to help make mothers independent in the sense of having a secure job at a decent wage. Instead, it forces more people into the status of working poor, a group whose numbers swell annually. Thus, the legislation further limits the autonomy of many poor mothers at the same time that it fails to address the dependence of tens of millions of Americans on a labor market in which full-time employment at living wages is increasingly scarce. The equation of independence with having a job here allows both the public and private sectors to avoid responsibilities to parents and children.

4. Full Employment and Guaranteed Income

Capitalism has some virtues, but after 300 years it should be clear that one of them is not employing all able-bodied people at decent wages. A liberal capitalist society can expect all citizens to make contributions only if it makes opportunities available to all at a level of compensation sufficient to support themselves and their children in a decent life. Where the private labor market does not have enough jobs for all those able and willing to work, the public sector should provide useful work at a decent wage.

Either employers should be required to raise their wages so that every worker can live at least a minimally decent life or public funds should supplement the incomes of poorly paid workers.[41] Part of any such wage adjustment policy should be efforts to raise wages for typically female jobs to levels more typical of decently paid men's jobs. A liberal democratic society that gives equal respect to all citizens would institute an income policy that guaranteed public support to all able-bodied persons to make social contributions that the private market only poorly supports: for example, care of dependents, whether inside or outside the home, provision of social service, building and maintaining affordable housing, community enhancement and empowerment organizing, and the facilitation of citizen participation in civic and political activities.

Within such a full employment and guaranteed income framework, dependency work done in the home ought to be recognized as a social contribution. As much as possible, families ought to be able to choose to care for their young children, elderly or disabled relatives, and close friends in their homes; they should not be forced to do so, however, by lack of good affordable alternative care. People who do dependency work, whether in or outside the home, should be materially supported. Public policy should promote flexible work hours in private and public jobs, moreover, so that dependency workers can combine their home-care responsibilities with out-of-home contributions. If dependency work were recognized and supported in these ways, many men would probably do more of it.

5. Mothers' Houses

People who parent alone by choice or circumstances should be respected as equal citizens. Even with adequate material support, however, it is more difficult for many people to raise children on their own than cooperatively with others. One way to recognize and appreciate single-mother families is to promote living arrangements for them that ensure privacy and at the same time facilitate cooperation and support in child-rearing responsibilities. Some liberal democratic governments have promoted or supported such cooperative living arrangements among single mothers.[42]

I have argued that a family-values rhetoric that finds married couple families the most morally valuable fails to recognize mothers as equal citizens. Holding independence in the sense of self-sufficiency as a primary norm of citizenship accounts for this devaluation of women, who in the current gender structure are doubly disadvantaged by poor wages and primary responsibility for society's dependency work. A society that recognizes all its members as equal citizens and expects them all to make meaningful contributions must recognize and support the contribution of dependency work and publicly support many other opportunities for making social contributions.

Notes

1. William Galston, *Liberal Purposes* (Cambridge, England: Cambridge University Press, 1991), chapters 1 through 7.

2. U.S. Bureau of the Census. *Statistical Abstract of the United States, 1993–94* (Austin, Tex.: The Reference Press), 101–2.

3. Judith S. Wallerstein and Sandra Blakeslee, *Second Chances: Men, Women and Children a Decade After Divorce* (New York: Ticknor & Fields, 1989).

4. Andrew Cherlin and Frank Furstenburg, "Divorce Doesn't Always Hurt the Kids," *Washington Post* (March 19, 1989), C3.

5. See Rosemary Dunlop and Alisa Burns, "The Sleeper Effect—Myth or Reality? Findings from a Ten-Year Study of the Effects of Parental Divorce at Adolescence" (paper presented at the Fourth Australian Family Research Conference, Manly, NSW, February 1993).

6. P. R. Amato and B. Keith, "Parental Divorce and the Well-Being of Children: A Meta-analysis," *Psychological Bulletin* 110 (1991): 26–46.

7. Dunlop and Burns, "The Sleeper Effect." Cherlin also finds that the adverse effects observed in children are often prior to divorce and can be attributed to a hostile family environment; Andrew Cherlin, "Longitudinal Studies of Effects of Divorce on Children in Great Britain and the United States," *Science* (June 7, 1991), 1386–89.

8. Dunlop and Burns suggest that one reason that they find lower levels of emotional distress in their study of children of divorce than do some American studies may be that Australian divorce procedures rely on family court counseling and mediation much more than do those in the United States, which relies on a highly charged adversarial system of divorce settlement.

9. *Statistical Abstract,* 61. These statistics may obscure the fact that unmarried parents may nevertheless be coparenting with other adults in the household. Lesbian parents, for example, usually appear as single mothers in statistics, even when they live in long-term partnerships with another woman.

10. *Statistical Abstract,* 64.

11. Ibid., 77–78.

12. Christopher Jenks, *Rethinking Social Policy: Race, Poverty and the Underclass* (New York: Harper Perennial, 1992), 198; Herbert L. Smith and Phillips Cutright, "Thinking about Change in Illegitimacy Ratios: United States, 1963–1983," *Demography* 25 (1988): 235–47.

13. *Statistical Abstract,* 78.

14. Larry Bumpass, "Children and Marital Disruption: A Replication and Update," *Demography* 21 (February 1984): 71–82.

15. See, for example, Amitai Etzioni, *The Spirit of Community* (New York: Crown, 1993), chapter 2.

16. Nan Marie Astone and Sara McLanahan, "Family Structure and High School Completion: The Role of Parental Practices," Institute for Research on Poverty discussion paper no. 905–909 (Madison, Wis., 1989).

17. Stephanie Coontz, *The Way We Never Were* (New York: Basic Books, 1992), 224.

18. Sharyne Merritt and Linda Steiner, *And Baby Makes Two: Motherhood Without Marriage* (New York: Franklin Watts, 1984), 160.

19. Sara McLanahan, "The Consequences of Single Parenthood for Subsequent Generations," *Focus* (University of Wisconsin, Institute for Research on Poverty) 11 (1988): 16–24.

20. Diana Pearce, "Welfare Is Not *for* Women: Why the War on Poverty Cannot Conquer the Feminization of Poverty," in *Women, the State, and Welfare,* Linda Gordon, ed. (Madison: University of Wisconsin Press, 1990), 265–79.

21. Laurence E. Lynn, Jr., "Ending Welfare Reform As We Know It," *American Prospect* (Fall 1993), 88.

22. Pearce, "Welfare Is Not *for* Women."

23. *Statistical Abstract,* 131.

24. Pearce, "Welfare Is Not *for* Women."

25. Jenks, *Rethinking Social Policy,* 235.

26. Teresa L. Amot, "Black Women and AFDC: Making Entitlement Out of Necessity," in *Women, the State, and Welfare,* Gordon, ed.

27. Jenks, *Rethinking Social Policy,* 149.

28. *Statistical Abstract,* 133.

29. Susan Okin, *Justice, Gender and the Family* (New York: Basic Books, 1989).

30. For an account of the role of "republican motherhood" in American history and its continued effects on reinforcing the inequality of women, see Rogers M. Smith, " 'One United People': Second Class Female Citizenship and the American Quest for Community," *Yale Journal of Law and the Humanities* 1 (1989): 229–93.

31. On the masculinity of independence as a citizen virtue, see Carole Pateman, "The Patriarchal Welfare State," in *The Disorder of Women* (Cambridge: Polity, 1989); see also Anna Yeatman, "Beyond Natural Right: The Conditions for Universal Citizenship," *Social Concept* 4 (1988): 3–32.

32. Jeremy Waldron well summarizes this rationale for independence as a virtue of early modern citizenship in "Social Citizen and the Defense of Welfare Provision," in *Liberal Rights* (Cambridge, England: Cambridge University Press, 1993); see also Susan James, "The Good-Enough Citizen: Female Citizenship and Independence," in *Beyond Equality and Difference: Citizenship, Feminist Politics and Female Subjectivity,* Gisela Bock and Susan James, eds. (London: Routledge, 1992).

33. On the paradoxes of women's incorporation into the modern polity and their implications for women's contemporary standing, see Carole Pateman,

"Equality, Difference, Subordination: The Politics of Motherhood and Women's Citizenship," in *Beyond Equality and Difference*, Bock and James, eds., 17–29.

34. See Eva Feder Kittay, "Equality, Rawls, and the Dependency Critique," in *Love's Labor: Essays on Women, Equality, and Dependency* (New York: Routledge, 1999).

35. For an important account of the changes in the meaning of dependence and the way the term is increasingly confined to single mothers, see Nancy Faser and Linda Gordon, "A Genealogy of *Dependency*: Tracing a Keyword of the U.S. Welfare State," *Signs: A Journal of Women in Culture and Society* 19 (1994): 1–29.

36. For an important account of a concept of autonomy along these lines, see Jennifer Nedelsky, "Reconceiving Autonomy," *Yale Journal of Law and Feminism* 1 (1989): 7–35.

37. In "Social Citizen and the Defense of Welfare Provision," Jeremy Waldron gives an important normative argument for this idea of social citizenship originated by Marshall. See also Barry Hindess, "Multiculturalism and Citizenship," in *Multicultural Citizens: The Philosophy and Politics of Identity*, Chandran Kukathas, ed. (Canberra: Center for Independent Studies, 1993), 31–46.

38. Deborah A. Stone, "Caring Work in a Liberal Polity," *Journal of Health Politics, Policy and Law* 16 (1991): 547–52.

39. See Harry Boyte, *Community Is Possible* (New York: Harper & Row, 1984).

40. See Frederick W. Bozett, ed., *Gay and Lesbian Parents* (New York: Praeger, 1987).

41. A number of writers have pointed out that a consistent commitment encouraging all able-bodied people to make meaningful social contributions entails expanding welfare supports to the working poor, rather than reducing welfare supports. That is, because so many people's wages are too little to give them a decent life, justice requires that they be dependent on public support. See Sar A. Levitan, Frank Gall, and Isaac Shapir, *Working But Poor*, rev. ed. (Baltimore: Johns Hopkins University Press, 1993).

42. Delores Hayden, *Redesigning the American Dream* (New York: Norton, 1984), 137–38; Gerda R. Wekerle, "Responding to Diversity: Housing Development by and for Women," in *Shelter, Women, and Development: First and Third World Perspectives*, ed. Hemalata C. Dandekar (Ann Arbor, Mich.: George Wahr, 1991), 178–86.

11

Domestic Abuse and Locke's Liberal (Mis)Treatment of Family

Matthew R. Silliman

There are at least two ways of accounting for the peculiar inconsistencies of Locke's comments on family relations in the *Second Treatise of Government.* I shall argue that the liberal, charitable reading, though it would perhaps have appealed to Locke himself, fails to explain crucial features of his account of human nature, politics, and family relations. A more critical reading is required to make sense of Locke's project, and to do so involves raising questions that are barely imaginable in a philosophical tradition uninformed by the past few decades of feminist thinking, for even the most thoroughgoing Marxist interpretations and critiques of Locke, I believe, fail adequately to comprehend the implications of Locke's treatment of women and families.

In the interpretation that follows, what look like lapses in an essentially egalitarian treatment of family actually reveal tensions in the philosophical commitments behind Locke's project itself. I take Locke's use of the "natural" family for social contractarian purposes to be, rather, an "abuse" of family relations, reflected in the sinister outcome for our own time that an ideological commitment to equality masks a durable system of thought and organization sustaining violent domestic abuse at epidemic levels.

I thus reject the liberal view that such problems are lamentable accidents, persisting *despite* the liberatory thinking of the tradition beginning with Locke, and argue that domestic abuse is only one extreme manifestation of tensions built into the metaphysics of liberty itself as

Locke and most of his successors conceive it. I will suggest, in fact, that the wholly autonomous individual, as this mythical creature has been understood in the Liberal tradition, is coextensive with a person (paradigmatically a *male* person—a woman fitting this description is considered anomalous or "masculinized"), whose liberty is secured only through the private domination of others, and thus whose liberty cannot consistently be described in a way that is not conceptually abusive of women and families.

|

Chapter VI of the *Second Treatise*, "Of Paternal Power" begins auspiciously, with Locke, in effect, deconstructing the title. Because men and women share equally in the production of children, he claims, and thus have equal power and authority over them and are equally responsible for them, the precise term would be "parental" power. Moreover, he says, this conventional usage of "paternal" is apt to mislead people into the assumption that the family is "naturally" structured like a monarchy and hence that nature sanctions monarchy, neither of which is the case. Locke thus seems to signal that he intends to apply to family relations his analysis of all rational persons as equal, in the sense of having an equal right to natural freedom without arbitrary subjection to the will or authority of anyone else. Such apparent willingness to challenge conventional gender roles in an institution notorious for its putatively natural inequality marks Locke as more than just a political revolutionary in his time.

Much of what this chapter of the Second Treatise and the next say about family reinforces this impression: He reiterates that parents are equal partners in the exercise of their duty to nurture, support, and educate their children so that they become capable of reason and independence. A late-twentieth-century reader is struck, perhaps, by Locke's frequent use of "man" and "he" as apparent though ambiguous generic terms for human persons, by his retention of the conventional term "Paternal Power" after all his protestations, and by such comments as: "A *Child* is *Free* by his Father's Title, by his Father's Understanding, which is to govern him, till he hath it of his own" (paragraph 61, emphasis and capitalization Locke's). Nevertheless, the preponderance of the discussion treats parents as moral and political equals, down to the legal and contractual rights of the wife in the event of a rationally justifiable separation or divorce. But then (paragraph 82) Locke makes the following odd claim:

> But the Husband and Wife, though they have but one common Concern, yet having different understandings, will unavoidably sometimes have different wills too; it therefore being necessary, that the last Determination, i.e., the Rule, should be placed somewhere, it naturally falls to the Man's share, as the abler and the stronger.

Locke immediately backpedals, hoping to avoid the inegalitarian consequences of this position:

> But this reaching but to the things of their common Interest and Property, leaves the Wife in the full and free possession of what by Contract is her peculiar Right, and gives the Husband no more power over her Life, than she has over his.

This hardly solves the problem, however. Nothing in the idea of a partnership implies that partners should have equal say except when they disagree, when one of them then automatically has the right to decide. As John Stuart Mill later observes, no one would freely enter into such a "partnership."[1] The logical consequence of Locke's position is that the wife gets her way if and only if she agrees with her husband, and this "rule of thumb"[2] is based on criteria ("abler and stronger") which Locke has previously rejected explicitly as morally irrelevant. It is cold comfort that in some abstract way this stops short of giving the husband absolute, monarchical power over her; the wife remains in the most important respect a second-class citizen, if in fact she is really a citizen at all.

There are at least two ways to interpret this odd contradiction. The liberal, charitable interpretation is that Locke is on the verge of developing a thorough-going gender-egalitarian social theory, consistent with his antimonarchist political position and the respect for the lives and liberties of individual persons which supports it. He sets out to reexamine family relations for the purpose of illustrating an account of nature that will make his political theory believable but soon finds that the rejection of patriarchy in the family, though it admirably parallels and supports the rejection of monarchy in government, raises some problems both for his elite, male audience and perhaps for his own intuitive sensibilities. Locke's occasional lapses into misogynist bias, inconsistent with his otherwise clear egalitarian principles, thus appear as either hedges for the sake of a sexist audience or simply a not-yet-complete commitment on the author's part to the full consequences of the powerful idea to which he is evidently committed. The liberal reading concludes that Locke's inconsistency is a personal—or perhaps historical, but not a philosophical—failing and may safely be overlooked.

Locke does at least raise the question of gender equality, according to the liberal reading, even if he is unable, for various reasons, to follow it through. Because we in the twentieth century are not constrained, as Locke was, by seventeenth-century gender-bias and a lack of audible female voices, we can follow his lead and complete the project he started. Locke's account of family seems, on principle, a powerfully liberating one: He describes the "conjugal society" between wives and husbands as the original and paradigmatic political relationship, and views it as both commendably natural and commendably artificial: the natural model for mutually empowering contractual relations freely chosen by independent rational individuals.

II

It is a struggle not to see some disingenuity in Locke's facile attribution to women of free, rational choice with respect to the institution of marriage, in a society which offered women few other choices (none particularly desirable). But we might grant him the benefit of the doubt on the grounds that his account is less descriptive than prescriptive, and that coming to understand families as egalitarian partnerships and incubators for free, informed citizens could help to bring it about. However, the culture seems to have assimilated much more of Locke's political program than it has his putative reform of the family. Somehow we have decoupled Locke's political conclusions from where he seems to think his arguments lead, and established states at least rhetorically based on the rights of freely consenting individuals without effecting a similar revolution in the power relations within families. An allegedly wholesale movement for human liberation, inspired in part by Locke, has proved remarkably exclusionary in practice. Liberal feminists since the eighteenth century have struggled to apply the apparently simple logic of political equality to women as well as to men and have received for their pains massive and vicious backlash against the most modest and incremental of gains.[3]

One measure of this failure of the liberal project is the persistently epidemic levels of abuse of women by men in domestic contexts, a phenomenon which distributes widely over all sectors of modern society and is highly resistant to political or legal remedy (for reasons stated later). Even according to conservative, official estimates, a woman is beaten in the United States every 15 seconds, most often by a husband or boyfriend.[4] Despite centuries of liberal rhetoric and reform, shockingly large numbers of men still feel entitled to treat their spouses (and spouse equivalents) as property, and the problem seems to get worse rather than better, at least as recognition of the problem leads to more widespread reporting of cases.

It is not easy for Lockean liberals to explain this persistence; we tend to point to the progress women have made, deplore the "senseless" violence, and hope improvements in legal protection and education (eliciting the essential goodness of human nature) will eventually, and gradually, solve it. Women's economic and political equality, however, not to mention safety, is consigned by this rhetoric to an indefinite future, with the Enlightenment assurance that because our reasoning is correct, bigotry will eventually run its course and the logic of equality will win out. This faith would be hollow, however, if the Liberal principle of equality itself were not what it seems. What if Locke's odd "lapses" result, not from the vagaries of his immediate history and personality, but from characteristics and contradictions built directly into his assumptions and philosophical commitments? The remainder of my comments will explore this possibility and argue that it is, in fact, the case.

III

We should note, in the first place, that Locke's interest in family relations in the *Second Treatise* is largely ad hoc, subordinated to his project of understanding the nature and origin of political power. From the beginning (paragraph 2) he proposes to redefine political power such that

> the power of a *Magistrate* over a Subject, may be distinguished from that of a *Father* over his Children, a *Master* over his Servant, a *Husband* over his Wife, and a *Lord* over his slave.

Although it is tempting to think that the book represents a first stage in a feminist reexamination of the political implications of the personal, it may in fact be one of the sources of the notion that the two are distinct and incommensurable. Locke devotes considerably more attention to property rights and civil relations than to family. His interest in family seems to arise primarily as a reaction to Filmer's justification of monarchy by the paternity of Adam; to the extent that Locke actually reexamines family, he does so in terms of a narrowly contractual and legalistic framework.

Thus, while he is not neglectful of children's need for nurture (he emphasizes the parents' responsibility to teach their children to reason and shift for themselves), Locke is oddly inattentive to the social consequence of this process. He does not remark that, owing to the length of time needed for children to develop into relatively autonomous adults, and the linguistic and relational sophistication of this process, even in his imaginary "state of nature" there would be complex kith-and-kinship, obligation and power relations, both within the nuclear "family" and among members of the wider support community. Locke speaks as though a successful, functioning family could be founded ex nihilo by two people, without social histories or outside support. This thus appears less like an independent project aimed at restructuring the concept of family than a deliberate *abuse* of that concept, which ignores the actual needs, purposes, and relationships which define it in practice.

I think, however, that there is a deeper reason Locke does not, and cannot, undertake this latter project, having to do with his conception of the human individual. Locke is a Cartesian dualist, which is to say that he asserts a radical distinction between mental and bodily existence. He conceives a "person," generally, as a *proprietor*, that is, a mind conjoined with all of the bodily possessions and characteristics which are *proper* to it, to which it naturally has a right (described collectively by Locke as "Life, Liberty, and Estate"). The person is thus a composite creature, defined by the intimately related rights, needs, and actions implied by its embodiment (such as the "labor" which separates objects from nature and make them the person's own). The sphere of influence which a person rightly creates through the "investment" of labor becomes that person's property, his "realm."

I use the masculine pronoun advisedly, and the latter term, "realm," is revealing, for the model underlying Locke's conception of the individual is that of a feudal lord, who owns and is responsible for a well-defined hereditary realm or estate (which, not incidentally, bears his ancestral name). Locke attempts, I think, to democratize this model, to generalize it to apply to all human persons capable of reason, but in doing so he fails to see that, just as a lord needs subjects to be a lord, and a proprietor needs property to be a proprietor, both generally need wives to support them and provide them with progeny. The Lockean proprietor is viable as an "independent" person only because his very definition *includes* an elaborate system of social support, normally including at least a nuclear family. He is able to think of himself as independent only because, as head of a household, he relies for many things on those who bear his name. Such ignorance is easy to sustain because from his perspective they are, properly speaking, *part of him.*

George Gale argues that Locke's political theory of property is "territorial" in precisely this feudal sense, that Locke thus transforms "the social and political arrangements of feudalism into the terms of modern states."[5] This is particularly evident with respect to the status of women. Thus while rejecting monarchism and attempting to redefine just political relations, Locke retains an essentially feudal and patriarchal conception of personhood which is in significant tension with the notion that women could qualify for it, insofar as they fill their conventionally mandated roles.[6]

Nor is this merely an idiosyncratic quirk of Locke's personal moral views. Silliman[7] argues for a close conceptual connection between the argument of the *Second Treatise* and the physical theory of Locke's *Essay Concerning Human Understanding*. The link between Locke's description of personhood and what we might call "feudal patriarchy" is reinforced by a striking analogy between the ontological relation of a person to his property, on the one hand, and of a physical object to its properties on the other. Briefly, in Boyle and Locke's "corpuscular" theory of matter, perceivable (secondary) qualities "flow" from the "real internal constitution" of an object, and thus although they are not an inherent part of its essence, they are connected to it intrinsically (one might even say "inalienably"). Similarly, what properly belongs to a person (understood as a proprietor), flows from that person's exercise of his liberty in fulfillment of his needs (that is, his labor). In this way he builds his estate and thus makes himself (and makes a name for himself), and is thereby known in the world. Thus, natural objects and natural individuals share a common structure in Locke's thinking: that of a ruling presence creating and controlling a defined sphere of influence beyond itself.

To the extent, therefore, that this structure informs and pervades the work of Locke and those who follow him, dependence and domination are irreducible parts of what it means to be a full-fledged person, and liberty must be understood as the exercise of prerogatives within a sphere of subordination. Locke famously insists that my liberty stops where it infringes on the like freedom of another, but this is not an achievable criterion if my liberty springs from an unacknowledged dependence on and power over others. It is as absurd to imagine that each and every rational human person could achieve the isolated, autonomous self-sufficiency demanded by Locke's vision as it is to imagine that the essence of the privileges and prerogatives of a king or feudal lord could be generalized into equal and inalienable rights for the entire population. Yet this is precisely what Locke, and liberal social theorists generally, attempts to do.

It will not be possible to "liberate" women in a culture if liberty is so defined by that culture that one can secure it only by privately dominating women. Locke's image of a free person does not readily generalize to all human persons, because one cannot be a lord or king without a realm and subjects. To reconceptualize the free individual to avoid this contradiction would involve an attention to nurturance relations and support communities which make the individual possible, as well as a basic reexamination of the contexts within which choices become relatively free. Locke shows no interest in or capacity for such a project. His sympathies seem to lie, rather, with an ideal that is still common coin: the "self-made man." The mythic power of this abstraction exacts a draconian price, not only from the inevitable losers in so-called free market competition but especially from his invisible network of (largely female) support.

IV

Had Locke known of, or acknowledged, the (probably then also) widespread problem of domestic violence against women, he would surely have called for educational and legal remedies. These would probably have been as inadequate and ineffective as such efforts are today, because Locke's liberal theory of consensual politics leaves intact, and even strengthens, a "private realm" of home and family, understood simultaneously as a natural need, a basic right, and a prerequisite for a stable and sustainable civil society. The result is a remarkable stability of *inequality*, enshrined in a cheery rhetoric and ideology of equal rights. Family violence resists political and legal remedies because such violence occurs, by definition, *outside* of the political sphere, in the axiomatically private domains of the persons who make up civil society, and such an axiom is prescribed by the metaphysical constitution of the "autonomous individual." The problem is thus perennially difficult to address, not only because every head of household assumes the right to the kind of privacy within which such violence occurs ("A man's home is his castle") but also because to challenge that privacy is to undermine the conceptual basis of the liberal state itself, as it has developed since Locke.

It is fair to ask: Why beat a dead philosopher? In the first place, the least we can say about Locke is that, with all his flaws, he casts a marvelous psychological profile of much of what has come after. The sorts of incoherences that Locke gets himself into tend to be our own characteristic incoherences, and what seems "common sense" to him is an acute reflection of what is common to us even, or especially, if it is not exactly sense. Moreover, many of the basic philosophical commitments and mental pictures of society and personhood which, I have argued, make Locke's theory what it is and obstruct its evolution into a gender-egalitarian social order, continue to characterize liberal theory and practice in the twentieth century. Alison Jaggar[8] observes that, whereas John Rawls and other liberal theorists are not explicitly committed to mind-body dualism in the metaphysical, Cartesian sense, they nonetheless subscribe to what she calls "normative dualism," whereby a narrowly mental notion of reason is given an elevated status, and its physical basis deemed irrelevant. Nor am I the first to notice that the deliberative process of Rawls's "original position" abstracts from precisely the sorts of nurturance and support relationships, the contexts which create liberty and within which it is exercised, which mark Locke's misappropriation of family.[9] (Pateman includes a detailed discussion of many of these issues.)

Whatever Locke's conscious intentions, therefore, both the theoretical and the political consequences of his account of gender equality have been vicious. Locke's faint acknowledgment of the issue effectively conceals the problem and legitimates a metaphysical and a social order committed to the perpetuation of gendered power relations in families and elsewhere. The reinterpretation of family on egalitarian grounds which Locke purports to attempt, while heuristically useful in rejecting Filmer and logically implied by the ideology of human equality, cannot be sustained by the philosophical commitments underlying his general project, and so issues inevitably in textual lapses and inconsistencies. Locke's seminal work (pun intended) is thus a metaphor for the juxtaposition of the rhetoric of equality and respect with a pattern of violence toward women, especially within the family. When contemporary Liberal politicians (by which I mean practically everyone in mainstream American politics) invoke "family values," I cannot help but suspect that it is really women's traditional condition of oppression, as rhetorically obscured in the Liberal tradition, that they really have in mind.[10]

Notes

I am grateful to many people for their advice and suggestions on this project, including Greta Phinney, Alison Jaggar, and David K. Johnson.

1. See John Stuart Mill, *The Subjection of Women* (Indianapolis, Ind.: Hackett Publishing Co., 1988), 41–42. Mill is not explicitly commenting on Locke here, though he certainly could be.

2. I use this expression here advisedly; the "rule of thumb" was an English law in Locke's own century that sought to protect wives by forbidding their husbands to beat them with sticks larger than the husband's thumb.

3. See Susan Faludi's account of historical cycles of reaction against the equality of women. Susan Faludi, *Blacklash: The Undeclared War Against American Women* (New York: Crown Publishers, 1991). A prime and early example is the venomous response to Mary Wollstonecraft's 1792 *A Vindication of the Rights of Woman* by, among many others, my ancestor Benjamin Silliman. It contrasts strikingly with the enthusiastic reception given her *Vindication of the Rights of Men* two years earlier.

4. Data on the extent and durability of domestic and other violence against women is widely available. See, for example, Kathleen J. Ferraro and John M. Johnson, "How Women Experience Battering: The Process of Victimization," *Social Problems* 30, 3: 325–39; A. H. Flitcraft, "Violence, Values and Gender," *Journal of the American Medical Association* (June 17, 1992), 267 (23): 3194–95; and J. Hoffman, "When Men Hit Women" *New York Times Magazine* (February 16, 1992): 22.

5. George Gale, "John Locke on Territoriality: An Unnoticed Aspect of the Second Treatise," *Political Theory* 1: 472–85.

6. Locke's tortured preservation of primogeniture in the *First Treatise*, his rejection of Filmer's hereditary monarchical right notwithstanding, underscores his allegiance not to family, but to an essentially feudal vision of personhood. By and large, the male head of a patriarchal household best fits Locke's description of a person.

7. Matthew R. Silliman, *The Concept of Property in John Locke's Epistemology and Politics* (Ph.D. dissertation, Department of Philosophy, Purdue University, William L. McBride, director), 1986.

8. Alison Jaggar, *Feminist Politics and Human Nature* (Sussex, England: The Harvester Press, 1983), 28–35.

9. Jaggar, *Feminist Politics,* 221; and Carol Pateman, *The Sexual Contract* (Stanford, Calif.: Stanford University Press, 1988).

10. It is ironic, in this light, that this appeal comes with a program for increased state control of putatively private issues, such as reproduction. Most of these controls, however, are aimed primarily at controlling women; the right wing of modern liberalism perceives, correctly I think, that the patriarchal family, hence the building block of the liberal state, is threatened by the aspiration of women to independent "estate." By contrast, the liberal center and left incoherently uphold freedom and equality for all persons while defending existing property relations and conceptual and institutional structures which make its realization impossible.

12

Marx, Irigaray, and the Politics of Reproduction

Alys Eve Weinbaum

I n the United States it has become commonplace in recent feminist
discussions of reproductive politics to express alarm and then outrage
about the commodification of babies and motherhood which has
resulted from the ascendance of paid surrogate labor. For more than
a decade it has simultaneously become a staple of feminist pro-abortion
arguments to emphasize a conception of the mother and fetus as involved
in a relationship in which they are inextricably intertwined. These are
two of the dominant positions within feminist reproductive debates;
indeed, if there are only a few feminists who would defend surrogacy as
a contractual arrangement in which reproductive labor and its products
ought to be bought and sold, there are fewer still who challenge the narration of the mother/fetus relationship as an essential and merged one.[1]
What is so striking about current feminist scholarship and the rhetoric
of reproductive activism, however, is that these two dominant feminist
positions, although often articulated by the same scholar/activist, are
strangely at odds. When feminists talk about the exploitation of surrogate
labor they do not explore the implications of this economic permutation
in relation to their conceptualization of abortion; whereas those that
posit an essential and knowable mother/fetus relationship in order to
justify their pro-abortion stance mysteriously refrain from analyzing the
impact of the transformed economic parameters of reproduction on pro-
abortion orientations to pregnancy.

Today both the concept and practice of reproduction have been newly configured. In the current historical conjuncture reproductive labor has assumed an abstract value as social labor, and women around the globe are presently working to produce baby commodities that are entering the market alongside other domestic products and imports.[2] Given this situation, the economic metamorphosis of reproduction heralded by surrogacy cannot be treated as an aberration but rather requires a necessary reconceptualization of the maternal body as a reproductive resource, and in turn of the mother/fetus relationship. This essay attempts to develop a materialist analysis of reproductive labor by offering a strategy for renarrativizing the mother. It does this in two ways. First it briefly examines what feminists involved in the pro-abortion movement could gain by incorporating a Marxist understanding of reproductive labor as productive in the strictest sense. Second it suggests, through an analysis of the work of Luce Irigaray, the simultaneous need for a self-reflexive renarrativization of the maternal body that might account for women's role as reproductive laborers.

Historically, capitalist culture has benefited from the reduction of womanhood to an essential function. In the 1990s the equation of womanhood with motherhood persists despite the potentially liberatory changes precipitated by new reproductive technologies. Whether she is an underpaid surrogate stripped of legal recourse or an infertile or older woman paying dearly to use the growing array of reproductive technologies in the hope of conceiving, women's activity as consumers functions as the flip side of their role as reproductive laborers insofar as the technologies that some women purchase (in vitro fertilization, artificial insemination, embryo transfer, GIFT, ZIFT) are also the ones that make the reproductive labor power of all women commodifiable. Quite simply, as they are deployed, the new reproductive technologies are used to render more women mothers and to enclose more mothers within the ideological rubric of the nuclear family. Within this enclosure it is the same formulation of woman's maternal essence that is invoked when the medical industry insists that the so-called infertile woman cannot conscientiously elect not to pay for the scientific expertise and medical procedures that will transform her into a mother even as she labors without compensation to produce a child, as it is when the legal system creates obstacles to women's access to abortion or denies surrogate mothers their rights as laborers by refusing to recognize the value and specificity of reproductive work.

As feminists we have accounted for the ways in which capitalism mobilizes an essential definition of motherhood. It is perhaps time that we also comprehend that it is capital that opens up the abstraction necessary to antiessentialist thinking. This has been put elegantly by Gayatri Chakravorty Spivak, who in conversation with Ellen Rooney suggests the two-pronged axiom that "Capital is antiessentializing because it is the abstract as such . . . [and that essences] are deployed by capitalisms for the political management of capital."[3] Following Spivak, what I will suggest here is that pro-abortion feminists begin to capitalize on Capital's abstractions. For those involved in the reproductive debates have yet to explore what it might mean to comprehend reproductive labor as socially valued in the very process of searching for new narratives of the mother that locate the specificity of the maternal body, without falling back on essential, reified representations of the relationship between mothers and their products. If one thread of this project weaves an argument for rethinking the usefulness of Marxism for pro-abortion feminism, another embroiders this more Marxist understanding of reproduction as productive with a feminist psychoanalytic discussion of the possibilities for renarrativizing the materiality of the maternal body. The project of articulating two disparate theoretical styles—modes of thinking that are perceived by many to be incompatible—is no doubt difficult if not awkward. It is, however, the dissonance catalyzed by their interarticulation that lends this project its force. Without a Marxist understanding of reproductive labor there is little reason to renarrativize the maternal body; without the insights of feminist psychoanalysis the proposed renarrativization remains unintelligible.

If it is Marxism that allows women to become conscious of the exploitation of their reproductive labor, it is feminist psychoanalysis that constitutes a lever into reclaiming the maternal body as the appropriable means of production. Through a persistent return to the materiality of the body feminist psychoanalysis has opened up the body as a site for radical discursive intervention. In the texts that I will analyze, I am particularly concerned with how Irigaray both describes and performs such a return. As Judith Butler has observed of Irigaray's work, in it "matter occurs in two modalities: first as a metaphysical concept that serves phallogocentrism; [and] second, as an ungrounded figure, worrisomely speculative and catachrestic, that marks . . . the possible linguistic site of a critical mime."[4] When capitalism insists on reducing all women to their role as mothers, it helps to shore up phallogocentrism; when Irigaray approaches the maternal body in order to reconsider its materiality, phallogocentrism and capitalism begin to become unmoored. It is thus that I put to use what Butler and others have identified as Irigaray's practice of critical mime, explicating and then developing her psychoanalytics as the principal means for renarrativizing the maternal body's materiality. For it is my premise that the possibility of altering the power relations that condition the now-limited conceptualization of the "right to abortion" lie in renarrativizing the mother in the very process of collectively pursuing the social and abstract recognition of (re)productive labor.

(Re)Production

When babies have price tags the public discussion of abortion cannot afford to remain narrowly focused on the Fourteenth Amendment and privacy. Rather, we need a systematic critique that can redefine the concept of reproduction in pro-abortion parlance. In 1986, when surrogate mother Mary Beth Whithead refused to turn her baby, Sara Elizabeth, over to William Stern who had contracted Mary Beth's (re)productive labor, surrogacy entered public debate as the watershed case of Baby M. Although, at the time, the reaction of morally disgusted feminist critics was to insist that babies and women's reproductive labor power could simply not be sold, there was already a growing consensus that this case signaled a new social constellation, the entrance of numbers of enterprising poor women into this newly found cottage industry.[5] For those willing to admit it, Mary Beth Whithead was a woman who had entered the market to sell her labor power as a commodity to the baby broker Noel Keane and produced a product, Baby M, who was then sold to Mr. Stern, the donor of the sperm, at a profit. In this transaction labor was exploited, surplus value extracted, and a commodity produced: the total cost of production was $25,000; Mary Beth Whithead's wages a mere $10,000; whereas the profit of $15,000 went to Keane. Although the episode is often invoked, what is so important about the Baby M case for the purposes of this argument is that it reveals the extent to which surrogacy as commodified labor power is the exceptional case that compels the redefinition of all forms of biological reproduction. For it is with the advent of surrogacy that reproduction begins to function along lines similar to other forms of market production, subject to mechanisms of extraction of surplus value similar to those engaged by other forms of paid work. If one pursues this observation, the challenge that arises with surrogacy is that of reconfiguring the meaning of reproduction wherever and whenever it appears.[6]

In the 1970s some Marxist feminists began exploring related, if decidedly distinct, propositions. These feminists pointed to the problems of a traditional Marxist analysis which failed to systematize the exploitation of women's reproductive labor in the private sphere.[7] Their critique revealed that women's work, both in the household and in the reproduction of workers, is problematically subsumed by most classical

Marxist texts under and within the analysis of production. As a consequence of its relegation to the home, these feminists have argued, the mechanisms by which reproductive labor is exploited remain unanalyzed, and, needless to say, this private labor continues to be unpaid. Ironically, the remuneration of surrogates can be seen as a perverse redress for these early Marxist feminist concerns. And yet there are serious problems with this, not the least of which being that $10,000 is hardly adequate compensation for nine months of strenuous physical work.

The key issue is that in the current situation surrogacy as paid reproductive labor that produces babies with price tags exists side by side with women whose labor goes unpaid and whose babies appear to have no price. When surrogates' babies and babies without price tags exist together on the market and in the home, it becomes evident that both have a relation of equivalence dependent on abstract reproductive labor. Indeed, with the advent of paid surrogacy we have entered an age of biotechnological reproduction in which the erosion of the divisions between public and private accompany the rupture of the production/reproduction binarism. Both unpaid mothers and gestational surrogate mothers exist in the public sphere as, even in the former instance, the idea of the private is increasingly revealed as a pretense. To be biologically female is to be feminized, since no matter where reproductive labor is performed its feminization ensures that women's labor is exploited.

What the earlier insights of Marxist feminist analysis cannot address in today's economy is the fact that women's reproductive work can no longer be calculated within the confines of the economy of family/market/factory as registered in Marx's text and replicated in their own. As it stands, the reproductive economy is emerging as nearly synonymous with the productive one, highlighting not only the exploitation of the unpaid home-worker but also that of the underpaid surrogate. Despite its contributions, the earlier Marxist feminist project is confounded by surrogacy, as this rent-a-womb economy signals the difficulty of applying productive metaphors to describe reproductive activity, if only because with surrogacy reproduction definitively surfaces as wage work.

In turning briefly to Marx, I am not proposing an extension of the early Marxist feminist critique so much as an incorporation of Marx's insights about production into a feminist redelineation of reproduction as it is cast in both Marx's and Marxist feminist texts. In chapter 1 of volume 1 of *Capital* Marx is most instructive. He writes:

> It is only the expression of equivalence between different sorts of commodities which brings to view the specific character of value-creating labour, by actually reducing the different kinds of labour embedded in the

different kinds of commodities to their common quality of being human
labour in general.
　　However . . . [h]uman labour-power in its fluid state, or human labour,
creates value, but is not itself value. It becomes value in its coagulated state,
in objective form. The value of the linen as a congealed mass of human
labour can be expressed only as an "objectivity" [*Gegenstandlichkeit*], a
thing which is materially different from the linen itself and yet common
to the linen and all other commodities.[8]

From this passage one can extract three general formulations: first,
the value of a commodity is an expression of the congealed quantity of
labor that has gone into its production; second, labor power, like other
commodities, is reduced to and expressed as a quantity of abstract human
labor in the process of exchange; and, third, through the operations of
equivalence that constitute exchange, the value of the commodity object
is produced. When the worker realizes that it is the consumed quantity
of abstract labor involved in commodity production that is expressed
in the commodity's value-form, "the problem," says Marx, "is already
solved."
　　The production of the baby commodity follows the same logic,
a logic that exposes the baby commodity as a congealed quantity of
reproductive labor, and reproductive labor as concrete labor expressible
as a quantity of abstract human labor. But perhaps most pressingly, it is
a logic that women who function as reproductive laborers have available
to them. It is in pursuing this line of reasoning that the significance of
the baby commodity becomes clear:

> Remember that commodities possess an objective character as values only
> in so far as they are all expressions of an identical social substance, human
> labor, [and] that their objective character as value is therefore purely
> social.[9]

One way of reading *Capital,* then, the way in which I am choosing to read
it here, is to look at how Marx tries to give to all workers in the capitalist
relation an understanding of that relation in terms of the flow of labor
power. He does this by rendering the commodity in such a guise that
workers can recognize in its value form that the labor embodied is their
social labor.
　　The political project that might take root in this alternative feminist
incorporation of Marxism calls for women's right to abortion as the
right to take reproductive labor out of circulation, a strategy that also
implies the recrafting of the idea of "the right to abortion" as it is now
articulated. Yet, what would it really entail for women to affirm that Marx's

critique of the commodity form is applicable to the products of their reproductive labor? On the one hand, it would mean understanding the baby commodity as inextricably connected to the socially valued labor that produced it, a recognition of the suprasensible baby commodity as the objective expression of social labor. On the other hand, it would suggest that in order to reanimate the idea of "the right to abortion" we urgently need to calculate abortion as a social need in an emphatic and double sense.[10] For example, when reproductive activist and scholar Rosalind Petchesky writes that abortion is a "social right," the analysis of reproduction as productive presented here would require the insertion of a second dimension of "social" into her already nuanced text. She writes:

> If abortion is to be understood as a "social right"—a necessary service that society ought to make available to all women—and not just an individual right, much less a fatality or a duty, it must be connected to women's social power. There is a basis for making this connection in popular consciousness by relating the "morality" of abortion to the "morality"—and power—of motherhood as a social practice.[11]

In Petchesky's analysis the mother is the active agent of the fetus's personhood because she is the one who puts it into the social relation. It is her consciousness that is the condition of the fetus's eventual humanization; thus it is the mother's right to see her motherhood as a "social practice." Through the lens of Marx's text Petchesky's ideas of motherhood as a "social practice" and abortion as a "social right" take on an additional facet. For the second dimension of "social" that I have worked to cull from Marx's text allows the idea of "social right" as Petchesky understands it to reemerge outside the confines of the discourse of rights, as more of a demand than a right; in fact, it emerges as the double demand to claim the social power of the flow of reproductive labor and to claim abortion as the vehicle for seizing control of the means of reproduction.

Having proposed this reformulation of reproduction as (re)production, I must avow my discomfort with a political project that has as its goal the making of all women into rationalists able to deconstruct the social as the flow of their (re)productive labor power. To do so is to glaringly avoid grappling with the emotional effect of abortion, to sever the complex issues involved in the reproductive experience from the project of abstracting (re)productive labor.[12] And yet it seems that in the present moment feminists involved in reproductive politics need to claim the rational project as their own, while at the same time carefully tracking the inevitable political gains and losses. When, as feminists, we think of reproduction as (re)productive, we lose the ability to articulate women's concerns from a specifically gendered space. With the conceptual collapse of the binarism of production/reproduction, reproduction as a gendered activity ceases to exist. As in Marx's text, labor can only be computed as a quantity, not a quality and, therefore, the specificity of women's reproductive experience is lost. In the remainder of this essay I will examine this last observation in order to attend to this loss. For even though it may be useful to understand reproduction as continually exploited labor on loan to a capitalist system that prefers to maintain control over women's pregnancies by making gestation into involuntary servitude, it may also be crucial to hold on to the specificity of the maternal body as the cornerstone of (re)productive politics. In order to attend to this loss, then, I turn to Irigaray who, through a brand of feminist psychoanalysis with dual emphases on renarrativizing the mother and on sexuate rights, provides an invaluable theoretical tool for usurping the means (re)production while at the same time retaining the maternal body as a supplement to the problematic genderlessness of (re)productive labor.

Maternal as Mimetic Matrix

I should say at the outset that to turn to Irigaray in the manner just proposed is to take a double risk: first, that of returning to the maternal body in order to think through the specificity of the feminine in a context in which such returns have tended to deleteriously collapse femininity into femaleness; and, second, the related risk of being radically misunderstood, since the often-rehearsed criticism of Irigaray in the United States (still!) focuses on her purported essentialism. When Irigaray is read as an essentialist—someone who believes that woman has an essence and can be specified accordingly across time and cultures[13]—she paradoxically tends to resemble proponents of feminist psychoanalysis such as Nancy Chodorow. In Chodorow's version of object relations the reproduction of mothering is the consequence of overidentification between mother and daughter, their merging. For Chodorow, the daughter's strong pre-oedipal relation to the mother is continued into the oedipal period, and indeed may never end, because the daughter's ego is understood to be shaped through her fusional relation to her mother as primary object. In contrast, the boy child, who has been pushed out of the preoedipal relationship, more successfully engages in individuation. The result of these different trajectories, Chodorow argues, is that

[a]s long as women mother, we can expect that girl's preoedipal period will be longer than that of a boy and that women, more than men, will be open to and preoccupied with those very relational issues that go into mothering—feelings of primary identification, lack of separateness or differentiation, ego and body-ego boundary issues . . .[14]

In the conclusion to her book Chodorow summarizes, "[W]omen's mothering . . . produces psychological self-definition and capacities appropriate to mothering in women, and curtails and inhibits these and this self-definition in men."[15] Because Chodorow argues that mothering is a social formation, she believes that the situation will change when men learn to mother. The problem with her argument is that she in the end embraces the idea that psychic structures emerge out of the biological facts of gestation and nursing, and are the only structures that are possible in response to these "facts." Rather than complicating our interpretation of biology and our understanding of the psyche, Chodorow recommends transforming our social behavior. In her critique of object relations, Drucilla Cornell suggests that the difficulty with this theory is that it conflates psychic structures with social reality.[16] I would go on to tease out of this critique a more explicit recognition of the extent to which this conflation is enabled by a further tacit reduction of psychic structures to biological, material ones.[17]

According to some critics, this reading of Chodorow's fusion of mother and daughter indicates the convergence of her theories with Irigaray's, a convergence I wish to challenge by demonstrating that Irigaray is neither a biological essentialist who regards anatomy as destiny, nor a psychic essentialist who attributes to women in a glorifying manner all that exceeds the symbolic.[18] Instead, in Irigaray's work the biological ground of the mother's body is renarrativized in such a way that it is rendered as material as opposed to essential, and thus comes to hold the possibility for a variety of psychic structures and the ensuing alteration of the social relations among subjects.

This said, it is also important to take note of Irigaray's insistence that the genealogical proposition that we have all had mothers is irreducible in the present moment of technological development.[19] Lacanian psychoanalysis, with its phallogocentric debt to Western metaphysics (and thus its consonance with global patriarchy), has described one possible outcome of this "truth." Irigaray agrees that this outcome is ordinarily, if detrimentally, experienced as social reality, and as a result, her depiction of the maternal is at times descriptive of women's position in the present symbolic order. At other times, she takes the inverse tack, insisting that this particular coding of the woman as the mother is not the only one and that the same body which is appropriated and then misunderstood by Lacan can be salvaged for more emancipatory ends. In a recent interview, Irigaray discusses this problem and inquires into the alternatives:

> The culture, the language, the imaginary and the mythology in which we live at the moment. . . . I say to myself . . . let's have a look . . . this edifice that looks so clean and subtle . . . let's see what ground it is built on. Is it all that acceptable?
>
> The substratum is the woman who reproduces the social order, who is made this order's infrastructure: the whole of our western culture is based upon the murder of the mother. The man—god—father killed the mother in order to take power. . . . [But] isn't there a fluidity, some flood, that could shake this social order? . . . [If] we make the foundations of the social order shift, then everything will shift. That is why they are so careful to keep us on a leash.[20]

Here culture as Westerners know it is revealed to be contingent on matricide; in turn matricide emerges as Irigaray's shorthand for the idea that the mother is the objectified matrix out of which the male subject, his signifiers, and language spring. For Irigaray, mothers are as good as dead in this description, because this construction is grounded in the equation of woman with mother, an operation of equivalence that effectively erases woman's subjectivity and renders maternity a form of symbolic death. As Irigaray elaborates in her more explicit exposures of Lacanian logic, the formulation that the woman's body as maternal body must be constructed as Other in order to give birth to the subject is an extremely violent one.[21] Precisely what matricide erases is the possibility that there is some "fluidity," some "flood that could shake this social order" and allow the "woman-mother" to imagine a different social flow in which she might give birth to herself and other women. Irigaray puts this more suggestively still, querying,

> Doesn't the phallic erection occur at the place where the umbilical cord once was? The phallus becomes the organizer of the world through the man-father at the very place where the umbilical cord, that primal link to the mother, once gave birth to man and woman.[22]

Again, the symbolic order's stability and the subject's coherence are seen as contingent on the denial of the mother as generative of subjects of both genders and of herself. And thus, it is only when this primary relation, or "primal link," is rethought that it becomes possible to narrate a genealogy in terms of the mother, a genealogy that begins to realize the possibility of another logic of subjectivity that might be enabled by this very different vision of the subject's relation to its first home and first love, its relation to the mother.

This exploration of the maternal body as a new sort of symbolically generative node is most forcefully undertaken in Irigaray's rewriting of the relationship between mothers and daughters. In contrast to Chodorow, who presents this relationship as inevitably merged, Irigaray diagnoses this representation as the cause of women's *déréliction*,[23] not because it is a representation that tells the "truth" about mothers and daughters, but because other truths made possible by this relationship cannot be symbolized in ways that allow women to conceive of themselves as subjects emerging out of it:

> Unable to create their own words, women remain and move in an immediacy without any transitional, transactional object. They take-give without mediation, commune without knowing it with and in a flesh they do not recognize: maternal flesh not reducible to a reproductive body, more or less shapeless amorous matter to which there could be no debt, no possible return.[24]

In this passage Irigaray describes the experience of being a woman in relation to the clinical account of the mother and daughter; but once again she goes on to insist that this is not the only description and that one way of contesting it is to represent this relationship by differentiating and thus refusing to reduce the reproductive body to this image of the fused maternal one.

Irigaray develops two procedures in order to represent the maternal body as a mimetic matrix. First, she looks at the manner in which the analytic session mirrors the mother-daughter relationship and offers an arena in which to rework it. Second, she describes this reworking as explicitly dependent on a return to the maternal body. In several essays on the analytic session and clinical practice she argues that successful analysis for women is contingent on creating a new ethics in the process of analysis, a new relational mode in which both the analyst and analysand can recognize each other as subjects. In the traditional therapeutic situation the analyst sits behind the analysand and is hidden and physically separated from her. Quite literally the analyst's position vis-à-vis the subject is a projection of the supposedly ideal relation of separation between mother and child, a relation that the analyst is ostensibly helping the analysand to move toward. The patient like the child is prodded to turn away from the mother; and yet, Irigaray asks, what if the analysand

and analyst were to position themselves face to face, were to engage in an other kind of interaction that did not symbolically repeat the annihilation or castigation of either one? Surely such an about-face would produce different results. In fact, such a turn and its articulation become the only means of foregrounding transference:

> We . . . need to find, rediscover, invent the words, the sentences that speak of the most ancient and most current relationship we know—the relationship to the mother's body, to our body—sentences that translate the bond between our body, her body the body of our daughter. We need to discover a language that is not a substitute for the experience of *corps-à-corps* as the paternal language seeks to be, but which accompanies that bodily experience, clothing it in words that do not erase the body but speak the body.[25]

Recognizing that the symbolization of the relationship between mothers and daughters is central to extricating women from *déréliction,* Irigaray suggests that women stop thinking of the maternal body as mother, and the mother-daughter relationship as one of pathological fusion. What is so significant about her renarrativization of this relationship is that it effectively sees the maternal body as a relational situation rather than as a threatening or devouring unity. To renarrativize is to shift from an idea of the mother as object-matrix of the subject and his signifiers to thinking, instead, of the mother as a site that instantiates the possibility of an ethical relationship between two subjects. To renarrativize the mother is to read the maternal body as the potential site of ethical instantiation.[26] What is most striking about this new psychoanalytic ethics is that in Irigaray's schema it emerges out of the biological body itself:

> Whilst it is relatively commonplace to talk of relations of merging or fusion, we still have to arrive at a different interpretation of what is in play in these fusional relationships. The placentary abode and the adhesion of the placenta to the mother's womb obey another economy and are liberated otherwise.[27]

Or, similarly,

> No image has been formed for the placenta and hence we are constantly in danger of retreating into the original matrix, of seeking refuge in any open body, and forever nestling into the body of the other woman.[28]

> The placental economy is . . . an organized economy, one not in a state of fusion, which respects the one and the other. Unfortunately, our culture,

split off from the natural order . . . neglect[s] or fail[s] to recognize the almost ethical character of the fetal relation.[29]

In the majority of her essays on the analytic session, Irigaray invokes the womb as the site, and the placenta as the organ, that operates as the threshold for instantiating an "almost ethical" relationship between subjects. In so doing she slips during the course of these discussions from the constellation of analyst-analysand to mother-daughter and then enters the body itself to speak of the mother-fetus. These elisions of important distinctions make one wonder whether Irigaray is renarrativizing the maternal body or just a particular part of it, and whether the fetus can only be female within the logic of her text. Those readers who have argued against viewing Irigaray as an essentialist find this an especially confusing set of moves that require explaining away the body she returns to as a metaphorical description, or seeing its invocation as an intervention into the Lacanian account of the relationship between the symbolic and imaginary.[30] Here, I am suggesting that Irigaray leaves a renegotiated tension between the imaginary and symbolic in place, and that it is more useful to begin to read the maternal body to which Irigaray continually returns in all of its materiality than to yield to an automatic aversion to the body's appearance in her work. For Irigaray approaches the mother and fetus through neither metonymy nor metaphor, but through an operation of radical mime that calls the epistemological and ontological status of both into question.

Few scholars who work on Irigaray have missed the opportunity to talk about mimicry in her texts as both a key concept and a primary method of philosophical investigation. As Elizabeth Weed argues, there is virtually no text of Irigaray's that can be read outside of her mimetic reading and writing practice.[31] For Naomi Schor it is through mimesis that Irigaray enacts the risky procedure of transvaluating rather than repudiating misogyny. According to Schor, mimesis names Irigaray's deconstructive and paleonymic strategy of using, as Derrida has put it, an " 'old name in order to launch a new concept' "; and thus, when Irigaray mimes, Schor recommends that we read her as "signify[ing] difference as positivity."[32] As Irigaray explains in her most often quoted passage on mimicry, for women mimicry is the deliberate conversion of a form "of subordination into an affirmation . . ." because by assuming the feminine role, women make " 'visible,' by an effect of playful repetition, what was supposed to remain invisible."[33] Responding to Schor, Judith Butler discusses mimicry as the strategy whereby Irigaray enters the philosophers' phallogocentric system in order to "mime and repeat the gestures of . . . [their] operation until . . . [the] emergence of the outside within the system calls into question its systematic closure and its pretension to be self-grounding."[34] Butler sees this as a piece of what Schor is getting at when Schor claims that "Irigaray mimes mimesis itself."

Following Weed, Schor, and Butler, in this reading, I use mimicry to succinctly describe the strategy that Irigaray deploys when rethinking the materiality of the biological reproductive body as a body capable of producing a new set of psychic structures and social relations. In fact, it is precisely through a return to the body in the act of critical linguistic mime that Irigaray can both expose its process of materialization and intervene in this process. Insofar as Irigaray teaches us to assume that living tissue can be read as text, she also asks us to participate in the possibility of renarrativization. In turning to the placenta, Irigaray refuses to posit a single cut between the signifier and signified, referent and reference. The two terms of this binary are rather imbricated within each other, and mimicry becomes her method of disclosing this overlap and convergence. Linking reproduction to mimicry, Irigaray writes:

> To play with mimesis is . . . for a woman, to try and recover the place of her exploitation by discourse, without allowing herself to be simply reduced to it. It means to resubmit herself . . . to make "visible," by an effect of playful repetition. . . .
>
> If women can play with mimesis, it is because they are capable of bringing new nourishment to its operation. Because they have always nourished this operation? Is not the "first" stake in mimesis that of re-producing (from) nature? Of giving it form in order to appropriate it for oneself?[35]

Once again, as the guardians of nature, women have been confined to a reproductive function that only serves the male subject and logos. And yet, it is just this reproductive capacity that is identified by Irigaray as a mimetic one. As Irigaray elaborates in this passage, reproduction itself is intimately associated with mimicry, because reproduction ventriloquizes mimetic repetition on the biological level. Indeed, the term "reproduction" itself assumes a paleonymic function. Insofar as "reproduction" signifies both the biological process that Western metaphysics and capitalism use to reduce women to mothers, as well as women's mimetic proclivity, it is the term over which Irigaray lingers. It is this term that best expresses women's potential to disrupt the violent and essentializing codification of their biological selves. In turning to her own body as biological ground, that same body which is said to be the source of subordination is repeated or reproduced with a difference. It is no longer the body assigned to woman to buttress the representation of male sexuality, but a body that allows woman to articulate her own subjective specificity and that of other women.

In her most recent work, Irigaray has "simplified [her] formerly . . . sibylline prose," according to critics such as Margaret Whitford, and has begun to convey her message by writing as directly as possible about the materiality of bodily relationships. Irigaray now states rather than alludes to the material implications of her arguments, and thus Whitford is concerned that "there is a real danger that the . . . less subtle and more programmatic elements of the later work could close off rather than open up dialogue with other women."[36] Although Whitford is justified in seeing the sharp stylistic break from Irigaray's earlier more recognizably philosophical texts as constituting a risk to readers who will be tempted to interpret these seemingly simplified statements at face value, I am proposing that if Irigaray's new approach is a gamble, it is also the most provocative development in her theory. Indeed, it is this new unabashed body talk that allows her to look to the mother, return to her in all of her corporeality, and then repeat her body's representation in order to produce a different material effect. In an interview in which Irigaray asks questions of Hélène Rouch, whom she identifies as a biology teacher at the *Lycée Colbert* in Paris, this new mimetic strategy is practiced with astonishing virtuosity.

"On the Maternal Order" begins with Irigaray's assertion that our culture is subject to two behavioral models, the Darwinian and the Pavlovian, which force a "fatal repetition" of the representation of the external environment as something that needs to be struggled against and/or adapted to. However, instead of accepting these representations, Irigaray indicates how their limitations can be interrogated by considering corporeal identity, especially the relationship between mother and fetus in utero. Although this relationship (as I have been arguing) is often presented in a state of fusion, the placenta, she explains, can actually be understood to play a mediating role during the intrauterine period, a role which can be comprehended as "respectful of the life of both" mother and fetus as distinct entities. The placenta, in other words, need not lend itself to representations of the mother as an external environment that is either hostile or hospitable to the fetus.

Rouch begins her explanation of the placenta by reminding us that it is a tissue formed by the embryo which, while imbricated in the uterine mucosa, remains separate from it. It plays a mediating role in the space between mother and fetus in two ways: on the one hand it prevents a fusion of maternal and embryonic tissues; on the other, it regulates the exchanges of nutrients and wastes, and simultaneously modifies the maternal metabolism. Comparing pregnancy to a successful organ transplant, Rouch further explores the placenta's participation in the exchanges between the immune systems of mother and fetus:

> The placenta isn't some sort of automatic reaction system, which would suppress all the mother's reactions by preventing her from recognizing the embryo-fetus as other. On the contrary, there has to be a recognition of the other, of the non-self, by the mother, and therefore an initial reaction from her, in order for placental factors to be produced. The difference between the "self" and other is, so to speak, continuously negotiated. It's as if the mother always knew that the embryo (and thus the placenta) was other, and that she lets the placenta know this, which then produces the factors enabling the maternal organism to accept it as other.[37]

At moments it seems that Rouch and Irigaray are speaking different disciplinary languages, but what is so noteworthy about the interview is that this hardly puts them at cross purposes. Whereas Irigaray asks questions posed in psychoanalytic terms that beg answers that speak to psychoanalysis, Rouch's ripostes are coached in biological terms which can be interpreted as equally psychoanalytic. Through this interview, through this exchange between analyst and biologist, a renegotiation of the relationship between biology and culture effectively takes place. The upshot of this communication is the revelation of "the almost ethical character" of the relationship between mother and fetus.[38] As Rouch explains, the placenta tells us "that the differentiation between the mother's self and the other of the child, and vice versa, is in place well before it's given meaning in and by language, and the forms it takes don't necessarily accord with those our cultural imaginary relays."[39]

In Chodorow's work "the fact" of fusion between mother and child can only indicate the necessity of reconfiguring social relationships through behavioral reform; Irigaray, in contrast, proposes that it is possible to look to the biological "origin" to find a different set of biological "facts." As Rouch suggests, to look to this corporeal "origin" as a place before language is to refuse to *over*look the scientific account of the material body as the ground for a different set of ethicopolitical configurations. In a very particular sense, what Irigaray and Rouch together enact is a foundational ruse; for in returning to the corporeal as "origin," they displace its status as origin and in turn reveal just how unoriginary it is. By refusing to separate tissue from text, they mimic the material body's operations in the interest of repeating and thus effectively renarrativizing its materiality.

And yet, the question remains, what does this mimetic renarrativiza-tion of the mother's body have to offer those seeking to secure women's access to abortion? Does not the idea of the placenta as the threshold of an ethical relation in utero run the risk of granting subject status to the fetus in exactly the way in which reproductive activists have warded against by insisting on mother-fetus fusion? Compare, for example, pro-abortionist Barbara Katz Rothman's account of the situation in utero to Rouch's: "Mothers and fetuses are not just connected chemically," Rothman writes. Rather, "the placenta is the point at which their fluids meet, . . . [and] there are other points of meeting: heads rest on bladders in pregnancy, feet dance against ribs. The mother holds her fetus within her."[40] Rothman continues in a different context, "The baby [is] not planted within the mother, but [is] flesh of her flesh, part of her."[41] Rouch's ideas are certainly separated by a gulf from Rothman's and on first glance quite close to those of the anti-abortion lobby. Bernard Nathanson, a key anti-abortion advocate, casts the mother-fetus relationship on the microbiological level in the following terms:

> When a pregnancy implants itself into the wall of the uterus at the eighth day following conception, the defense mechanisms of the body . . . sense that this creature now settling down for a lengthy stay is an intruder, an alien, and must be expelled. Therefore an intense immunological attack is mounted on the pregnancy by the white blood cell elements, and through an ingenious and extraordinarily efficient defense system the unborn child succeeds in repelling the attack. In ten percent or so of the cases the defensive system fails and the pregnancy is lost as a spontaneous abortion or miscarriage. Think how fundamental a lesson there is for us here: Even on the most minute microscopic scale *the body has trained itself, or somehow in some inchoate way knows, how to recognize self from non-self.*[42]

Although Nathanson's fetal war stories portray the maternal environment as the hostile enemy camp, the mother's white blood cells attacking the sentient "unborn child," who, in the end, is generally the better military strategist, Nathanson (like Rouch) explicitly depicts the womb as the place where the recognition of a difference of "self from nonself" occurs. Furthermore, like Rouch, Nathanson grounds his argument in the material body. With evident confidence he presents fetal personhood not as a moral, religious, or philosophical question, but as a scientifically knowable fact. Nathanson views science as simply revealing of the fetus as the "unborn child," a scientific revelation dictated by his politics.

For Cynthia Daniels, the feminist scholar from whose book on fetal politics this comment from Nathanson is borrowed, Nathanson is one among many anti-abortionists who have used the power of the new scientific technologies to furnish an array of visual images of the fetus which make it tangible, knowable, and which have helped endow it "with independent life," thus facilitating a shift of "the power of procreation and pregnancy away from women and toward the social institutions of science and the state."[43] Daniels correctly identifies this shift; and yet, the very terms of her argument indicate the problems residing in the feminist pro-abortion image of a fusional relationship between mother and fetus. Although Daniels, Rothman, and other feminist strategists are willing to narrate the maternal body for their political ends, they have implicitly conceded the scientific terms and definitions that make meaning of the materiality of the pregnant body. In concluding her discussion of Nathanson, Daniels asserts,

> politicized characterizations of the biological processes of reproduction, in ancient times and today, have informed our understanding of the maternal-fetal relationship. The science of reproduction reflects assumptions about male power, rights, and ownership of the fetus as well as of the pregnant woman's body.[44]

Certainly Daniels is right once again. However, what is problematic about her comments is that at the precise moment of recognizing the politicized terrain of science and its control by what she loosely labels "male power," she simultaneously marshals her contrasting fusional image of the mother-fetus relationship as an absolute and essential truth. As pro-abortion feminists disavow the scientific finding of the fetus's autonomy as "bad" science and represent the biological tissue that is the placenta as a truly comprehensible point of maternal-fetal fusion, they essentialize this tissue and neglect the option of rendering a different *scientific* account of it, as well as a different account of science. The unfortunate outcome of these seemingly pragmatic decisions is that there is little room left in pro-abortion arguments for unsettling or denaturalizing the very process of materialization in which these feminists are so deeply engaged. Unwittingly conceding that in this instance biology is destiny, even as they recognize that the biological body is consistently misrepresented, they cover over the traces of the processes by which the maternal body is materialized in their own rhetoric. The idea of a fusional relationship between mother and fetus is implicitly posited as a biological reality, not recognized or purposely dismissed by patriarchal science, and thus the pro-abortion account of mother-fetus fusion obscures the very unstable conditions of this narrative's possibility. As Daniels concludes in the last chapter of her book,

> the interests of the fetus and the pregnant woman are unitary. When a pregnant woman acts in ways that are damaging to the health of the fetus,

she is engaged not in fetal abuse but in self-abuse. Her health and the health of the fetus are inseparable. . . . In this sense, pregnancy stands as a metaphor for all relations of human dependency . . .[45]

The pregnant woman represents the interdependence of human life and the difficulty, even impossibility, of distinguishing self from other.[46]

It is not that pro-abortion feminists do not turn to the body to renarrate it (or in Daniel's case metaphorize it), but rather that, in contrast to Irigaray, they relinquish a potential form of control over the material body which they so effortlessly and apodictically invoke. Although Rouch is no more critical of the idea that the pregnant body has a meaning that "is in place well before it's given meaning in and by language"[47] than are the pro-abortionists in question, by entering into conversation with Rouch, Irigaray reenters the pregnant body as Rouch presents it to her, exposing through mimicry (in contrast to metaphor) its very materialization within the scientific discourse she is coinhabiting throughout the duration of their dialogue. What distinguishes Irigaray from Rothman, Daniels, and other pro-abortionists who insist on mother-fetus fusion is not only the specific narration of the maternal body that she proffers but her unwillingness to abandon science as a tool of critical mime, as just the tool that opens up the possibility of self-reflexively rematerializing the maternal body's operations and contours.

Reproductive Ethics and Sexuate Rights

In the conversation between Irigaray and Rouch, Irigaray clearly takes science very seriously, consistently attempting to secure her narrative of the maternal body in Rouche's scientific one.[48] If one effect of this mimicry is the revelation that there is no anatomy that can serve as a stable referent, another is the realization that the mimic's access to the body is always tenuous. Other feminists working on the representation of bodily materiality have argued similarly.[49] Judith Butler explains the problem of the body's accessibility in terms of the relationship between materiality and language:

> To posit a materiality outside of language, where that materiality is considered ontologically distinct from language, is to undermine the possibility that language might be able to indicate or correspond to that domain of radical alterity. Hence, the absolute distinction between language and materiality which was to secure the referential function of language undermines that function radically.[50]

The idea of materiality as a space separate from language, *the space* that pro-abortion feminists, anti-abortionists, and Rouch all believe they are indicating when discussing the maternal-fetal relation, is in Butler's view external to language only fantasmatically because the very idea of a clean break between language and materiality is one that is manufactured by the language of materiality itself. Butler continues, "There can be no reference to a pure materiality except via materiality," and, therefore, materiality and language are not opposed; "what is material never fully escapes from the process by which it is signified."[51]

Butler's analysis coincides with Irigaray's understanding of the materiality of the maternal body in Rouch's scientific account of it. Irigaray is not suggesting that there is a maternal body that can simply be known (as Rouch, in contrast, does), but rather that there is an irresolvable tension between the maternal body's materiality and its representation.

For Irigaray, science is an important and powerful coding system, one that allows women to stake a claim in the highly politicized struggle to define the body. Mimicry is the philosophical method that lets one inhabit this system; but mimicry has a double edge. It is both a method that tampers with the representation of the body's materiality by intervening into the process of representing it, and at the same time a method that exhibits the potentially fraught and endlessly deferred connection between the body's materiality and its representation. To extend this point further, it is not only that mimicry exposes the body as discursively inscribed but also that it points to the materiality of the signifier, to the necessary role that representation plays in the process of materializing the body. With respect to the dominant rhetoric of pro-abortionists, this understanding of mimicry's double edge alerts one to what is so troubling about the feminist rejection of science as a coding system. In conceding science to the dominant symbolic, in refusing to appropriate the power of mimicry, pro-abortionists refuse to participate in the scientific materialization of the body, confining themselves to engagement in the body's "representations." The unfortunate result of this confinement is that the materiality of the body actually begins to evaporate in pro-abortion accounts of it, as the complex relationship between materiality and representation has been seriously neglected.[52] What Irigaray's brand of feminist psychoanalysis can offer, then, when we desire the reappropriation of the maternal body as a means of reproduction, is a strategic lesson in pilfering the power of scientific discourse to rematerialize this controversial body as well as to make meaning of it.

In Irigaray's vision of sexuate rights she most forcefully suggests why it is that the mother must be renarrativized. Her reasoning resonates with that of feminist legal theorists who have also begun to debate the need for jurisprudence that emphasizes the specificity of the feminine within sexual difference by theorizing and, in fact, making the pregnant body exceptional. For several of these legal scholars it is explicitly the precariousness of *Roe v. Wade* that has sparked a quest to redefine equal rights as "equivalent rights," as rights that can guarantee women's reproductive freedom as part of a larger legislative framework that promises to protect women's right to "bodily integrity."[53] Like feminist legal theorists, Irigaray too has as her primary concern the theorizing of sexual difference as distinct from an idea of difference within sameness. Like these scholars, she turns to the specificity of the maternal body in order to ground the possibility of what she labels "sexuate rights," rights that symbolically institute sexual difference. And yet, although Irigaray's insistent demand for a renarrativization of the maternal body's materiality is consistent with legal theory that seeks to make the pregnant body visible in the eyes of the law, her renarrativization of the scientific, phallogocentric, and metaphysical symbolization of the mother situates the maternal body as a site for critical mime. Thus Irigaray challenges the metaphysical understanding of the body's materiality in a way in which feminist legal theorists, who must work at least partially within the legal edifice, cannot.

According to Irigaray, sexuate rights are not simply legal rights (though they may also be that), but rather the rights accorded to women so that their bodies may be adequately imagined and symbolized in and by a culture (and a legal system) which has until now been preoccupied with the symbolization of one sex and one sex alone. When Irigaray calls for sexuate rights she is calling for the symbolization of two distinct sexes rather than one. She realizes that all ethical positions require a universalization of the singular but additionally comprehends that when there is only one universal (as now there is a male one) it cannot be inclusive of difference. For this reason she finds it necessary to make the logistically impossible move of positing two universals. In most of her writing this involves looking at how phallogocentric culture erases woman's sexuality, sexual pleasure, and the symbolization of the existing relationships among women, including those between mothers and daughters; it involves reexamining the relationship between the female body and the law of the symbolic in order to redress injustice. In a prescriptive essay, "The Culture of Difference," Irigaray argues that culture has nearly inverted the meaning of what is distinct about the female body and its toleration of the other's growth within. As she puts it, "civilization" forgets that the female body "engenders respect for difference"[54] and plods on by endlessly repeating two injustices or anomalies: first, the exclusion of the reproductive body as a site of differentiation; and, second, the repression of the girl child so that she remains outside of culture, a natural body only good for procreation.

It is with these two formulations in mind that Irigaray calls for a rethinking of the biological body. She cautions that "the difficulties women have in gaining recognition for their social and political rights are rooted in . . . [an] insufficiently thought out relation between biology and culture."[55] In our present moment, "To deny all explanations of a biological kind—because biology has paradoxically been used to exploit women—is to deny the key to interpreting this exploitation."[56] To fight injustice, in striving to give women subjective status, Irigaray insists on returning to bodily tissue in order to renarrativize this tissue and explore the bodily text as the site of women's emergence as subjects able to symbolize themselves in the public space of culture.

Such a project is decisively distinct from either a liberalism that demands the sort of equality that obliterates all varieties of difference, or a politics based on ideas of choice and privacy that takes as given a certain set of metaphysical assumptions about the subject as substance, presuppositions that have historically reinforced rather than countered discriminatory legal practices.[57] In contrast to these misdirected tactics, through her discourse on sexuate rights, Irigaray offers her readers the option of basing these rights in what I will label "reproductive ethics." In forging this term I pull together Irigaray's ideas about the mother as a relational situation and her mimicry of the maternal body. I cite Irigaray's prompting to her fellow analysts at a recent convention in order to indicate what might be a stake in mobilizing this synthetic label:

> Our urgent task is to refuse to submit to a desubjectivized social role, the role of mother, which is dictated by an order subject to the division of labor—he produces, she reproduces—that walls us up in the ghetto of a single function. When did society ever ask fathers to choose between being men or citizens? We don't have to give up being women to be mothers.[58]

Here Irigaray seamlessly slips into the language of rights and citizenship in order to implore women to claim their status as both women and mothers in the eyes of the law, symbolic and legal. She indicates that the maternal must be reappropriated as the place from which to argue for women's right to self-symbolization because mothers do not have to give up being women (that is, subject-citizens) just because they have until now been used to buttress the male economies of both desire and production.

But perhaps Irigaray's most daring move lies in rephrasing and inverting this idea. She directly continues, We "need to discover and declare that we are always mothers just by being women."[59] Such a statement would certainly be impossible within the logic of the pro-abortion movement's understanding of "the right to abortion" as it is now being articulated. For Irigaray's inverted formulation gives all women license to understand themselves as mothers, regardless of whether they have children, want to have children, are infertile, sterilized, use contraceptives, or choose to abort. Indeed, it is the statement that makes a pro-abortion coalition held together by a shared renarrativization of the mother's body as a-essential (rather than essentialized), thinkable. It is a formulation that implicates all people who *identify as women* in the articulation of the demand for abortion, the demand to control reproductive labor power. At the same time, it is an axiom whose flexible logic suggests that one might conceivably regard oneself as a mother even if one does not identify as a woman. Finally, it is this formulation that makes it possible to use *Capital*'s antiessentializing abstractions in the interest of wresting from capitalism the control of essences that have until now been used to justify and perpetuate reproductive exploitation.

To incorporate Marxism and supplement it with psychoanalysis is to comprehend how reproductive rights might be based in an a-essential maternal body that shares in the abstracted social relations of reproduction. It is this feminist psychoanalytic incorporation of Marxism, moreover, that compels one to imagine a united front politics that recognizes the specificity of the reproductive experience without essentializing it. This is in turn the future justice that will be brought closer by the liberation of all people from the hegemonic reduction of their bodies to essential roles. Although Irigaray very rarely talks about abortion, this use of the renarrativized maternal body resonates with her larger project. The reverberations are clearly audible:

> In a sense we need to say good-bye to maternal omnipotence (the last refuge) and establish a woman-to-woman relationship of reciprocity with our mothers in which they might possibly also feel themselves to be our daughters. In a word, liberate ourselves along with our mothers. That is an indispensable precondition for our emancipation from the authority of fathers. In our societies, the mother-daughter, daughter-mother relationship constitutes a highly explosive nucleus. Thinking it, and changing it, is equivalent to shaking the foundations of the patriarchal order.[60]

Following Irigaray's lead, one might venture the generalization (in a not-too-millennial tone) that we are all potentially mothers—whether we choose to mother or are biologically able to or not—as it is the abstracted reproductive relation that allows all of us to grasp the social as the flow of our reproductive labor power. And thus, perhaps the question that we, as pro-abortionists, need to begin to ask is what it would mean to think about "the right to abortion" as a demand grounded in a recognition of the maternal bodies that call for economic sexuate justice as material if a-essential?

Notes

This article was first published in *differences: A Journal of Feminist Cultural Studies* 6, no. 1 (1994).

1. A fusional narration of pregnancy has allowed pro-abortionists to assert the primacy of the mother as life-giving subject within a context in which anti-abortion forces attempt to cast the fetus as "the newest social actor in the American conservative imagination." (See Cynthia R. Daniels, *At Women's Expense: State Power and Politics of Fetal Rights* [Cambridge, Mass.: Harvard University Press, 1993], 3.) Even though it is increasingly common to question the category of "woman" within feminism and speculate about how a feminism that refuses to ground itself in this category might look, pro-abortion feminists have decidedly neglected to raise similar concerns about their own reliance on an essentialized understanding of maternity. It is this situation that motivates the intervention I hope to make here.

Carmel Shalev is one of the only U.S. scholars who advocates wages for reproduction and the establishment of a free market in surrogacy. Shalev's perspective—that it is necessary for feminists to be self-critical about the reactive moralizing response to women controlling their bodily resources—is important. This said, her liberal faith in the legal system's ability to protect surrogates through contractual laws that guarantee commensurate pay tends to subsume her argument's other insights.

2. The mainstream press has been quick to quip that in the United States in the 1990s "babies have price tags" (Ellen Hopkins, "Tales from the Baby Factory," *The New York Times Magazine* [March 15, 1992]: 40ff.). The problem with such coverage is twofold: (1) it hides the exploitation of reproductive laborers by insisting that the commodification of babies and reproductive labor is separate; (2) it obscures the fact that baby production occurs within a global context formed by the unequal division of labor and uneven development. U.S. feminists urgently need an international analytic frame in order to account for reproductive exploitation within the global baby market. Such an analysis also must consider (especially in relation to the Conference on Population and Development in Cairo) the vexing question of population control as it functions as a coercive force through the action of both international agencies and national states. See Farida Akhter, "On the Question of the Reproductive Right: A Personal Reflection," in *Declaration of Comilla* (Bangladesh: UBINIG, 1991): 45–49; Betsy Hartmann,

Reproductive Rights and Wrongs (New York: Harper & Row, 1987); and Maria Mies, "Sexist and Racist Implications of the New Reproductive Technologies," *Alternatives XII* (1987): 323–42.

3. Gayatri Chakravorty Spivak, *Outside in the Teaching Machine* (New York: Routledge, 1993), 13.

4. Judith Butler, *Bodies That Matter: On the Discursive Limits of "Sex"* (New York: Routledge, 1993), 47.

5. Katha Pollitt, Barbara Katz Rothman, and Ellen Hopkins all share this concern, and are especially suspicious of the racist dimensions of surrogate exploitation, as the new reproductive technologies make it possible for women of color to bear genetically unrelated "white" children. From the other side of the political divide, the development of the free market argument (not unlike Shalev's) has been under way since the 1970s. Its proponents urge the state to intervene in order to balance the supply of white adoptable babies with the growing demand. Although Elisabeth Landes and Richard Posner's early article on the adoption market does not deal with surrogacy, it explicitly recommends that a free market in adoption should be established by inducing white women contemplating abortion to go through with their pregnancies and then give up their babies for adoption.

6. Workplace legislation ostensibly directed at the protection of the fetus effectively prohibits women from "choosing" to reproduce if they want to retain certain higher paying jobs. Such legislation reveals the exact dimensions of the (re)productive nature of women's work. Consider, for example, the famous case of the American Cyanamid plant in West Virginia at which women were given the option of sterilization or losing their positions. Although it is true that women were being asked to "choose" between having a child and their jobs, less visible was the way in which, in being coerced into making this decision, they were also being recruited into the (re)productive labor force, where their labor was still being regulated by their bosses.

7. The essays collected in the 1979 anthology edited by Zillah Eisenstein are exemplary of this Marxist feminist trend. Note, however, that by no means all Marxist feminist work sustains the criticism I am making here. To name only a few exceptions, Swasti Mitter's international framework complicates the distinctions between public and private, while Donna Haraway's "Cyborg Manifesto" compellingly elaborates on the cybernetic character of women's labor in a global market. These problematizations of the division between public and private inform my analysis throughout.

8. Karl Marx, *Capital*, vol. 1, Ben Fowkes, trans. (New York: Vintage, 1977), 142.

9. Ibid., 138–39.

10. Bangladeshi reproductive activist Farida Akhter argues that it is only in bourgeois society that women can be said to have a "right" to their bodies and that the demand for "rights" in the context of the reproductive rights movement must be understood as a demand to submit the individual body to the laws of Capital: "The reproduction of the human species is primarily a social activity

which is realized through individuals, but it is never an individual affair" (Akhter, "On the Question of the Reproductive Right," 47). Akhter concludes that with a new "material basis for human history" women would no longer need to demand the right to their bodies (ibid., 48). I am partially aligned with Akhter but am in addition suggesting that it is just this understanding of "right" that needs to be reappropriated and abused by abortion rights activists in the United States. It is true that woman is "naturally an owner of her body," but it is exactly this property relation that has been obscured by the anti-abortion lobby and by capitalism alike. What is at stake in the U.S. context is certainly an eventual transformation of this state of ownership, but first a recognition of it is needed. Thus, my argument also resonates with Patricia Williams's imbrication of rights and needs. For Williams rights are a very usable discourse: "what is needed . . . is not the abandonment of rights language for all purposes, but an attempt to become multilingual in the semantics of evaluating rights" (Patricia Williams, *The Alchemy of Race and Rights* [Cambridge, Mass.: Harvard University Press, 1991], 149). I will return to the question of rights shortly.

11. Rosalind Pollack Petchesky, *Abortion and Woman's Choice* (London: Verso, 1984), 375.

12. This project of abstraction is not meant to detract from but rather to supplement the kind of ideological work that other feminists have undertaken in their cogent attacks on family values and attention to the often highly charged emotive experiences of pregnancy, child rearing, and abortion.

13. Naomi Schor provides an excellent working definition of essentialism and a careful examination of its various critiques ("This Essentialism Which Is Not One: Coming to Grips with Irigaray," *differences: A Journal of Feminist Cultural Studies* 1, no. 2 [1989]: 41–42). Her definition is also the one with which Drucilla Cornell works (*Beyond Accommodation: Ethical Feminism, Deconstruction, and the Law* [New York: Routledge, 1991], 15–16).

14. Nancy Chodorow, *The Reproduction of Mothering: Psychoanalysis and the Sociology of Gender* (Berkeley: University of California Press, 1978), 110.

15. Ibid., 208.

16. Cornell, *Beyond Accommodation*, 50–51.

17. Chodorow's biological essentialism stems from her misreading of Freud. For Chodorow Freud is a biological determinist; although she undertakes to repair his theory by insisting that gender is a purely social construct, she ends up producing psychoanalysis in the deterministic way that she argues Freud himself does.

18. E. Ann Kaplan's work on motherhood and representation focuses on the liberatory potential of the maternal body invoked by Irigaray, and typically refuses to consider how for Irigaray women's biological bodies might produce different psychic effects without being essentialized: "Because [Irigaray] ultimately [has] to rely on the biological structuring of the female body to arrive at a new female 'language,' a new female way of relating to the world, to other woman, Irigaray . . . [has], like Chodorow, been accused of essentialism. The biological determinism apparently underlying Irigaray's theories is a problem. . . . [I] think it is hard

to escape essentialist traps" (*Motherhood and Representation: The Mother in Popular Culture and Melodrama* [New York: Routledge, 1992], 39).

19. Melanie Klein's insistence that we have all had mothers allows her to read the biological ground of the maternal body as a terrain for multiple significations. In this respect, Klein is Irigaray's precursor (*Envy and Gratitude and Other Works* [New York: Delacorte, 1975]).

20. Luce Irigaray, "Women-Mothers, The Silent Substratum of the Social Order," in *The Irigaray Reader,* Margaret Whitford, ed., 47.

21. Irigaray launches into her dialogue with Lacan at the point at which he factors gender into his conceptualization of the fantastical desiring self/Other dialectic. In *Seminar XX, Encore,* he explicitly negotiates the relationship of The woman to *jouissance* and then to the phallus as signifier of lack par excellence. As the bar through the "The" that Lacan uses to preface the term "woman" suggests, for him "The woman" names the lacking Other, or is this lack. Phallic sexuality based on a signifying economy of oneness posits woman as its Other; and, thus, her lack is the fantasy on which its unity and the possibility of the constitution of the subject rests. Woman, Lacan argues, is the "signifier of the lack of a signifier" (Jacques Lacan, *Seminar XX, Encore,* translated as "God and the *jouissance* of The Woman" in *Feminine Sexuality: Jacques Lacan and the école freudienne.* Juliet Mitchell and Jacqueline Rose, eds. Jacqueline Rose, trans. [New York: W. W. Norton, 1985], 144). She is the empty sign, the "not-all" which "can only be written with *The* crossed through . . . [as] there is no such thing as *The* woman, where the definite article stands for the universal." But if woman is not-at-all she is also something more in this equation—a supplement with a surplus attached to it—a *jouissance* beyond the phallus. This surplus is what defies representation and is not symbolizable within a logic and language constructed around the identity and oneness of the subject. In her critique of Lacan this is where Irigaray steps in. She objects that the only way in which the female body can enter discourse in Lacan's schema is in its maternal function, as a generative womb which is the matrix of the subject's signifiers, or the receptacle of the process of signification's excess. It is beyond the scope of this paper to provide a more detailed explication of Lacan's schema, but I hope that this summary will suffice to situate my argument.

22. Luce Irigaray, *Sexes and Genealogies,* Gillian C. Gill, trans. (New York: Columbia University Press, 1993), 14.

23. *Déréliction* is the state in which women remain in the absence of symbolization of their subjectivity and intersubjective relationships. There is an ongoing debate about the status of the mother-daughter relationship in Irigaray's text. For Margaret Whitford this bond must be symbolized in order for women to enter the social as subjects and thus avoid psychosis (Margaret Whitford, *Luce Irigaray: Philosophy in the Feminine* [New York: Routledge, 1991], 77–78). Drucilla Cornell takes a different view, suggesting that *déréliction* is not necessarily the result of the unsymbolized fusional relationship between mother and daughter. Cornell argues that to attribute this to Irigaray is to equate her with object relations theory as I suggested Kaplan does above (*Beyond,* 74–76). I am sympathetic to Whitford's reading of *déréliction* as a symptom of the unsymbolized mother-

daughter bond, but am more in agreement with Cornell that reinterpreting this so-called overidentification is the way to achieve identification that affirms sexual difference.

24. Luce Irigaray, "The Limits of Transference," in *The Irigaray Reader,* Margaret Whitford, ed. (Oxford, England: Basil Blackwell, 1991), 108.

25. Irigaray, *Sexes and Genealogies,* 15.

26. In discussing Irigaray's essay on Levinas, "The Fecundity of the Caress," (Luce Irigaray, *An Ethics of Sexual Difference,* Carolyn Burke and Gillian C. Gill, trans. [Ithaca, N.Y.: Cornell University Press, 1993], 185–217) Gayatri Spivak writes, "Irigaray exhorts lover and beloved to give the woman to the other, indeed to rememorate being-in-the-mother as the impossible threshold of ethics, rather than inaugurate it as the law of the father. Not all of us are mothers, but we have all been children" ("French Feminism Revisited: Ethics and Politics," in *Feminists Theorize the Political,* Judith Butler and Joan W. Scott, eds. [New York: Rutledge, 1992], 75–78). Spivak sees the maternal relation as the impossible threshold of ethics rememorated by the lovers in Irigaray's text. She additionally sees childhood rather than motherhood as the operative role in rememorating this impossible ethical relation. In the parts of Irigaray's work that I am analyzing here, she shifts her emphasis, taking the risk of regarding the maternal body as a possible site for instantiating ethical relationships between subjects. Rather than focusing on the notion that we have all been children, I look to Irigaray's idea that we "are all mothers just by being women" (Irigaray, *Sexes and Genealogies,* 18), a point I turn to in the last section of this paper.

27. Irigaray, "Limits of Transference," 108.

28. Irigaray, *Sexes and Genealogies,* 15.

29. Irigaray, *Je, tu, nous,* 41.

30. These arguments are made by Whitford and Cornell, although Cornell's approach differs in its reliance on a more deconstructive understanding of metaphor. Cornell claims that the idea that one can reach woman's essence is impossible because woman can only be invoked through metaphor; in short, there is no essence of woman that can be abstracted from the metaphorics of the representation of woman (*Beyond Accommodation,* 31–33). Whitford is more interested in renegotiating the relationship between the symbolic and imaginary through an analysis of Irigaray's reworking of this pair in Lacan's texts (*Luce Irigaray: Philosophy in the Feminine,* 89–97).

31. Elizabeth Weed, "The Question of Style," in *Engaging with Irigaray: Feminist Philosophy and Modern European Thought* (New York: Columbia University Press, 1994).

32. Schor, "This Essentialism," 48.

33. Luce Irigaray, *This Sex Which Is Not One,* Catherine Porter with Carolyn Burke, trans. (Ithaca, N.Y.: Cornell University Press, 1985), 76.

34. Butler, *Bodies That Matter,* 45.

35. Irigaray, *This Sex,* 76–77.

36. Whitford, *Luce Irigaray,* 12.

37. Irigaray, *Je, tu, nous,* 41.

38. Ibid.

39. Ibid., 42.

40. Barbara Katz Rothman, *Recreating Motherhood: Ideology and Technology in a Patriarchal Society* (New York: W. W. Norton, 1989), 97.

41. Ibid., 161.

42. Daniels, *At Women's Expense,* 21.

43. Ibid., 19.

44. Ibid., 22.

45. Ibid., 137.

46. Ibid., 139.

47. Irigaray, *Je, tu, nous,* 42.

48. Schor points out that Irigaray relies heavily on the universe of rational science, especially physics and chemistry. She suggests that it might be precisely this privileging of the scientific that allows Irigaray's readers to see her as unwittingly demonstrating the complicity of essentialism and scientism, but argues that this is a hysterical response that is blind to the crucial intervention into materialism that Irigaray is making by taking science so seriously (*This Essentialism,* 50–51).

49. For example, Spivak explains, "The body, like all other things, cannot be thought, as such. I take the extreme ecological view that the body as such has no possible outline. As body it is a repetition of nature. It is in the rupture with nature when it is a signifier of immediacy for the staging of the self. As a text, the inside of the body (imbricated with the outside) is mysterious and unreadable except by way of thinking of the systematicity of the body, value coding of the body. It is through the significance of my body and others' bodies that cultures become gendered, economicopolitic, selved, substantive" (*Outside,* 20). Judith Butler begins her argument about materiality by citing an earlier version of this passage as an epigraph.

50. Butler, *Bodies That Matter,* 68.

51. Ibid.

52. Another way of understanding the difference between the pro-abortionist's preoccupation with images or representations of the pregnant body and Irigaray's insistence on negotiating its materiality lies in distinguishing between historical work on the body, which traces the history of the body's representations as instrumental reflections of the social (see, for example, Laqueur's work on the representation of female genitals in *Making Sex: Body and Gender from the Greeks to Freud* [Cambridge: Harvard University Press, 1990]), and analyses that posit a more dialectical or reciprocal relationship between discursive power and materiality. Foucault is of course the best example of the latter (*The History of Sexuality, Volume 1: An Introduction,* Robert Hurley, trans. [New York: Vintage Books, 1990]). The body is not only inscribed by power but produces material effects, rendering knowledge itself material; on this point Foucault and Irigaray are of one mind.

53. For example, Zillah Eisenstein uses the "reality" of the pregnant body as the cornerstone of a theory of sexual equality that reveals that sameness as

a standard for equality is inadequate. Like Eisenstein, Grbich is concerned with finding a way to theorize the specific experiences of women by making women's bodily experience legally authoritative. Cornell's work develops the concepts of both "equivalent rights" and "bodily integrity" and is explicitly engaged in a dialogue with Irigaray and her discourse on sexuate rights (Zillah R. Eisenstein, *The Female Body and the Law* [Berkeley: University of California Press, 1988]; Judith E. Grbich, "The Body in Legal Theory," in *At the Boundaries of Law*, Martha Albertson Fineman and Nancy Sweet Thomadsen, eds. [New York: Routledge, 1991], 61–76; and Drucilla Cornell, *Transformations: Recollective Imagination and Sexual Difference* [New York: Routledge, 1993], 143–46 and "Gender," 280–96).

54. Irigaray, *Je, tu, nous*, 45.

55. Ibid., 46.

56. Ibid.

57. Mary Poovey argues that a metaphysics of substance can encompass no real idea of sexual difference. She has called on women to rethink the gendered assumptions to which the ideals of choice, privacy, and rights are wed. She writes, "In the metaphysics of substance . . . the idea of individual rights is not separable from the idea of individual identity, and this, in turn, is inextricably bound to a binary system of gendered norms that seems to but does not derive from sexual difference" ("The Abortion Question and the Death of Man," 243). Poovey calls for laws that comprehend sexual difference, as do the feminist legal theorists I refer to here. For an especially trenchant analysis of the problems with the privacy principle and an elaboration of the reasons to shift from an analysis of personal rights (wed as they are to the sedimented history of privacy), to an analysis of political power viewed in relational rather than institutional terms, see Kendall Thomas, "Beyond the Privacy Principle," *Columbia Law Review* 92 (1992): 1431–516.

58. Irigaray, *Sexes and Genealogies*, 18.

59. Ibid.

60. Irigaray, "Women-Mothers," 50.

Bibliography

Akhter, Farida. "On the Question of the Reproductive Right: A Personal Reflection." *Declaration of Comilla: Proceedings of FINRRAGE-UBINIG International Conference 1989*. Bangladesh: UBINIG, 1991: 45–49.

Butler, Judith. *Bodies that Matter: On the Discursive Limits of "Sex."* New York: Routledge, 1993.

Chodorow, Nancy. *The Reproduction of Mothering: Psychoanalysis and the Sociology of Gender*. Berkeley: University of California Press, 1978.

Cornell, Drucilla. *Beyond Accommodation: Ethical Feminism, Deconstruction, and the Law*. New York: Routledge, 1991.

———. *Transformations: Recollective Imagination and Sexual Difference*. New York: Routledge, 1993.

Daniels, Cynthia R. *At Women's Expense: State Power and the Politics of Fetal Rights.*
Cambridge: Harvard University Press, 1993.

Eisenstein, Zillah R. *The Female Body and the Law.* Berkeley: University of California
Press, 1988.

———, ed. *Capitalist Patriarchy and the Case for Socialist Feminism.* New York:
Monthly Review, 1979.

Foucault, Michel. *The History of Sexuality, Volume 1: An Introduction.* Robert Hurley,
trans. New York: Vintage Books, 1990.

Grbich, Judith E. "The Body in Legal Theory." In Martha Albertson Fineman and
Nancy Sweet Thomadsen, eds. *At the Boundaries of Law: Feminism and Legal
Theory.* New York: Routledge, 1991, 61–76.

Haraway, Donna. "A Manifesto for Cyborgs: Science Technology, and Socialist
Feminism in 1980s." *Socialist Review* 80 (1985): 65–107.

Hartmann, Betsy. *Reproductive Rights and Wrongs: The Global Politics of Population
Control and Contraceptive Choice.* New York: Harper & Row, 1987.

Hopkins, Ellen. "Tales from the Baby Factory." *The New York Times Magazine*
(March 15, 1992): 40ff.

Irigaray, Luce. *This Sex Which Is Not One.* Catherine Porter with Carolyn Burke,
trans. Ithaca: Cornell University Press, 1985.

———. "The Limits of Transference." In *The Irigaray Reader.* Margaret Whitford,
ed. Oxford, England: Basil Blackwell, 1991, 105–17.

———. "Women-Mothers, The Silent Substratum of the Social Order." In *The
Irigaray Reader.* Margaret Whitford, ed. Oxford, England: Basil Blackwell,
1991, 47–52.

———. *An Ethics of Sexual Difference.* Carolyn Burke and Gillian C. Gill, trans.
Ithaca: Cornell University Press, 1993.

———. *Je, tu, nous: Toward a Culture of Difference.* Alison Martin, trans. New York:
Routledge, 1993.

———. *Sexes and Genealogies.* Gillian C. Gill, trans. New York: Columbia University
Press, 1993.

Kaplan, E. Ann. *Motherhood and Representation: The Mother in Popular Culture and
Melodrama.* New York: Routledge, 1992.

Klein, Melanie. "Envy and Gratitude." *Envy and Gratitude and Other Works 1946–
1963.* New York: Delacorte, 1975, 176–235.

Lacan, Jacques. *Feminine Sexuality: Jacques Lacan and the école freudienne.* Juliet
Mitchell and Jacqueline Rose, eds. Jacqueline Rose, trans. New York: W. W.
Norton, 1985.

———. *Seminar XX, Encore.* Translated as "God and the *jouissance* of The Woman"
in *Feminine Sexuality: Jacques Lacan and the école freudienne,* Juliet Mitchell and
Jacqueline Rose, eds. Jacqueline Rose, trans., 144. New York: W. W. Norton,
1985.

Landes, Elisabeth, and Richard Posner. "The Economics of the Baby Shortage."
Journal of Legal Studies 7 (1978): 323–48.

Laqueur, Thomas. *Making Sex: Body and Gender from the Greeks to Freud.* Cambridge,
Mass.: Harvard University Press, 1990.

Marx, Karl. *Capital.* Vol. 1. Ben Fowkes, trans. New York: Vintage, 1977.

Mies, Maria. "Sexist and Racist Implications of the New Reproductive Technologies." *Alternatives* XII (1987): 323–42.

Mitter, Swasti. *Common Fate, Common Bond: Women in the Global Economy.* London: Pluto, 1986.

Petchesky, Rosalind Pollack. *Abortion and Woman's Choice: The State, Sexuality, and Reproductive Freedom.* London: Verso, 1984.

Pollitt, Katha. "Contracts and Apple Pie: The Strange Case of Baby M." *The Nation* 23 (May 1987): 667, 682–88.

Poovey, Mary. "The Abortion Question and the Death of Man." In *Feminists Theorize the Political.* Judith Butler and Joan W. Scott, eds. New York: Routledge, 1992, 239–56.

Rothman, Barbara Katz. *Recreating Motherhood: Ideology and Technology in a Patriarchal Society.* New York: W. W. Norton, 1989.

Schor, Naomi. "This Essentialism Which Is Not One: Coming to Grips with Irigaray." *differences: A Journal of Feminist Cultural Studies* 1, no. 2 (1989): 38–58.

Shalev, Carmel. *Birth Power: The Case for Surrogacy.* New Haven: Yale University Press, 1989.

Spivak, Gayatri Chakravorty. "French Feminism Revisited: Ethics and Politics." In *Feminists Theorize the Political.* Judith Butler and Joan W. Scott, eds. New York: Routledge, 1992, 54–85.

———. *Outside in the Teaching Machine.* New York: Routledge, 1993.

Thomas, Kendall. "Beyond The Privacy Principle." *Columbia Law Review* 92 (1992): 1431–516.

Weed, Elizabeth. "The Question of Style." In *Engaging with Irigaray: Feminist Philosophy and Modern European Thought.* New York: Columbia University Press, 1994.

Whitford, Margaret. *Luce Irigaray: Philosophy in the Feminine.* New York: Routledge, 1991.

———, ed. and introduction. *The Irigaray Reader.* Oxford: Basil Blackwell, 1991.

Williams, Patricia. *The Alchemy of Race and Rights.* Cambridge, Mass.: Harvard University Press, 1991.

PART 4

ANALYTIC APPROACHES AND FEMINIST THEORY

13

The Very Idea of Feminist Epistemology

Lynn Hankinson Nelson

The Limits of Analysis

This essay attempts to redirect, among feminists representing a variety of philosophical traditions, a discussion of feminist epistemology and feminist philosophy of science.[1] I pursue two lines of argument. The first is that critiques of feminist epistemology offered by feminist theorists and mainstream epistemologists have relied on questionable views of both epistemology and feminist epistemology. The second line of argument builds on the first to advocate the view that epistemology is radically interdependent with other knowledge, undertakings, and interests—a view I claim is commensurate with epistemology's history and is promising for feminist theory.

In the course of these arguments, three ironies emerge. One is that, their different motivations notwithstanding, it is on the basis of premises they share that many feminists and mainstream epistemologists have been led to the view that the very idea of feminist epistemology is incongruous. A second irony is that some of these shared premises are effectively undermined by feminist analyses and critiques of epistemology. The third is that some of these premises are incommensurate with the standards their mainstream advocates claim to uphold.

I begin by noting a fourth irony. The more interesting and vexing issues at the intersections of feminism, epistemology, and the philosophy of science will not be resolved by conceptual analysis alone. The juxtapositions encompassed in the phrases "feminist epistemology" and "feminist philosophy of science," for example, which strike some feminist theorists and mainstream epistemologists as incongruous, strike others of us as only *apparently* incongruous and as roughly locating research agendas whose pursuit will help us become clearer about the nature of knowledge, of science, and of theories about them.[2] These juxtapositions often signal the view that epistemology and the philosophy of science are not (and perhaps could not be) what some of their practitioners and advocates have wanted or claimed them to be—but also are not "dead," as some of their critics proclaim.

In the end, the worth of research undertaken under these rubrics will be determined not by discussions such as this, but by criteria appropriate to judging any research program carrying substantial empirical content. Such criteria include whether the results achieved are commensurate with our experiences—including women's experiences—or, alternatively, point to more coherent reconstructions of these; and the contributions made to more viable accounts of knowledge and epistemic communities, and to better knowledge and epistemic practices.[3] Although feminist scholarship provides sufficient warrant for forays into the nature of knowledge, science, and theories about them, final judgments of the significance of these forays are not yet possible. And it would be less than forthright not to acknowledge that the impact of these forays will be determined in part by factors other than the criteria just outlined. Claims to knowledge and about it constitute claims to cognitive authority, and these are political and socially mediated.

Why, then, engage in the kind of analysis undertaken here? Because here, in the interim, we ask ourselves and are asked by our nonfeminist colleagues about the nature of the relationships among feminist analyses of knowledge, feminist politics, and epistemology and the philosophy of science "proper." Our answers, however qualified and tentative, have some bearing on how our work is received and on our own practices.

Consider, for example, the recent call for papers for a special issue of *The Monist* devoted to the astonishing topic "Feminist Epistemology— For and Against," which suggested that whether one is "for" or "against" "feminist epistemology" is a matter of subscribing to one of two clearly delineated, complete, and mutually exclusive sets of tenets.[4] I contend that the call badly mischaracterized much of the work at the intersections of feminism, epistemology, and the philosophy of science. But I am also concerned that some of us working at these intersections have offered arguments which imply much the same.[5]

Our tentative answers to questions about the relationship between feminist analyses of knowledge and epistemology "proper" also shape our evaluation of and openness to each other's approaches. Consider, for example, our apparent acceptance of the analytic/continental and other divides—an acceptance reflected in debates within feminist theory about the future of epistemology—and of the dismissiveness that has characterized debates "across" philosophical traditions.[6] On one hand, this acceptance is curious. The efforts some of us have undertaken to create conceptual and empirical frameworks for investigating knowledge and theories about it have led us to draw simultaneously on the analytic, continental, pragmatist, and other traditions. We have crossed what some would maintain as hard and fast boundaries because one implication of feminist scholarship is that a framework adequate for investigating knowledge will be substantively related to the concrete circumstances within which knowledge is made (circumstances that are characterized by gender relations, historically specific and political), no less than it will be related to the notions of evidence, truth, and objectivity which have been at the heart of both epistemology and feminism.

On the other hand (and as soon as the last point is articulated), our acceptance of traditional divides can be seen to reflect substantive tensions. A further implication of two decades of feminist research into epistemology and the philosophy of science is that, contra a long tradition in epistemology, any universal, abstract, and "value-free" formulations of epistemological notions may be neither possible nor desirable.[7]

Developing understandings and formulations of epistemological notions commensurate with feminist research, as well as the conceptual space within which to do so, is hard work. Given the tensions just noted, this work is increasingly decried by some of our feminist and mainstream colleagues. Although I will challenge some of the assumptions central to these critiques, I will also acknowledge and work within some of the tensions that motivate them. The issues explored carry implications for the relationship between feminism and "analytic philosophy," but these remain implicit until my concluding remarks.

The Incongruity of Feminist Epistemology: Two Arguments

From the perspective of mainstream epistemology, Susan Haack maintains, "The very rubric of feminist epistemology is incongruous on its face" in somewhat the way that "Republican epistemology" would be.[8] The bases for Haack's charge are multiple. She starts out from the claim that feminist epistemologies presume as core tenets the views "that oppressed, disadvantaged, and marginalized people are epistemically privileged" and "that there are distinctively female . . . or feminist 'ways of knowing.' "[9] A charitable interpretation of this generalization is that Haack believes that whatever the stated assumptions of feminist research intersecting epistemology and the philosophy of science (and Haack does not distinguish between these two disciplines),[10] any such research *must* presuppose these tenets. It is also worth noting that Haack does not attribute much if any significance to the difference between the two claims she subsumes under the second "tenet."[11] *Prima facie*, these are significantly different; as much to the point, they are viewed as different and their relationship is explored and worried about in many of the discussions Haack is analyzing.[12]

In any event, Haack contends that there is little reason to assume these tenets (two by her count, three by mine) are warranted (but her discussion also suggests that feminists advance them as "first principles"— that is, without argument) and that an obvious reason not to advance the second is that it involves a "reversion to the notion of 'thinking like a woman' . . . disquietingly reminiscent of old, sexist stereotypes."[13] Third, Haack maintains that both the tenets and interests motivating them are inconsistent with epistemology and the philosophy of science because they represent an effort to politicize epistemological and scientific inquiry. Such inquiry, according to Haack, serves as a remaining defense against relativism.

What is most troubling about feminist epistemology, Haack maintains, is:

> The label is designed to convey the idea that *inquiry should be politicized.* And *that* is not only mistaken, but dangerously so. . . . Inquiry aims at the truth . . . [and] this should remind us that those who despair of honest inquiry cannot be in the truth-seeking business; . . . they are in the propaganda business. [It] is dangerously mistaken, also, from a political point of view, because of the potential for tyranny of calls for "politically adequate research and scholarship."[14]

Finally, Haack contends that feminist epistemology requires an implausible inference from "ought" to "is."[15]

Although not motivated by an interest in saving epistemology or the philosophy of science, Lorraine Code expressed similar doubts about the possibility of feminist epistemology in the final chapter of her *What Can She Know? Feminist Theory and the Construction of Knowledge.*[16] Code's doubts were motivated by her understanding of feminists' interests and goals, but aspects of her arguments overlap with Haack's. Like Haack, Code identified epistemology as a project to construct a monolithic, comprehensive theory of knowledge.[17] She was also concerned that a feminist theory of knowledge "would seem to require a basis in assumptions about the essence of women." But here Code's and Haack's arguments for the incongruity of feminist epistemology diverge. In Code's analysis, epistemology emerged as inimical to feminism, rather than vice versa.

The assumption that "Academic women, from their privileged place, can speak for other women and show them how they ought to live," Code argued, "would be as pernicious as any of the paternalistic practices feminists deplore."[18] Additionally, Code maintained, epistemology has produced "particular and distinct kinds of subordination for women's knowledge and women's positions on the philosophical-epistemological terrain" and derives from "a specific set of interests: the interests of a privileged group of white men." Support for these claims emerged within Code's larger discussion, which analyzed alignments between epistemic ideals (rationality, for example, and objectivity) and traits associated with (stereotypical) masculinity, and the consequences of these alignments for women's abilities to claim and exercise cognitive authority.[19] It was partly on the basis of such alignments and consequences, and epistemology's pretensions despite them to "occupy a neutral, transcendent place outside the epistemic struggles . . . central to people's lives,"[20] that Code concluded that "it would not be possible to develop a feminist theory of knowledge that retained allegiance to the pivotal ideas around which epistemology—for all its variations—has defined itself."[21]

I take the two arguments just summarized to be representative of those offered by mainstream epistemologists and feminist theorists against the very idea of feminist epistemology. Three assumptions emerge as common to these arguments: that it is obvious what epistemology *aspires* to be (although feminist and mainstream critics of feminist epistemology typically disagree about whether this aspiration has been or could be fulfilled), that feminist epistemology could not fall within the scope of this enterprise, and that feminist epistemology presupposes distinctively female or gender-specific "ways of knowing"—an assumption many find unwarranted if not dangerous. I focus on the first and second of these assumptions, but some comments about how "feminist epistemology" is functioning in these arguments and about the third assumption are in order.

A survey of work at the intersections of feminist theory, epistemology, and the philosophy of science would indicate that the research assumptions and projects engaged in under the rubric "feminist epistemology" are diverse (and not always compatible), dynamic, and far from complete—let alone completed.[22] It would also indicate that the phrase "feminist epistemology" is ambiguous. The phrase has come to serve as shorthand for any analysis which engages epistemology "proper," or the issues with which the latter has been concerned, or science and/or the philosophy of science, or virtually any issue concerning knowledge or rationality, from a feminist perspective—of which, of course, there are many. This generality might not be problematic (provided we remained mindful of it), but the phrase has also come to serve as shorthand for a distinctive, comprehensive feminist theory of knowledge or science or project whose aim is the development of such a theory. Although such theories are envisioned and sought by some,[23] there is no single vision these efforts represent.

As much to the point, the project of developing a feminist theory of knowledge is one that many of the analyses undertaken at the intersections of feminist theory, epistemology, and the philosophy of science neither represent nor allow. Code's analysis, for example, constitutes a critical engagement with philosophical epistemology, but as outlined, it concludes with doubts about both the possibility and the desirability of a feminist theory of knowledge. Feminists who have drawn on or advocated naturalized epistemologies also reject the vision of a universal theory of knowledge but are not convinced that epistemology of *any kind* is incompatible with feminism.[24]

When the diversity and ambiguities just noted are not acknowledged, issues become muddled—and they are in danger of being muddled here. It is in the narrow sense of a distinctive theory of knowledge that Code used "feminist epistemology" to discuss a project about which she harbored doubts. Haack consistently conflates the two senses, with the result that she fails to distinguish what are different and not always compatible projects. Some of the difficulties this poses for her analysis become clearer below. The moral I am drawing here is that locating a project using "feminist epistemology" or "feminist philosophy of science" requires considerable care.

Caution is also warranted when someone attributes the assumption of "gender-specific ways of knowing" to any analysis or theory of knowledge or science starting out from a feminist perspective. A number of arguments have been advanced against the view that "feminist epistemology" in either sense presupposes this assumption, and there are substantive and unsettled issues here. It remains an open issue, for example, among feminist standpoint epistemologists, empiricists, and pragmatists, whether maintaining the epistemological significance of gender and other social relations requires essentialist views of either selves or gender. This is in part because it remains an open issue whether the loci of knowledge are individuals; whether gender is a trait of individuals;

whether the notion of "selves" as stable entities is coherent; what the content or role of "experience" is that can or should be related to knowledge; and (for these reasons and others) how relationships between knowledge and gender, including science and gender, should be construed.[25]

Things are no less complicated when we turn to the first and second points on which critics of feminist epistemology agree: that it is obvious what epistemology aspires to be and that a feminist theory of knowledge could not fall within the scope of this enterprise. I contend that neither point is obvious and that there are far-reaching costs associated with their assumption by feminists. I begin to make the case for these claims by exploring the assumptions underlying Haack's analysis and here follow Haack in subsuming the philosophy of science under epistemology.[26]

Haack's contention that feminist epistemology is incongruous is plausible only if one assumes that epistemology is and must be what contemporary mainstream epistemologists take it to be. It is the latter understanding—more correctly, it is *one view* of this understanding—that Haack's arguments privilege. It is not the appeal to a community's practices, standards, and assumptions that is problematic here; short of an appeal to Platonic forms or alleged a priori truths, I know of no other way to define epistemology or anything else. What is problematic in Haack's analysis and what feminists need to be in a position to criticize are two things. First, Haack fails to acknowledge that once we give up treating the standards and assumptions that inform epistemology as alleged a priori truths (and she repeatedly makes the claim that epistemology is "very hard work"), we are committed to the refinement or wholesale abandonment of these standards and assumptions should experience and knowledge so advise. Second, an assumption implicit in Haack's arguments that feminist epistemology is incongruous is that (real) epistemology is itself a monolithic discipline. This assumption is wholly unfounded. Among "mainstream epistemologists" there are advocates of naturalized epistemology (and more than one understanding of the latter) as well as a variety of other projects and assumptions. But, as efforts to naturalize epistemology attest, there is nothing like unanimity concerning the *nature* or *role*, let alone the details, of a theory of knowledge or of science.

Feminists' doubts about the possibility of "feminist epistemology" are also motivated by the view that there are standards, assumptions, and aspirations common to the various projects that have been undertaken under the rubric of epistemology. Code argues, for example, that assumptions about cognitive agents and knowing that inform the "*S* knows that *p*" tradition in contemporary epistemology—for example, that persons are interchangeable in their epistemic activities, that claims about middle-sized physical objects are paradigmatic knowledge claims, that science constitutes the only endeavor worth epistemological notice—would make it difficult (if not impossible) to pose questions about relationships among knowledge, gender, and politics. Hence, Code contends, the dominant tradition in mainstream epistemology does not allow the questions of concern to those (such as women) who want to know well, questions which would also reveal the parochialism of epistemology's emphases. It is for both reasons that Code is led to the view that epistemology may be incommensurate in principle with feminists' goals.[27]

Although I concur that the assumptions Code identifies are features of much work in contemporary epistemology and philosophy of science (including naturalized projects in these fields) and incommensurate with the results of feminist analyses of knowledge, I am not convinced that these assumptions are necessary to epistemology or the philosophy of science. As much to the point, I am not convinced that there are reasons to grant that what epistemology is or could be has been settled.

An Alternate View

One implication of the discussion of Haack's and Code's arguments is that neither position is itself obvious. We found each to rely on a web of assumptions, standards, knowledge, and practices—a point that can also be made by noting that there is an obvious third alternative: that virtually all the categories directly implicated in the question of whether a feminist theory of knowledge is possible or desirable, as well as the issue of what criteria, interests, and traditions should be privileged in addressing this question, are contestable. I have argued elsewhere that a number of considerations support this view.[28]

First, it is true that some issues feminists address and some questions they identify have been deemed at least irrelevant to epistemology and the philosophy of science "proper" (if not, in fact, incommensurate with these enterprises). These include the questions "*Whose* knowledge?" and "*Whose* science?"[29]; the emphasis placed on the historical, sociopolitical, and (often less than tidy) concrete circumstances in which knowledge is constructed; and the claims made of deep relationships between power and knowledge. But other issues and questions on which feminists focus are surely not outside the bounds of these enterprises. They include the question of who or what is the primary bearer of knowledge (and whether, indeed, anyone or anything is); the question of the nature and scope of the evidence supporting our claims; and the issue of the relationships among epistemology and other theories, practices, and interests.[30]

A second consideration which suggests that the categories at issue are contestable has been alluded to in several arguments advanced above. Feminist critiques and the history of epistemology indicate that epistemology is and always has been an evolving enterprise. Answers to the questions with which it has been concerned—"What are the grounds for knowledge claims?" "Who knows?" and "What can I/we know?" no less than the answer to Code's question "What can she know?"—are not and have never been obvious.[31] Both the questions and answers to them have emerged, and persistently reemerged, concomitantly with other questions asked, other things known, and other projects undertaken within historically and culturally specific contexts.[32] So, too, the view of epistemology as a project to construct a comprehensive theory of knowledge to stand in a foundational relationship to other theories is subject to refinement or abandonment, as evidenced in naturalistic epistemology and philosophy of science, of which there are now several feminist versions.[33]

What sense is to be made, then, of the claim that epistemology is *complete*?

And if epistemology is *not* complete, what sense is to be made of the alleged incongruity of feminist epistemology in either the narrow sense (that is, a feminist theory of knowledge) or broad sense (that is, an analysis of knowledge and/or epistemology which starts out from a feminist perspective)? Let us start again.

The general claim underlying mainstream arguments for such incongruity is best parsed as: "Analyses or theories of knowledge which are informed by feminism are incongruous because they constitute a mix of politics and apolitical inquiry and knowledge." This claim is implicit in Haack's charge that feminist epistemology (hence, by implication, not "real" epistemology) presupposes that one can derive "is" from "ought." But this construal of the tension between feminist analyses and epistemology or philosophy of science "proper" (or of their alleged incommensurability) begs the question. It presumes that the latter *are* apolitical and in general "value-free" (at least free of values not taken to be "constitutive" of inquiry), a view many feminists reject in the light of substantial counter evidence.[34] At the very least, the apolitical or value-free status of epistemology, the philosophy of science, and/or the sciences is not a function of our declaring it (nor even of our subscribing to it as an ideal).

Closer to the mark in terms of the issues so far considered is Linda Alcoff and Elizabeth Potter's identification of a general tension between feminists' interest in the concrete ("the impact of social status as well as the sexed body of the knower upon the production of knowledge"), and the "universality" sought and claimed by epistemology and the philosophy of science "proper."[35] Contemporary epistemology and philosophy of science have been informed by the assumption that the social status and sexed bodies of knowers are not of epistemological significance. And in more general terms, many (but not all) traditions in epistemology and the philosophy of science have resisted efforts to historicize knowledge claims, epistemological notions, or epistemology itself. "[The] conception of proper epistemology leaves unchallenged the premise that a general account of knowledge . . . is *possible*. But this is precisely the premise that feminist epistemologists have called into question. Feminists . . . have insisted on the significance and particularity of the context of theory."[36]

Perhaps we are getting somewhere. Alcoff and Potter's analysis suggests that a general problem with "mainstream" epistemology and philosophy of science from feminist perspectives is not that either project is political and parochial. The problem is, rather, that those engaged in these projects do not recognize or acknowledge these features of their undertakings and allow the insight to inform their analyses and claims. This point is at the heart of Code's critique of epistemology and borne out by Haack's presentation and defense of it. One way of construing the question before us, then, is what feminists should make of this tension.

From here, two strategies seem plausible. One strategy is for feminists engaged in analyses of knowledge and theories about it to view ourselves as engaged in something other than—and in principle distinct from—epistemology and/or the philosophy of science. In *What Can She Know?* for example, Code suggested that rather than attempting to develop a feminist theory of knowledge, feminists undertake critical interventions of the theories generated by, and the self-presentation of, epistemology so as to "unmask its claims to universality," and work to create practices (in academic, therapeutic, and social policy arenas, for example) which will enable women to know well.[37]

An obvious benefit of this strategy is that it would enable us to focus our attention on the kinds of question with which we began: for example, "What have feminist analyses of knowledge and epistemology accomplished or promised to accomplish?" and "What is their relationship to and potential impact on women's lives?" These questions surely warrant as much attention as answering the charges leveled by mainstream epistemologists that our questions and analyses violate "the" rules, or wrestling with some precise articulation of the relationships between our work and epistemology or the philosophy of science "proper." Moreover, the latter undertakings have served to divide us along lines not of our own making and arguably more deserving of challenge than allegiance.[38] So, too, abandoning epistemology might prompt more attention to the development of concrete practices which would enable women to know well and to exercise cognitive authority.

But it remains unclear that the only way to avoid elitism or undue attention to intradisciplinary or academic squabbles or to contribute to the development of epistemic practices that will enable women to know well is to abandon epistemology. To assume this, we need to assume that epistemology could only be what its most abstract, nonempirical, universalist, and elitist versions have been, and could only aspire to what these versions aspired to.

Nor is this strategy without costs, some of which are relevant to Code's concerns about the relationship between academic feminism and women's lives. One implication of feminist analyses of epistemology and philosophy of science "proper," including Code's, is that in their historical and contemporary variants, the theories developed within these enterprises play a significant role in shaping and legitimating the methodologies, self-understandings, and knowledge claims of various institutions granted cognitive authority (the sciences, academic disciplines, and other institutions that define the grounds for and shape social policy). Another implication is that the institutions so legitimized have had substantial and deleterious consequences for women and others who have not enjoyed cognitive authority, as well as for the content of knowledge. Abandoning epistemology—vowing to intervene only from the sidelines in the role of "spoilers" or whistle blowers—threatens to minimize the force of feminist critiques aimed at revealing these consequences and identifying their sources and implications. Consider, for example, where analyses devoted to such interventions might be published, who would read them, and whose work might be informed by them. And despite assurances from many quarters that "epistemology is dead," a survey of journals and conference programs in our discipline, and of the appeals made by scientists and others granted cognitive authority to views developed within epistemology, would suggest that this message (even if warranted) has not gotten through.

These concerns can be phrased less abstractly. Proclaiming the death of epistemology might be a cutting-edge position in intellectual circles, but it is not clear that epistemology *is* dead or that feminist philosophers take a responsible position by assuming this. A division of labor among us—and efforts to enable a range of feminist perspectives to inform mainstream approaches, the development of better epistemic practices, and one another—seems an equally responsible way of responding to the tensions Code, Alcoff and Potter, and others identify.[39]

There is another and deeper cost attendant to abandoning epistemology on the grounds so far considered. If we claim that our analyses of
knowledge and of science are not epistemology, we make it plausible for
"mainstream" epistemologists, philosophers of science, and enthusiasts
of epistemology to feel justified in ignoring the insights feminist analyses
afford. Suppose we insist that our ways of asking the questions of interest
to epistemologists and philosophers of science, and/or the new questions
we ask, and/or the empirical and normative considerations we identify
and privilege, indicate that we are not engaged in epistemology. We
thereby blunt the argument that knowledge and theories thereof are
always informed by the historically specific interests, projects, values,
and traditions of inquiry and practice of their makers. We effectively
sanction the view that a theory of knowledge concerned with the actual
circumstances within which knowledge is generated, including the relationships between knowledge, gender, and power, is in principle distinct
from (if not incommensurable with) a theory concerned with criteria
for distinguishing among claims and theories that are more and less
warranted.[40]

This view is common among those who find the divide between
analytic and continental approaches to knowledge unbridgeable. But
like others, I see no reason why feminists should maintain it.[41] One of
the lessons of the last three decades would seem to be that any *viable*
theory of knowledge or science would encompass relationships between
knowledge and power, including its own relationship(s) to power, and
other features of the circumstances within which knowledge is generated.

An example might make these concerns clear. One of the central
claims advanced in Code's *What Can She Know?* is that there is a need for a
"remapping of the epistemic terrain" so as to incorporate what Code calls
"subjective factors."[42] Among the factors Code cites are the particularity
of cognitive agents, their embodiment, their "location" in specific and
concrete circumstances, and their emotions and interests.[43] In insisting
on the need for attention to these factors, Code explains, her point is
not "to denigrate projects of establishing the best foundations possible
or of developing workable criteria of coherence." It is to argue that
the questions addressed in such projects do not exhaust the important
questions to be asked about knowledge "whose answers matter to people
who are concerned to know well":

> Among them are questions that bear *not just* on criteria of evidence,
> justification, and warrantability, *but* on the "nature" of cognitive agents:
> questions about their character; their material, historical, cultural
> circumstances; their interests in the inquiry at issue.[44]

I have emphasized portions of this passage to draw attention to an implicit distinction between questions concerning evidence, justification, and warrantability—the recognized "domain" of epistemology—and the questions that Code identifies as important but neglected or suppressed in the discipline, which are questions concerning the material, historical, and cultural circumstances of cognitive agents and their interests. If we recognize such a distinction and assume that epistemology is concerned only with questions of the first group, then arguably feminist analyses that raise questions of the second group are outside the domain of epistemology.

The question I am raising is whether feminists should grant this distinction. It would appear to rely on views of cognitive agents, cognitive agency, and epistemic communities that feminist analyses, including Code's, effectively undermine. On the basis of such analyses, we now ask, "Could a viable theory of evidence not take into account the material and cultural circumstances of cognitive agents? Not take into account the divisions in cognitive labor and authority that characterize epistemic communities (our largest social community, science research facilities, academic disciplines, and so on)? Could a viable account of evidential warrant not recognize the 'situated-ness' of cognitive agents—including epistemologists, scientists, and philosophers of science?" It would appear that questions such as those to which Code draws our attention would need to be addressed within anything purporting to be a viable account of evidential warrant.

Again, the alternative response to the tensions that have emerged is to insist that epistemology as it is and as it can be is contestable, because a theory of knowledge is radically interdependent with other current theories, practices, and undertakings.[45] One straightforward benefit of this view of epistemology has already been noted: It is commensurate with the history of the enterprise, including its recent history, and feminist critiques of it. Both indicate significant relationships among theories of knowledge and the broader theoretical, social, and political contexts within such theories are generated.

There are other benefits. Acknowledging such interdependence provides the grounds for defending feminist analyses against charges that imply that one can know in advance (on the basis, for example, of "received views" within or about epistemology) that the assumptions guiding feminist analyses of knowledge are wrongheaded, and against the (related) charge that these assumptions are being advanced (or can be judged) as "first principles." In this view of epistemology, many of these assumptions are empirical hypotheses. These include the assumption that there are "women's ways of knowing," which guides some (but by no means all) feminist research; the assumption that beginning research from the lives of those marginalized can produce better knowledge, as Sandra Harding and other standpoint epistemologists argue[46]; and the assumption that social relations such as gender are epistemologically significant, which guides research undertaken by feminist empiricists and pragmatists. These are hypotheses which emerged concomitantly with feminist scholarship and politics and are interdependent with them. Their viability will be determined on the basis of criteria appropriate to judging any empirical hypothesis: their explanatory power, their success in explaining and predicting experience, and their contributions to better knowledge and the development or refinement of notions of evidence, cognitive agency, objectivity, and so on.[47]

A third benefit is that, on this view, the assumptions that inform what Haack and other mainstream critics of feminist epistemology suggest we should think of as "real epistemology"—that persons are virtually inter-changeable in their epistemic activities, that evidence can be construed ahistorically, that "good" theorizing has nothing to do with gender, and so on—are not different in kind from those informing feminist research and analyses. They are also empirical hypotheses that emerged apace with other knowledge and projects and remain subject to refinement or abandonment when changes in other knowledge and experience, such as those feminists claim, advise.

And on the basis of these several lines of argument, feminists can insist that reasonable judgments about the coherency and/or viability of the several and diverse research projects currently underway at the intersections of feminism, epistemology, and the philosophy of science require as much hard work as serious judgments in any other area of philosophy—an idea which the current debates surrounding feminist philosophy suggest is timely, if not overdue.

False Dichotomies

One would be hard put to categorize the view of epistemology I have advocated or other aspects of this discussion as constituting a defense of analytic philosophy, including feminist analytic philosophy, or as an attack on it.[48] At least so I hope. I have attempted at various points to raise doubts about the "either/or"'s which inform such defenses and attacks, and continue to do so in this section.

The claim that epistemology is radically interdependent with other knowledge and projects—hence that epistemic notions are shaped by and evolve in response to historically specific traditions of inquiry and practice—is not new. Dewey and Rorty, among others, have advanced versions of it; so have those, including Quine, who advocate the naturalization of epistemology and the philosophy of science, including some feminist theorists.[49] But this claim is deeply incommensurate with the view of epistemology (or philosophy more broadly) as something like a "first knowledge": an enterprise which identifies first (that is, foundational and universal) principles and starting points, and which need not concern itself with the actual circumstances within which knowledge is generated. This claim is also incommensurate with the view that because there can be no such enterprise, epistemology is appropriately abandoned.

As the references to Dewey, Rorty, and Quine indicate, this view of epistemology is not uniquely feminist, although feminist analyses which reveal relationships among philosophical positions (including feminist positions) and specific sociopolitical contexts and interests further the case for it. Moreover, when informed by feminist research, projects informed by this understanding of epistemology have evolved to include attention to gender and other social relations; the responsibilities attendant on cognitive authority; and the relationships between philosophical theories and practice, and women's lives.[50] But recent journal issues and symposia devoted to the question of whether some aspect of feminist theory really is philosophy indicate that we run little risk of overemphasizing the status of this view of epistemology as a contender.[51]

The radical interdependence claimed for epistemology and other knowledge and interests might be interpreted as conducive to the "falsely innocent indifference" Christine Di Stefano and others attribute to postmodernism.[52] Alternatively, my attention to pragmatic issues might be interpreted as endorsing what Haack calls "sham reasoning"—that is, politics masquerading as inquiry—and attributes to feminist epistemologists and philosophers of science.[53] There are more false dichotomies presupposed in Haack's charge than I have space to address, but let me be still clearer about the views motivating the recommendations I have offered.

I am neither feigning nor advocating an indifference to evidence, to truth, or to power. Proclamations of indifference to these are rarely if ever politically innocent. In the present scheme of things, they appear at least disingenuous—a luxury perhaps available only to those in positions of privilege of various sorts, conducive to obfuscating the cognitive authority underlying their claims and to silencing or bracketing those approaches that would expose their political import.[54]

I also confess to feeling somewhat bemused when faced with claims to the effect that evidence and/or truth are notions now safely abandoned. Such claims are not commensurate with our experience; nor do they suggest an alternative and more coherent reconstruction of that experience. As much to the present point, recent formulations of these claims appear to presuppose the very dichotomies—of theory and practice, of language and world, of objectivism and relativism—that their advocates claim (correctly) are untenable.[55] In short, the motivations of their advocates notwithstanding, claims that notions of truth and evidence are vacuous are not epistemologically innocent.

The general view underlying the recommendations I have advanced is that theories of knowledge, like theories about anything, are tools to organize, explain, and reconstruct our present and past experiences, and to be used in the service of our efforts to develop better knowledge and epistemic practices. Such theories, like all theories, emerge and evolve concomitantly with others and with the interests, values, projects, and practices that motivate and shape our work to generate them.

From this view, feminists presently have choices to make about the very ideas of feminist epistemology and feminist philosophy of science, and these choices have implications—simultaneously epistemic and practical in the sense of how successfully we manage to understand, explain, or reconstruct our experience, simultaneously epistemic and political in the sense of what difference or effects our choices make. I have not argued, nor do I believe, that feminists must agree on the appropriate choice. But implicit in the foregoing is a case for less dismissiveness across— and more skepticism concerning—the lines alleged to divide us. Neither the grounds for making these choices nor the candidates we currently recognize are starting or end points, and as we consider them, we need to be as clear as we can about the assumptions and interests that inform them and their consequences.

Notes

Earlier versions of this essay were presented at a meeting of the Society for Women in Philosophy in Atlanta, December 1993; and at the Center for Women's Studies and Nordiskt Nätverk för Forskarstuderande inom Feministisk Epistemologi och Feministisk Vetenskapsteori at the University of Umeå, October 1994. I am grateful to members of these audiences and Ann Cudd, Hildur Kalman, Virginia Klenk, Ullaliina Lehtinen, and Jack Nelson for insightful and constructive criticisms.

1. For ease of explication, I subsume the philosophy of science under the rubric epistemology in much of what follows, for it is so subsumed in many of the discussions I consider. Although I cannot argue the point here, I think the philosophy of science is a distinguishable discipline. To the point here, I

think taking the philosophy of science to be a subdiscipline of epistemology has contributed to the ambiguity of the rubric "feminist epistemology" and to misrepresentations of work at the intersections of feminism, epistemology, and the philosophy of science in mainstream critiques. The issues of ambiguity and misrepresentation are addressed in this essay.

2. See, for example, Alcoff and Potter's introduction to *Feminist Epistemologies* (Linda Alcoff and Elizabeth Potter, eds. [New York: Routledge, 1993]); Louise Antony, "Quine as Feminist," in *A Mind of One's Own*, Louise M. Antony and Charlotte Witt, eds. (Boulder: Westview Press, 1993); Jane Duran, *Toward a Feminist Epistemology* (Totowa, N.J.: Rowman and Littlefield, 1991); Sandra Harding, *Whose Science? Whose Knowledge? Thinking from Women's Lives* (Ithaca, N.Y.: Cornell University Press, 1991); Helen E. Longino, *Science as Social Knowledge* (Princeton, N.J.: Princeton University Press, 1990); Jack Nelson and Lynn Hankinson Nelson, "No Rush to Judgment," *The Monist* 77, no. 4 (1994): 486–508; Phyllis Rooney, "Recent Work in Feminist Discussions of Reason," *American Philosophical Quarterly* 31, no. 1 (1994): 1–21; and Sarah Ruddick, "New Feminist Work on Knowledge, Reason and Objectivity" *Hypatia* 8, no. 4 (1993): 140–49.

3. Kathryn Pyne Addelson, "The Man of Professional Wisdom," in *Discovering Reality,* S. Harding and M. Hintikka, eds. (Dordrecht: D. Reidel, 1983); and Lorraine Code, *What Can She Know?* (Ithaca, N.Y.: Cornell University Press, 1991).

4. "The new 'feminist epistemologies,' " the call for papers maintained, "far from repudiating the 'feminine,' insist on its importance. Whether in the relatively modest versions . . . or in the most ambitious . . . [feminist epistemologies] presuppose a distinctive female (or, in some variants, feminist) 'way of knowing.' . . . The goal is that *The Monist* issue . . . should represent the arguments on *both sides* in as rigorous and detailed a fashion as possible" (mimeograph; emphasis added).

5. I do not deny that some recent mischaracterizations of feminist philosophy are deliberate. I contend that this makes it all the more important for feminist philosophers to be clear about what they take to be the "nature" and implications of their work.

6. Sandra Harding, "Feminism, Science, and the Anti-Enlightenment Critiques," in *Feminism/Postmodernism,* Linda J. Nicholson, ed. (New York: Routledge, 1990); and Linda J. Nicholson, ed., *Feminism/Postmodernism* (New York: Routledge, 1990).

7. See Addelson, "Man of Professional Wisdom"; Linda Alcoff and Elizabeth Porter, eds., *Feminist Epistemologies* (New York: Routledge, 1993); Code, *What Can She Know?;* Sandra Harding, *Whose Science? Whose Knowledge? Thinking from Women's Lives* (Ithaca, N.Y.: Cornell University Press, 1991); Helen E. Longino, *Science as Social Knowledge* (Princeton, N.J.: Princeton University Press, 1990) and "Subjects, Power, and Knowledge," in *Feminist Epistemologies;* and Lynn Hankinson Nelson, *Who Knows* (Philadelphia, Pa.: Temple University Press, 1990) and "Epistemological Communities," in *Feminist Epistemologies.*

8. Susan Haack, "Epistemological Reflections of an Old Feminist," *Reason Papers* 18 (1993): 31–43.

9. Ibid., 32–33.

10. Haack is not alone in viewing the philosophy of science as a subdiscipline of epistemology. I do not (see n. 1), but this is not what motivates my commenting on her failure to distinguish between feminist epistemology and feminist philosophy of science. One explanation of the misrepresentations of feminists' work in Haack's critiques is that she superimposes (one view of) the standards, assumptions, and goals of traditional epistemology on work that explicitly distinguishes its goals and core assumptions from these. Included in the latter category are analyses drawing on both feminist scholarship and naturalistic traditions in epistemology and the philosophy of science (for example, Jane Duran, *Toward a Feminist Epistemology* [Totowa, N.J.: Rowman and Littlefield, 1991]; and Nelson, *Who Knows*); feminist standpoint theories (Sandra Harding, *The Science Question in Feminism* [Ithaca, N.Y.: Cornell University Press, 1986], and *Whose Science?*); and analyses which critically engage epistemology but are skeptical of the possibility of a feminist theory of knowledge (Code, *What Can She Know?*).

11. Consider, for example, Haack's claim that "The profusion of incompatible themes proposed as '*feminist* epistemology' itself speaks against the idea of a distinctively *female* cognitive style" (Haack, "Epistemological Reflections," 33 [emphasis added]).

12. Indeed, aspects of Haack's analysis are curious. Immediately before enumerating "core tenets" of feminist epistemology, she launches another argument against feminist analyses of knowledge and science, the linchpin of which is that there is "a bewildering diversity of epistemological ideas described as 'feminist' " (Haack, "Epistemological Reflections," 32).

13. Ibid., 32.

14. Ibid., 37–38.

15. Ibid., 35.

16. Code notes (private correspondence) that her views about the fixed nature of epistemology have evolved since the publication of *What Can She Know?* I focus on the arguments offered in that work because they are representative of those feminists have advanced against feminist epistemology and I find them among the most compelling. It should also be noted that the issue of accountability was more central to *What Can She Know?* than the question of a feminist epistemology. I turn to the relationship between accountability and epistemology in the third section of this essay.

17. Code, *What Can She Know?* 1–26.

18. Ibid., 288.

19. See especially Code's chapters 2 and 3; see also Susan Bordo, *The Flight to Objectivity* (Albany, N.Y.: State University of New York Press, 1987), and Naomi Scheman, "Though This Be Method, Yet There Is Madness in It," in *A Mind of One's Own*, Louis M. Antony and Charlotte Witt, eds. (Boulder, Colo.: Westview Press, 1993).

20. Code, *What Can She Know?* xii.

21. See also n. 16. As I mention later in this essay, Code also cites the assumptions about cognitive agency and paradigmatic knowledge claims which

inform the dominant tradition in contemporary epistemology as among the "pivotal ideas" that are in tension with feminists' interests, goals, and analyses of the circumstances in which knowledge is generated.

22. See also Alcoff and Potter, *Feminist Epistemologies,* 1–14; Antony and Witt, *A Mind of One's Own,* xiii–xvii; Phyllis Rooney, "Recent Work in Feminist Discussions of Reason," *American Philosophical Quarterly* 31, no. 1 (1994):1–21; and Sarah Ruddick, "New Feminist Work on Knowledge, Reason and Objectivity," *Hypatia* 8, no. 4 (1993): 140–49.

23. For example, Mary Belenky et al., *Women's Ways of Knowing* (New York: Basic Books, 1986); Duran, *Toward a Feminist Epistemology;* Nancy Harstock, "The Feminist Standpoint," in *Discovering Reality: Feminist Perspectives on Epistemology, Metaphysics, Methodology, and Philosophy of Science,* S. Harding and M. Hintikka, eds. (Dordrecht: D. Reidel, 1983); and Harding, *Whose Science?*

24. See also Addelson, "The Man of Professional Wisdom" and "Knower/ Doers and Their Moral Problems"; and Nelson, *Who Knows* and "A Feminist Naturalized Philosophy of Science," *Synthese* 104, no. 3 (1995).

25. See Addelson, "The Man of Professional Wisdom"; Linda Alcoff, "Cultural Feminism versus Post-Structuralism," *Signs* 13 (1988): 405–35; Alcoff and Potter, *Feminist Epistemologies*; Code, *What Can She Know?;* Harding, *Whose Science?;* Helen E. Longino, *Science as Social Knowledge* (Princeton, N.J.: Princeton University Press, 1990) and "Subjects, Power, and Knowledge," in Alcoff and Potter, *Feminist Epistemologies;* Nelson, *Who Knows,* and "Epistemological Communities"; Nicholson, *Feminism/Postmodernism;* Rooney, "Feminist Discussions of Reason"; and Ruddick, "New Feminist Work."

26. See n. 1.

27. Code, *What Can She Know?* ix–xii; 314–24, passim. In contrast to Haack, Code does distinguish between dominant traditions in epistemology and others.

28. Nelson, *Who Knows* and "Epistemological Communities"; Nelson and Nelson, "No Rush to Judgment"; see also Alcoff and Potter, *Feminist Epistemologies,* 1–14; Duran, *Toward a Feminist Epistemology*; Harding, *Whose Science?;* and Longino, *Science as Social Knowledge.*

29. Harding, *Whose Science?*

30. See, for example, Alcoff and Potter, *Feminist Epistemologies;* Antony and Witt, *A Mind of One's Own;* Code, *What Can She Know?;* Harding, *Whose Science?;* Longino, *Science as Social Knowledge;* Nelson, "Epistemological Communities"; and Rooney, "Feminist Discussions of Reason."

31. Indeed, Code's analyses of epistemic ideals in *What Can She Know?* reveal their "shifting and evolving history" and their relationships to the "subjectivity" of their creators. See especially 110–28.

32. Bordo, *The Flight to Objectivity;* Code, *What Can She Know?* especially 46–55 and 110–30; Nelson, "Epistemological Communities"; and Scheman, "Though This Be Method."

33. Addelson, "Knower/Doers" and "Notes Toward a Collectivist Moral Theory," presented at a meeting of Eastern SWIP in Atlanta, 1993; Louise M. Antony, "Quine as Feminist: The Radical Import of Naturalized Epistemology,"

in *A Mind of One's Own;* Duran, *Toward a Feminist Epistemology;* and Nelson, *Who Knows,* "A Feminist Naturalized Philosophy of Science," *Synthese* 104, no. 3 (1995), and "Empiricism Without Dogmas," in *Feminism, Science, and the Philosophy of Science,* L. H. Nelson and J. Nelson, eds. (Dordrecht: Kluwer Academic Publishers, 1996).

34. Nor is it obvious that the values embraced as "constitutive of inquiry" are not themselves interdependent with historically specific systems of theory and practice. See Harding, *Whose Science?;* Longino, *Science as Social Knowledge* and "Subjects, Power, and Knowledge"; and Lynn Hankinson Nelson and Jack Nelson, "Feminist Values and Cognitive Virtues," *PSA* 2 (1995).

35. Alcoff and Potter, *Feminist Epistemologies.*

36. Ibid., 1.

37. Code, *What Can She Know?* 314–24, passim.

38. Harding, "Feminism, Science, and the Anti-Enlightenment Critiques."

39. Addelson, "Knower/Doers," and *Moral Passages: Toward a Collectivist Moral Theory* (New York: Routledge, 1994).

40. See also Addelson, "The Man of Professional Wisdom"; Alcoff, "Cultural Feminism versus Post-Structuralism"; Harding, "Feminism, Science, and the Anti-Enlightenment Critiques"; Nelson, "Epistemological Communities"; and Nicholson, *Feminism/Postmodernism.*

41. Harding, "Feminism, Science, and the Anti-Enlightenment Critiques."

42. The next several paragraphs closely parallel arguments offered in Lynn Hankinson Nelson, "Critical Notice: Lorraine Code's *What Can She Know? Feminist Theory and the Construction of Knowledge,*" *Canadian Journal of Philosophy* 24, no. 2 (1994): 295–326.

43. Code, *What Can She Know?* 1–8, 27–70, passim.

44. Ibid., 7–8.

45. Addelson, "Knower/Doers" and "Notes Toward a Collectivity Moral Theory"; Antony, "Quine as Feminist"; and Duran, *Toward a Feminist Epistemology.*

46. Patricia Hill Collins, *Black Feminist Thought: Knowledge, Consciousness, and the Politics of Empowerment* (New York: Routledge, 1991); and Nelson, "Critical Notice."

47. See also Nelson and Nelson, "No Rush to Judgment." One long-standing objection to the view of epistemology I am advocating is that a theory of knowledge must be "free standing" in order to avoid circularity (see, for example, Harding, *The Science Question in Feminism*). The short response to this objection is that not all circles are vicious. The interdependence claimed here is not vicious if we assume that the claims made by feminists (and anyone else) will be justified, if they are, on the basis of their commensurability with experience and other current knowledge, rather than solely (or even primarily) by appeal to a current epistemology. See also Nelson, *Who Knows,* "Epistemological Communities," and "A Feminist Naturalized Philosophy of Science."

48. For example, the view that a theory of knowledge should be pursued as an empirical science has its roots in Quine's proposal that epistemology be naturalized. But I take Quine's relationship to analytic philosophy to be complex

and would not describe the body of his work (as suggested, for example, in Antony, "Quine as Feminist") as an exemplar of "analytic philosophy" (compare to Nelson, *Who Knows*).

49. Addelson, "Knower/Doers"; Antony, "Quine as Feminist"; and Duran, *Toward a Feminist Epistemology*.

50. See Addelson, "Knower/Doers"; Duran, *Toward a Feminist Epistemology;* and Nelson, *Who Knows.*

51. Nor, contra the claims of some mainstream critics of feminist philosophy, need the views informing feminist research be unique. Building on and synthesizing other approaches and results is a theoretical virtue and recognized as such in virtually every other context.

52. Christine Di Stefano, "Dilemmas of Difference," in *Feminism/Postmodernism,* Linda J. Nicholson, ed. (New York: Routledge, 1990). See also Nicholson, *Feminism/Postmodernism.*

53. Haack, "Epistemological Reflections," 37–38.

54. Di Stefano, "Dilemmas of Difference"; and Nicholson, *Feminism/Postmodernism.*

55. Harding, "Feminism, Science, and the Anti-Enlightenment Critiques."

Bibliography

Addelson, Kathryn Pyne. "The Man of Professional Wisdom." In *Discovering Reality*. S. Harding and M. Hintikka, eds. Dordrecht: D. Reidel, 1983.

———. "Knower/Doers and Their Moral Problems." In *Feminist Epistemologies*. Linda Alcoff and Elizabeth Potter, eds. New York: Routledge, 1993.

———. "Notes Toward a Collectivist Moral Theory." Presented at a meeting of Eastern SWIP in Atlanta honoring Kathryn Pyne Addelson as Distinguished Woman Philosopher, 1993.

———. *Moral Passages: Toward a Collectivist Moral Theory*. New York: Routledge, 1994.

Alcoff, Linda. "Cultural Feminism versus Post-Structuralism: The Identity Crisis in Feminist Theory." *Signs: Journal of Women in Culture and Society* 13 (1988): 405–35.

———. *Real Knowing: New Versions of the Coherence Theory*. Ithaca, N.Y.: Cornell University Press, 1995.

Alcoff, Linda, and Elizabeth Potter, eds. *Feminist Epistemologies*. New York: Routledge, 1993.

Antony, Louise M. "Quine as Feminist: The Radical Import of Naturalized Epistemology." In *A Mind of One's Own: Feminist Essays on Reason and Objectivity*. Louise M. Antony and Charlotte Witt, eds. Boulder, Colo.: Westview Press, 1993.

Antony, Louise M., and Charlotte Witt, eds. *A Mind of One's Own: Feminist Essays on Reason and Objectivity*. Boulder: Westview Press, 1993.

Bar On, Bat-Ami. "Marginality and Epistemic Privilege." In *Feminist Epistemologies*. Linda Alcoff and Elizabeth Potter, eds. New York: Routledge, 1993.

Belenky, Mary, et al. *Women's Ways of Knowing*. New York: Basic Books, 1986.

Bordo, Susan. *The Flight to Objectivity: Essays on Cartesianism and Culture*. Albany, N.Y.: State University of New York Press, 1987.

Code, Lorraine. *What Can She Know? Feminist Theory and the Construction of Knowledge*. Ithaca, N.Y.: Cornell University Press, 1991.

Collins, Patricia Hill. *Black Feminist Thought: Knowledge, Consciousness, and the Politics of Empowerment*. New York: Routledge, 1991.

Di Stefano, Christine. "Dilemmas of Difference." In *Feminism/Postmodernism*. Linda J. Nicholson, ed. New York: Routledge, 1990.

Duran, Jane. *Toward a Feminist Epistemology*. Totowa, N.J.: Rowman and Littlefield, 1991.

Haack, Susan. "Epistemological Reflections of an Old Feminist." *Reason Papers* 18 (1993): 31–43. Delivered at the symposium, "Feminist Philosophy Reconsidered," sponsored by the American Association for the Philosophic Study of Society, Washington, D.C., December 1992.

Harding, Sandra. *The Science Question in Feminism*. Ithaca, N.Y.: Cornell University Press, 1986.

———. "Feminism, Science, and the Anti-Enlightenment Critiques." In *Feminism/Postmodernism*, Linda J. Nicholson, ed. New York: Routledge, 1990.

———. *Whose Science? Whose Knowledge? Thinking from Women's Lives*. Ithaca, N.Y.: Cornell University Press, 1991.

Hartsock, Nancy. "The Feminist Standpoint: Developing the Grounds for a Specifically Feminist Historical Materialism." In *Discovering Reality: Feminist Perspectives on Epistemology, Metaphysics, Methodology, and Philosophy of Science*. S. Harding and M. Hintikka, eds. Dordrecht: D. Reidel, 1983.

Longino, Helen E. *Science as Social Knowledge: Values and Objectivity in Scientific Inquiry*. Princeton, N.J.: Princeton University Press, 1990.

———. "Essential Tensions—Phase Two: Feminist, Philosophical, and Social Studies of Science." In *A Mind of One's Own: Feminist Essays on Reason and Objectivity*. Louise M. Antony and Charlotte Witt, eds. Boulder, Colo.: Westview Press, 1993.

———. "Subjects, Power, and Knowledge: Description and Prescription in Feminist Philosophies of Science." In *Feminist Epistemologies*. Linda Alcoff and Elizabeth Potter, eds. New York: Routledge, 1993.

Nelson, Jack, and Lynn Hankinson Nelson. "No Rush to Judgment." *The Monist* 77, no. 4 (1994): 486–508.

Nelson, Lynn Hankinson. *Who Knows: From Quine to a Feminist Empiricism*. Philadelphia, Pa.: Temple University Press, 1990.

———. "Epistemological Communities." In *Feminist Epistemologies*. Linda Alcoff and Elizabeth Potter, eds. New York: Routledge, 1993.

———. "A Question of Evidence." *Hypatia* 8, no. 2 (1993): 172–89.

———. "Critical Notice: Lorraine Code's *What Can She Know? Feminist Theory and the Construction of Knowledge*." *Canadian Journal of Philosophy* 24, no. 2 (1994): 295–326.

————. "A Feminist Naturalized Philosophy of Science." *Synthese* 104, no. 3 (1995).

————. "Empiricism Without Dogmas." In *Feminism, Science, and the Philosophy of Science.* L. H. Nelson and J. Nelson, eds. Dordrecht: Kluwer Academic Publishers, 1996.

Nelson, Lynn Hankinson, and Jack Nelson. "Feminist Values and Cognitive Virtues." *PSA* 2 (1995).

Nicholson, Linda J., ed. *Feminism/Postmodernism.* New York: Routledge, 1990.

Rooney, Phyllis. "Recent Work in Feminist Discussions of Reason" *American Philosophical Quarterly* 31, no. 1 (1994): 1–21.

Ruddick, Sarah. "New Feminist Work on Knowledge, Reason and Objectivity." *Hypatia* 8, no. 4 (1993): 140–49.

Scheman, Naomi. "Though This Be Method, Yet There Is Madness in It." In *A Mind of One's Own: Feminist Essays on Reason and Objectivity.* Louise M. Antony and Charlotte Witt, eds. Boulder, Colo.: Westview Press, 1993.

14

Can There Be a Feminist Logic?

Marjorie Hass

Can there be a feminist logic? By most accounts the answer would be no. What I find remarkable is the great difference in the justifi- cations provided for this conclusion. The impossibility of feminist logic is defended, on the one hand, on the grounds that logic itself is most fundamentally a form of domination and so is inimical to feminist aims. Other philosophers, while also defending the impossibility of feminist logic, do so from the conviction that it is feminist theory rather than logic that is the problem. For these thinkers, feminism cannot make any interesting or important contribution to logic because feminist theory is fundamentally shallow or misguided. In this paper I will argue that both positions are mistaken: Logic is neither as totalizing as the one side believes nor is feminist theory as inconsequential for logic as the other pole would have it. In the course of these arguments, I describe the work of several feminist logicians, showing the possibility and value of feminist approaches to logic.

I

To identify feminist strands of antilogic sentiment, I turn to the most fully developed expression of the view that logic is inimical to feminism: Andrea Nye's groundbreaking book *Words of Power: A Feminist Reading of the History of Logic.*[1] Nye argues that an examination of the history of logic reveals logic as a totalizing and hence, dangerous, discourse. Far from the epic struggle to overcome ignorance through the discovery of ever-more-accurate means of representing logical form, Nye's history of logic is the story of the power to legitimize some ways of speaking at the expense of others.[2] Through her contextual readings of the work of the great men of logic, Nye contests the history of logic in which logic is portrayed as "the language that has detached itself from confusion and passion, the language which has transcended natural language embedded in sensual lives, mutably imprinted with social, economic, or personal concerns."[3] More specifically, Nye argues that logic embodies a suspect desire for certainty and power at the expense of an understanding of the context in which utterances are produced. And this is not, for Nye, merely an epistemic worry. The consequences of logical analysis are, she thinks, potentially dangerous in that logic becomes a form of oppressive power.

Nye's reading encompasses a variety of developments in the history of logic. To show the character of her critique more fully, I turn to two of the extended examples she considers. The first, from her reading of Aristotle, illustrates her concern that the emphasis on logical form creates an epistemic structure that disadvantages those from whom logical training is withheld. The second, a summation of part of her reading of Frege, shows a related point: the danger Nye sees in the relationship between abstraction and the desire for closure and totality.

In her reading of Aristotle's logic, Nye recalls one of Aristotle's examples of the structure of syllogistic logic:

> We may know, to use Aristotle's example, that "all mules are barren" and that "this animal here is a mule," and still not have put these two facts together. "Nothing prevents someone who knows that both A belongs to the whole of B and that B belongs to the whole of C, thinking that A does not belong to C" (Prior, II, 21 67a33–35). But once the statements are combined in a syllogism, the truth that "this animal will not give birth" becomes evident.[4]

Nye points out that examples such as these only serve to reveal the abstract nature of Aristotle's logic in that no farmer, no one with any experience of foals and mules, would be likely to make the mistake of thinking that the mule in the barn would be giving birth given that mules are barren. Syllogistic logic requires that the abstract structure of the inference takes precedence over the content and context of the utterance. "In fact," she says, "this defense of the syllogism is only intelligible when one takes into account that it was never meant that any farmer would have use of it."[5]

And so, Nye argues, Aristotle's logic is meant to clarify and formalize the argumentative projects of an elite class. Once separated from lived experience, through its emphasis on form over content, logic acquires a dangerous kind of power in that actual experience of foals and mules becomes understood as a lesser form of knowledge than the abstract reasoning of the logician. Nye suggests that once logic becomes the arbiter of truth, "Logic needs no respondent; it has reduced to silence any possible hearer and even the second thought of the logician himself. . . . Other voices have disappeared and there is only the logician's own."[6]

Nye makes a similar argument about Frege's logic by pointing to Frege's desire to erase difference and distance. She argues that for Frege, "logic offers only the approximation of understanding: a thought from which personal differences are erased, a thought which exists apart from any individual and which is graspable by all."[7] As the ultimate exemplar of logical abstraction, a language that has fully erased content, "a language without style, a language purged of the coloring, nuance, rhythm, metaphor, rhetoric that mark an individual voice," Frege's logic is also the one Nye finds most dangerous.[8] For in establishing this abstract language, Frege creates a "thought like a hammer," a thought detached from lived persons who suffer and bleed and who cannot now use their lived experience to respond to the logician. The logician's thought, expressed in the abstract language of logic will, Nye argues, point to a common action, an action that might be immune to the needs of individuals. Feeling, desire, and passion can all be ignored by the Fregean logician, much as Michael Dummett takes Frege's alleged anti-Semitism as irrelevant to Frege's logical program.[9]

Although Nye denies that the history of logic exhibits a single narrative thread, her own critiques identify a single underlying flaw: In allowing us to focus on abstract form over concrete content, logic erases difference in favor of unity and so disadvantages those on the margins for whom unity means erasure. I will call this problem, a problem that Nye identifies in the work of both Aristotle and Frege, "the problem of abstraction." In Nye's view, entry into the logical project is a form of participation in the politics of dominance and erasure. As feminists, she argues, we can never participate in the development of formal logic or even offer feminist revisions of logic. "If I am right," she says, "there can be no superior logic that will show up the mistakes of logicians; there can be no feminist logic that exposes masculine logic as sexist or authoritarian."[10] Nye calls instead for feminists to "read logic," that is, to put it in its historical and political contexts, and to "respond" to logic: "The antidote to logic is no supralogical metalanguage that will criticize and regulate the forms of logical thought, but language itself, the normality of human interchange that logic refuses."[11]

Much as I sympathize with Nye's emphasis on individual differences and primary experience, I am suspicious of this as a criticism of logic. The type of abstraction that logic exhibits cannot be easily discarded, even by feminists cognizant of the importance of recognizing individual differences. The ability to identify form independent of context, the very technique that formal logic requires, has been important for feminists and remains a seemingly essential element of collective political action. As Allison Weir argues, "In rejecting abstraction, feminist theorists forget that the capacity to abstract from particular relationships, from linguistic systems and social norms, is essential to a capacity to *criticize* those relationships, systems, and norms."[12]

This is not to say that the dangers of abstraction, which Nye has identified, do not exist. The very same process that allows us to see wife battering as a systematic and generalized cultural practice can lead us to ignore the ways that the meaning of battering might differ among women of differing ethnicities and/or social classes. The failure to mark these differences, and difference generally, does often lead to ineffective solutions. But our desire to guard against this error ought not lead us to an opposing error. Wholesale flight from generality would prevent us from inventing all but the most local of solutions. I think we must respect the tension between the need for generality and the need to respect differences, recognizing the full weight of both sides of the problem. In aiming to avoid the recognizable problems with abstractions, we must not imagine that we can retreat into a "purer," fully concrete form of description.

In this respect, Nye's tendency to hold up natural language as logic's purer other is problematic. For even natural language fails to offer a refuge from generality. The terms of natural language themselves depend on a willingness to move away from the particular. It is not only contested terms such as "woman," that are liable to distort the differences among particular women; the problem of abstraction emerges for ordinary terms as well. Even proper names, those terms most closely tied to an individual, require us to ignore differences in time and place. Sylvia remains "Sylvia" even as she changes in space and time. Far from opposing logic as a more particular form of expression, natural language itself requires a form of generality that produces anew the problem of abstraction.

If we cannot simply flee from generality, what are we to do about the problem of abstraction? The solution seems to me to lie in the development of new theories of generality that allow for distance and universality while at the same time respecting difference. Rather than turning our backs on logic, we can use the techniques and methods of the philosophical study of logic to enhance our understanding of generality and find new representations of generality that are respectful of difference. The challenge of balancing the claims of particularity and generality, far from foreclosing the possibility of feminist logic, opens the way for a variety of feminist approaches.

Cognitive scientist Rachel Joffe Falmagne has suggested that such a project might begin with a reconsideration of the dialectical logic developed by E. V. Ilyenkov.[13] Falmagne emphasizes the difference between standard and dialectical logic: "Whereas, within the standard view, conceptual unity among objects relies on the commonality of elements, it is the interrelatedness of diverse elements and the integration of opposites that creates unity within dialectics."[14] In other words, dialectical logic is not based on the relations between abstract concepts defined intensionally as those exhibiting or containing a common element or property, but rather depends on concrete concepts defined extensionally.

Falmagne contests the identification of abstract concepts with universality and the resulting demotion of concrete concepts. In Falmagne's view, Ilyenkov provides a model for developing universal concepts and judgments that are nonetheless grounded in concrete facts and descriptions. Falmagne suggests the following definition as an illustration of the notion of a concrete universal: "One might define a mother as a woman having primary relation to a child, a relation embedded in the social and historical context in which they live."[15] This "definition" does not identify some feature or activity purported to be common to all mothers, nor does it restrict mothering to biological motherhood or to a unique relationship between a single woman and a single child. For Falmagne, the concept of mothering, understood as a concrete universal, does not abstract away from particular forms of mothering but "remains concrete in that it sustains a dialectical relationship with those particulars."[16] It thus becomes possible to sustain theorizing and generality without losing sight of the particularities of lived experience.

Emphasizing concrete universals has radical consequences for logic and our understanding of the role logic plays in thought. Falmagne argues that we must develop models of cognition that encompass both formal inference processes and processes that depend on the grasping of content. Whereas Nye takes the problem of abstraction as insurmountable, Falmagne points to a way of developing logic by reinterpreting generality.

Responding to the problem of abstraction by investigating generality is one project that could count as a feminist approach to logic. But identifying ways that logic can further feminist theorizing addresses only one side of the objections to the idea of feminist logic. I turn now to an alternative set of criticisms in which it is not logic but feminism that is under attack.

II

In calling this section "antifeminism" I do not intend to imply that the representatives of this position are unsympathetic to feminism as a political movement. My title refers only to a particular type of critique of feminist theory, a critique which finds feminist theorizing inadequate. Susan Haack, in a recent series of papers, has argued that feminist philosophy of science and epistemology are fundamentally misguided.[17] Although she has commented on feminist logic only briefly and by extension, her arguments about these other domains flow from a general indictment of feminist theorizing and so must be addressed if feminist logic is to be defended.[18]

In Haack's paper, "Science 'from a Feminist Perspective,'" she argues that feminist theory has not shown that science has a masculine character. She dismisses several attempts on grounds such as the following: "[The paper] was so clotted with Marxist jargon as to be almost unreadable" and "[another paper] lost my sympathy by obliging me to struggle with the convoluted banalities of recent French philosophy."[19] Although I find this more invective, or perhaps humor, than argument, Haack's more substantive criticisms are certainly worth examining and provide a clear argument that feminist theory is fundamentally misguided.

Her central substantive charges, made in both "Science 'from a Feminist Perspective'" and "Knowledge and Propaganda: Reflections of an Old Feminist" are the following: (1) Feminist theory is based on the "New Cynicism," which falsely assumes there is no objective truth and thus that political values ought to determine theory choice, and (2) women do not have a distinctive way of knowing or thinking that could make theorizing distinctively feminist. Haack does allow that a feminist political orientation might serve the minor but useful function of ferreting out examples of misapplication of the standards of scientific or philosophical rigor, but she maintains that such work is often "fairly familiar stuff" or at best "a fine piece of detective work."[20] Even the best examples, she suggests, only serve to show that the traditional standards of intellectual rigor ought to be preserved and that feminist theorizing that aims to problematize or replace those standards is misguided.

With respect to the first charge, Haack argues that feminist philosophers are motivated by the destabilization of such concepts as "truth," "objectivity," and "reason" that arises in postmodern and deconstructive philosophy. Haack dismisses these concerns as instances of what she calls the "passes for" fallacy: concluding that there is no such thing as evidence, fact, or reality on the grounds that what passes for evidence, fact, and reality is often no such thing.[21] In other words, those who would reject these epistemological standards do so on the basis of faulty inductive reasoning.

Whatever the merits of this as a fallacy, it does not reflect the sort of work that I am identifying as feminist logic. Using Falmagne's work as a model, we can see possibilities for feminist approaches to logic that are reconstructive. Feminist logic does not require that we abandon epistemological standards in favor of politics, as Haack alleges is typical of feminist philosophy.[22] In the next section I describe the work of a variety of feminist logicians. Like Falmagne, their work is motivated by the same concerns that have motivated other logicians: the attempt to develop a rigorous and accurate understanding of validity.

Whereas Haack's first charge fails to characterize the majority of feminist writing on logic, her second charge is potentially more troubling. If formal logic presupposes that women have a special reasoning style and it is false that they do, then formal logic is certainly misguided. Haack says that she finds the notion that women have distinctive or special epistemic powers "embarrassing" and inimical to what she takes to be the aims of feminism. From this perspective, the attempt to find a distinctively *feminist* logic is at best unnecessary and at worst, counterproductive.

In a similar, though much less polemical vein, Sandra Menssen rejects the claim that Gilligan's work demonstrates that men and women use different logics.[23] Menssen argues that her interpretation of Gilligan, far from being antifeminist, is the one that best furthers feminist aims:

> If indeed the language of logic is universal, then it seems to be that the frequent failure of men to hear women should be set in a harsher light than that to which Gilligan and her followers are accustomed . . . women should labor to make the universality of the language of logic understood. This is a labor not only consistent with, but, I believe, supportive of an effort to end the oppression of women.[24]

For Menssen too, feminist logic presupposes "difference" feminism in which men and women have differing reasoning styles and hence a need for different formal logics. From this point of view, the development of a special "woman's logic" delays the cause of feminism by emphasizing nonexistent differences between men and women. This is a particular concern because any differences in logical style are apt to be taken as evidence of women's inferiority as reasoners. Additionally, the idea that women have need of a special logic seems to be based on essentialist underpinnings, returning us to the problem of abstraction.

I am not in principle opposed to the idea that women and men have different reasoning styles, nor does it seem to me that any difference between men and women must lead inevitably to prejudice against women, but there is no conclusive evidence that women and men think or reason in fundamentally different ways. Given this lack of evidence, a feminist logic that is intended as a woman's logic would appear to be on shaky ground. But for the majority of feminist logicians, feminist logic does not mean "women's logic." Feminists have challenged classical logic in ways that do not imply that women have a special capacity for reasoning that differs from men. In the next section, I describe the work of several such feminist logicians and explore a variety of feminist approaches to formal logic.

III

Sandra Harding, in examining feminist critiques of science, has suggested that two strands emerge.[25] On the one hand, there are feminist criticisms of "bad science" claiming that androcentric scientific culture regularly fails to adhere to its own scientific standards. More radical, she says, are feminist criticisms of "science as usual" which call into question the scientific standards themselves and provide the ground for a new feminist philosophy of science. In what follows, I will use Harding's distinction to map the parallel territory of feminist logic, arguing, contra Nye and Haack, that there can be both feminist *logic* and *feminist* logic.

A variety of feminist philosophers have offered criticisms of the type I will call "bad logic." Martha Nussbaum, in an essay for the *New Republic*, has emphasized the ways in which the norms of masculinity in our culture actively discourage logical thinking.[26] In contrast to our cultural image of manliness as the embodiment of reason, Nussbaum argues that:

> Unlike true Socratic reasoners, [the enforcers of hegemonic masculinity] are unwilling to be penetrated by new factual information . . . to follow reason in the Socratic way requires a form of vulnerability and even passivity. It means dropping the pose that one is always adequate to any occasion, always on top, always hard.[27]

Here Nussbaum is not undermining logic as it is properly practiced; indeed, she is calling for us to practice it with greater care. From this perspective, one of the virtues of feminism is that it may enable us to be *more* logical.

The claim that feminism can help us avoid bad logic has been developed by a variety of other feminist philosophers. Janice Moulton, for example, has argued that the feminist recognition that masculine pronouns are not really gender neutral in English helps us avoid the fallacy of equivocation.[28] In a similar vein, Trudy Govier has shown that the logical evaluation of testimony is best carried out with an attention to the social situation of the testifier, especially when she is part of an oppressed group.[29] Karen Warren argues that a patriarchal conceptual framework interferes with good reasoning and logical thinking in that it biases the reasoner.[30] In each of these cases, feminism serves not to undermine logic, but as an antidote to bad logic. Feminist theorizing reveals systematic ways that patriarchal bias and prejudice masquerade as logical reasoning. Importantly, these are not instances of "women's logic." None of the logicians mentioned here posits a special logical framework applicable to (only) women. The logical principles described are understood as applying equally well to men as to women and are intended as corrections to errors made in more standard accounts.

At first sight the "bad logic" aspect of feminist logic might seem to be remarkably akin to the narrow arena marked out by Haack for feminist philosophy of science—namely, the identification of isolated examples of masculine bias interfering with the correct application of standards. But the similarity is deceptive. On the "bad logic" side, gender bias impacts the application of logical standards, not merely accidentally (as Haack might have it) but in a deep and organized way: There is no way that the standards can be applied properly without a feminist analysis of gender. As we saw above, these philosophers point to systematic errors in the application of logical principles that arise from masculine bias. What is needed, then, according to these feminists, is an understanding of gender that will allow us to hold men (and women) to men's own professed standards of logical rigor.

This sort of work is but one type of feminist approach to logic. More radical are feminist critics of "logic as usual," feminists who find fault with elements of classical logic and seek alternative formal representations of basic logical concepts. Most of the work in this arena has focused on one of three elements of classical logic: quantification (generality), identity, and negation. Each of these topics has been the center of debate within both logic and feminism, and so it is perhaps not surprising that feminist logicians would center their analyses here. I have already described Falmagne's work on generality and the way that nonstandard logics may contribute to a resolution of the problem of abstraction. Negation, however, has been the subject of the most sustained feminist interest.

In her essay "The Politics of Reason: Towards a Feminist Logic" as well as in *Feminism and the Mastery of Nature*, Val Plumwood argues that relevance logic offers a better account of negation than classical logic, in that classical negation corresponds to the dualistic characterization of self/other lying at the heart of dominance relations.[31] In contrast, Plumwood argues, relevance logic characterizes negation as a nonhierarchical relation:

> It is neither a cancellation of nor a lack or absence of a specified condition, but another and further condition—a difference—yielding the concept of an other which is not just specified negatively but is independently characterized and with an independent role on its own behalf.[32]

For Plumwood, relevance logic offers an alternative conception of negation, one in keeping with the desire to escape conceptual dualisms and thus one more conducive to the feminist desire to end oppression. But it is not feminist politics alone which motivates the adoption of relevance logic. For Plumwood, nonhierarchical negation is more accurate in that it better characterizes the actual relation between self and other.

Feminist thinking about logic need not reject logic as dangerously abstract or hopelessly masculinist. As a central structure of the western conception of knowledge, formal logic deserves the same careful attention that feminists have given to science, epistemology, and rationality. The work of Falmagne, Plumwood, and the other feminist logicians discussed here forms the beginnings of a new direction for feminist theorizing. It remains to be seen whether this research will result in new technical developments or only in new justifications for already developed logics (such as relevance logic). My aim here has been to show that feminist logic is possible—indeed, is already underway. The arguments against it, both feminist and nonfeminist, fail to show that feminism and logic are incompatible. The conclusion I draw is even stronger: Feminist approaches to logic can enhance our understanding of generality, negation, and identity, concepts central to both fields.

Notes

1. Andrea Nye, *Words of Power: A Feminist Reading of the History of Logic* (New York: Routledge, 1990).

2. For a more traditional history of logic see William Kneale and Martha Kneale, *The Development of Logic* (Oxford: Oxford University Press, 1962).

3. Nye, *Words of Power,* 4.

4. Ibid., 41.

5. Ibid., 42.

6. Ibid., 59.

7. Ibid., 132.

8. Ibid., 154.

9. Nye argues that Dummett's discovery of Frege's anti-Semitic writings in an unpublished diary caused Dummett to hesitate but ultimately conclude that Frege's politics were irrelevant to his work in logic (Nye, *Words of Power,* 152, n. 6). For an argument that Frege's anti-Semitism is not connected to his logic, see Joan Weiner's review of *Words of Power* in *Journal of Symbolic Logic* 59, no. 2 (June 1994).

10. Nye, *Words of Power,* 175.

11. Ibid., 176.

12. Allison Weir, *Sacrificial Logics: Feminist Theory and the Critique of Identity* (New York: Routledge, 1996), 190.

13. Rachel Joffe Falmagne, "The Abstract and the Concrete," in *Sociocultural Psychology: Theory and Practice of Doing and Knowing,* L. Martin, K. Nelson, and E. Tobach, eds. (New York: Cambridge University Press, 1995), 205–28. See also E. V. Ilyenkov, *Dialectical Logic,* H. Campbell Creighton, trans. (Union of Soviet Socialist Republics: Progress Publishers, 1977), and *The Dialectics of the Abstract and the Concrete in Marx's Capital* (Moscow: Progress Publishers, 1982).

14. Falmagne, "The Abstract and the Concrete," 207.

15. Ibid., 209.

16. Ibid.

17. Susan Haack, "Knowledge and Propaganda: Reflections of an Old Feminist," *Partisan Review* (Fall 1993); "Science 'from a Feminist Perspective,' " *Philosophy* 67 (1992); and "Preposterism and its Consequences," *Social Philosophy and Policy* (Summer 1996). Haack also comments briefly on Nye's work and on the work of Val Plumwood in the introduction to *Deviant Logic, Fuzzy Logic: Beyond the Formalism* (University of Chicago Press, 1996).

18. "The vast recent literature of feminist approaches to ethics, epistemology, philosophy of science, philosophy of language, and lately even logic, is a striking manifestation of some consequences of preposterism. Reading in this vast literature, one can hardly fail to notice how endlessly it is repeated that feminism has radical consequences for this or that arena, and how frequently those radical consequences turn out to be trivial, or obviously derivative from some male philosopher, or manifestly false; how determinedly practitioners avert their attention from serious criticisms, and how lavishly they praise the work of others of their own persuasion" (Haack, "Preposterism and its Consequences," 313).

19. Haack, "Science 'from a Feminist Perspective,' " 16.

20. In "Science 'from a Feminist Perspective,' " Haack cites as examples Gardy's argument that sexist assumptions in sociobiology only came to be revised

when substantial numbers of women entered the field and Bleier's work on the history of research into sex differences in cognitive abilities.

21. Haack, "Knowledge and Propaganda," 562.

22. In responding in this way, I do not intend to imply that I accept Haack's dismissal of postmodernism as a form of preposterism, lacking intellectual rigor.

23. Sandra Menssen, "Do Men and Women Use Different Logics? A Reply to Carol Gilligan and Deborah Orr," *Informal Logic* XV, no. 2 (Spring 1993): 123–38.

24. Menssen, "Do Men and Women Use Different Logics?" 136.

25. Sandra Harding, *Whose Science? Whose Knowledge?* (Ithaca, N.Y.: Cornell University Press, 1991).

26. Martha Nussbaum, "The Softness of Reason," *The New Republic* (July 13, 1992): 26–27; (July 20, 1992).

27. Nussbaum, "The Softness of Reason," 27.

28. Janice Moulton, "The Myth of the Neutral 'Man,' " in *Sexist Language*, Mary Vetterling-Braggin, ed. (Totowa, N.J.: Littlefield, Adams and Company, 1981).

29. Trudy Govier, "When Logic Meets Politics: Testimony, Distrust and Rhetorical Disadvantage," *Informal Logic* XV, no. 2 (Spring 1993): 93–104.

30. Karen J. Warren, "Critical Thinking and Feminism," *Informal Logic* X, no. 1 (Winter 1988): 31–44.

31. Val Plumwood, "The Politics of Reason: Towards a Feminist Logic," *Australasian Journal of Philosophy* 71, no. 4 (December 1993): 436–62; and *Feminism and the Mastery of Nature* (New York: Routledge, 1993).

32. Plumwood, *Feminism and the Mastery of Nature*, 58.

15

Feminism and Mental Representation: Analytic Philosophy, Cultural Studies, and Narrow Content

David Golumbia

I n 1983, Naomi Scheman published an essay which neither she, nor, as far as I know, any other philosopher or feminist theorist has built upon in detail.[1] That essay, "Individualism and the Objects of Psychology," was included in the seminal volume of feminist philosophy edited by Sandra Harding and Merrill Hintikka called *Discovering Reality,* which appeared the same year. Since I first read it a number of years ago, Scheman's essay has remained a touchstone for me. It seems to embody the best of both analytic philosophy and feminist theory, and indeed to promise a merger between these two strands of thinking, a merger which this volume seeks both to encourage and, at the same time I think, to problematize. Indeed, along with Hilary Putnam's "The Meaning of 'Meaning' " and Tyler Burge's "Individualism and the Mental," I think of Scheman's essay as one of the most important essays in philosophy of mind to have appeared in recent times. So the question from which this paper begins is, why has Scheman's essay and the sort of analysis she propagates there exerted so little influence, whether on feminist theory or on traditional analytic philosophy?

This provocative question, which I will confess has interested me for quite a while now, will nevertheless not be the subject of the essay to follow—at least not in any direct way. That's in part because answers to the question seem relatively clear. Philosophy of mind is so technical, after all, so enmeshed with the scientific and scientistic character of much analytic philosophy, and for these reasons may be of less immediate interest or relevance to those of us who are concerned with problems of politics and culture and especially gender and race. Even more importantly, perhaps decisively important, of course, is the degree to which philosophy of mind is one of those heavily guarded fortresses of philosophy today. Those who occupy the fortress, or at least many of them, scorn those of us who do not, consider our work ultimately unphilosophical, and view our work (more invidiously) in some sense "not worthy" of the title Philosophy. Given the traditionalism and sexism of this position, and the technicality I've mentioned before, it's no wonder that feminists generally have avoided philosophy of mind.

As I've said, I don't consider these arguments about the topic of Scheman's essay especially instructive, and I'm aware that my map of the current philosophy scene is overly schematic. What interests me at this point is the fact that I think we're starting to see a way in to a feminist critique of the philosophy of mind along the lines of Scheman's argument, and it seems to me that the farther we push this critique the more we see how valuable it is; how much is at stake in that abstruse sphere we feminist and other cultural theorists have largely been willing to leave alone; and how much there is to be gained by storming the technical barricades. In short, I am suggesting that the time has come not for retrenchment of our clearly embattled forces, but rather for a kind of frontal assault, one that may well carry overtones of an intensified usefulness for feminist theory as a tool in the serious social battle with which we all cannot help but be engaged.

Now that I hope I've got your attention for the somewhat rarefied argument which follows, let me drop the military metaphor I've been awkwardly employing so far. I hope you'll share my conviction that that metaphor stems largely from the defenders of the tradition, as I've been describing them, but like many feminists I would prefer not to see the terms of our culture come down to terms of battle. What I'd like to do instead for the remainder of my paper is to rehearse some of the terms and contexts of Scheman's argument, and some other arguments in contemporary philosophy of mind, and then to discuss how a feminist critique of this argument may be useful both philosophically and for feminist theory in general, and even find some (perhaps partially) willing allies in certain strands of argument within that largely hermetic field. Philosophy of mind is neither as irrelevant as some of us may think, I will argue, nor is it by any means as neutral as its adherents implicitly (and sometimes explicitly) insist. Just what its putative neutrality consists in shall be an important topic in what follows.

I want to bring some much-needed focus to this large topic by focusing on a few specific aspects of the philosophy of mind, and especially one on which Scheman touches only in passing (indeed, it had largely not yet congealed as a philosophical topos when she wrote her essay and has in part been surpassed as of today; but it is an instructive topic nevertheless). That topic goes under the name of "wide and narrow content," and is associated largely with the late 1980s work of Jerry Fodor and his defenders and critics. In what follows I'll argue that Fodor's development of these concepts, his specific deployment of them and the responses we can bring to them out of feminist theory as well as feminist and other analytic philosophy, reveal much about the stakes of analytic philosophy today and the relevance of theory itself for the social and cultural exchanges which are wrought upon feminism by largely disingenuous conservatives.

I'm going to rehearse some of the history of the wide and narrow content issue, and I hope you'll forgive me if this is well-trodden territory for my readers. I'm trusting that for at least some of them it won't be, and in fact that's one of the interesting things about the larger question I'm raising, in that what I'm about to describe is, in some spheres at least, one of the best-known philosophical controversies of the last few decades. Yet I am not at all sure how familiar with it will be the philosophers reading this essay.

The controversy has its acknowledged origin in Hilary Putnam's 1976 essay (actually written in 1973),[2] "The Meaning of 'Meaning,'" although in part Tyler Burge's later essays "Individualism and the Mental" and "Individualism and Psychology"[3] played an important role in demonstrating the argument's importance for philosophy of mind. The argument runs as follows. The notion of meaning is supposed to be captured by straightforward analytic statements like:

1. The word "water" means H_2O.

Putnam famously devises what are now known as the Twin Earth thought experiments to show the difficulty in this assumption, that the word "water" does not mean H_2O in the ordinary sense of "mean." The experiment goes like this. The planet Twin Earth is molecule-for-molecule identical with its counterpart, our own earth, but for one important fact. Whereas we on Earth have H_2O, on Twin Earth they have XYZ; and without sophisticated chemical analysis, H_2O and XYZ are indistinguishable. So in cultures that lack this "sophistication" (say, Western culture before 1750), what does it mean—specifically, what does the word "water" mean—when I say "I want a glass of water" and my molecule-for-molecule identical doppelgänger says the same thing?

Putnam's intuition—one many philosophers share—is that they do not mean the same thing, even though to all physical appearances and all available experiments their consequences and truth conditions are identical. I don't want to get carried away with this science fiction example and I hope that my discussion of this topic won't get hung up, as some discussions of Putnam have, on the outlandish context of his thought experiment. Rather, I want to look at the broader context of Putnam's argument, to see whom or what he is arguing against and why. For that issue we can do no better than to turn to the end of Putnam's article, where he articulates why philosophers and linguists alike have been so mistaken in their discussions of meaning:

> If there is a reason for both learned and lay opinion having gone so far astray with respect to a topic which deals, after all, with matters which are in everyone's experience, matters concerning which we all have more data than we know what to do with, matters concerning which we have, if we shed preconceptions, pretty clear intuitions, it must be connected to the fact that the grotesquely mistaken views of language which are and always have been current reflect two specific and very central philosophical tendencies: the tendency to treat cognition as a purely *individual* matter and the tendency to ignore the *world,* insofar as it consists of more than the individual's "observations." Ignoring the division of linguistic labor is ignoring the social dimension of cognition; ignoring what we have called the *indexicality* of most words is ignoring the contribution of the environment. Traditional philosophy of language, like much traditional philosophy, leaves out other people and the world; a better philosophy and a better science of language must encompass both.[4]

Now that last sentence, along with Putnam's emphasis on "the social dimension of cognition," is not something many feminists (or at least those of us I'll call cultural-studies feminists, as I'll explain below) would disagree with, and I'll return to Putnam's usefulness for feminist thought at the end of this essay; but I want to spend a few moments sketching out what the traditional position is Putnam argues against here, as well as the response of those traditional forces to Putnam's arguments in "The Meaning of 'Meaning,' " and how that response is instructive and a good subject for feminist theory.

As I've just said, the context of Putnam's argument, and Burge's as well, is that analytic philosophy of mind, and, insofar as it follows a similar line of argument, cognitive science as well, concentrates too much on the individual's contribution to mental process. This is Scheman's point in "Individualism and the Objects of Psychology": In all three cases the point proceeds from an understanding that what we have been loosely referring to as "individualism" is not at all a given of empirical investigation but in fact a peculiarly Western phenomenon whose hold on Western science and (especially analytic) philosophy is very strong. Furthermore, as Scheman insists, it is a concept with a determinate masculinist history; keeping the notion in place, for reasons deeper than that of insisting on a problematic liberal humanism, seems a crucial part of masculinist culture.

So when a few incisive feminist scholars notice one of the gaping holes in individualism's cloak, a hole which, among other things—and as both Putnam and Scheman make clear—calls into question the specifically scientific and/or physicalist aspect of psychological investigation, it is no surprise that the response of the traditional philosophical establishment is defensive retrenchment. This is where narrow content comes into the picture, and with it the looming figure of Jerry Fodor. As Putnam points out, Fodor is a complex and provocative philosopher, and what is to follow may smack more than a little of caricature, but I am not sure that is inappropriate. After all, Fodor is explicit about the cultural (if not the political) commitments of his own philosophical work. He writes in the introduction to one of his books that

> I hate relativism. I think it affronts intellectual dignity. I am appalled that it is thought to be respectable. . . . The argument, *par excellence,* that purports to show that relativism is true is holism. So this book is an attempt to take away holism. Hate me, hate my dog.[5]

Of course, this is from the Introduction to *A Theory of Content,* and the word Fodor aligns here with relativism—holism—is on some readings at least just the opposite of what Putnam, Burge, and Scheman all call "individualism," namely the doctrine that the semantic content of psychological states can be explicated solely in terms of the persons whose heads they (apparently) occur in.

From a cultural, if not philosophical, standpoint what is remarkable is the tenacity with which Fodor opposes this idea, and the tone and social valence of the remarks he makes along the way to that opposition. And the first move in his opposition to holism was Fodor's creation of the idea of "narrow content." Narrow content, at first, picked out those "in the head" aspects of a belief, and was opposed to "wide content," which picks out the aspects of a belief, its contexts and referents and so on, that clearly are not in the head.[6]

Rather than concentrating on what Fodor says about narrow content (though such an investigation would be of great interest), we can get to some of those commitments and contexts more directly by seeing where the more general thrust of Fodor's theory points, and that is something we can accomplish by turning for just a moment to some of Fodor's other writings. For example, in the aptly named "Creation Myth," a somewhat fanciful appendix to his important 1987 volume *Psychosemantics,* Fodor assumes a position that probably seems ironic to him, in addressing what he calls the problem of "social coordination"— namely, the position of God:

> Here is what I would have done if I had been faced with this problem [of passing complex social knowledge from generation to generation] in designing *Homo Sapiens.* I would have made a knowledge of commonsense *Homo Sapiens* psychology *innate;* that way nobody would have to spend time learning it. And I would have made this innately apprehended commonsense psychology (at least approximately) *true,* so that the behavioral coordinations that it mediates would not depend on rigidly constraining the human behavioral repertoire or on accidental stabilities in the human ecology. Perhaps not *very much* would have to be innate and true to do the job; given the rudiments of commonsense Intentional Realism as a head start, you could maybe bootstrap the rest.[7]

Something profound occurs in Fodor's philosophy, something that the phrase "Intentional Realism" helps us to understand. I'm thinking about just what it is that Fodor hopes to naturalize in this theory. It isn't just intuitions about beliefs and desires, about human behavior, or about crude causality. Rather, Fodor's theory works to naturalize something far more specific, namely the notion of the person implicit in the theory of belief/desire psychology. That notion is a very Western, individualistic idea, an idea in which innate psychological processes lead pretty directly to the marks of civilization—for Fodor of course, the marks of Western civilization like Shakespeare and Sherlock Holmes. As he explains, the problem of social coordination is subordinate to the larger problem of Embodied Intelligence, which Fodor says can be put this way: "Shakespeare wouldn't have gotten around to writing *Hamlet* if he had had first to rediscover fire and reinvent the wheel."[8]

I have argued elsewhere that it is right to identify Realism with universalism, and therefore with the attempt to naturalize and eternalize the norms, methods, and metaphysics of Western culture as true for all human beings.[9] In this passage Fodor at least nominally identifies a species of Realism as itself an *innate* property, and this, I think, shows at least one of the underlying commitments in his philosophy—toward the discovery of the Western notion of the person in the very prewritten biology of human beings.[10] In this regard it seems more than coincidental that the image Fodor uses is the very image invoked by Hilary Putnam to indicate what is unacceptably universalist in Realism itself—that is, that Fodor identifies himself with the justly infamous "God's-Eye View."[11]

Indeed, in other writings, Fodor suggests that belief/desire psychology—which I am insisting is deeply implicated, on Fodor's story, in a very Western notion of the subject—should be written into the "ultimate fabric of the universe." My objection to this line of reasoning will probably seem very familiar, namely, that we should be wary of any attempts to tell just what are the ultimate constituents of the universe in the first place; and that when such attempts are written into the enterprise of Western science, we can see there a deep desire to write the terms of Western self-understanding into the descriptions of all human experience—to universalize our notions of who we are through the validating power which science has taken on itself.[12]

Now I suspect that most of my readers will have picked up on the explicitly feminist character of my criticisms of Fodor, but I'd like to spend my last few pages here making these more overt. The first thing I want to explain is that my views lead not just to feminist critique but to a particular brand of feminist critique which I will call "cultural studies feminism"; and I mean that term in part because it casts its net widely and finds room to include important critical work in African American studies, queer theory, and so on. It also includes most feminist work that sustains a meaningful theoretical component, so that I'm not going to be at pains to distinguish among materialist feminism, cultural feminism, radical feminism, and so forth. I hope to be able to speak to those of us who stick by any of those positions, or more than one of them. The one position this critique does tend to rule out is what Christina Hoff Sommers and her neoconservative like call "liberal feminism," and it does so precisely by calling into question whether that position deserves the name "feminism" in any manner we here may recognize.[13]

The theory of mind at which I mean to gesture here is seldom more than implicit and is constructed moreover out of discourses (such as psychoanalysis and Marxism) which lack the overtly philosophical character we have been invoking here. Nevertheless this work—in which I will want to include cultural theorists and feminists like Judith Butler, Gayatri Spivak, Hortense Spillers, Evelyn Fox Keller, Gloria Anzaldúa, and Donna Haraway, as well as feminist epistemologists and philosophers of science— all leads to a searching critique of what I have only glancingly here referred to as Western universalism. This critique has been developed by writers in other spheres of cultural studies as well as feminists. It rests on the recognition that Western culture continually seeks to establish a canon of cross-cultural and atemporal human truths, truths which do and will obtain regardless of our social and political contexts, truths about who we are, and—perhaps even more importantly who—we can become. Liberal humanism, in its most benign mode, rests on the most generalized form of this idea, namely that we are all "deserving human beings," an idea which most of us would find difficult to wrestle down altogether. But look how easily that idea translates into the disingenuous kind of "liberal feminism" Sommers continually invokes, as if it were not possible to discern everywhere in her writing, a desire to reestablish a stable, universal, and ultimately masculinist status quo.

In this sense, the abstruse work I've been advocating for most of this essay should, I hope, seem potentially more relevant than it might have previously. Like other philosophies critical of political oppression and repression, cultural studies and feminist theory strike me as most profound when they challenge our deepest preconceptions of our own identities and of the ways by which those identities are structured. Perhaps surprisingly, in the work of philosophers of mind like Jerry Fodor we discover some of our own culture's deepest determination to keep in place an oppressive and generally masculinist notion of identity, one which works at a very deep level to destabilize our own feminist ideas of diversity and flux. I hope to have suggested here, at least by association, that the general metaphysical picture I've associated with cultural studies and feminism on the one hand, and with Hilary Putnam's antirealist philosophy on the other, presents an alternative picture that is no less deep in its potential for explication of what goes on inside the mind. Indeed, the famous injunction philosophers remember and argue with from Putnam's essay is that "meanings ain't in the head." Feminist theory, I am suggesting, offers a far more unsettling picture, in which not just meanings but minds, in an important sense, aren't in the head—instead, they are part of the general social and cultural, which is to say political, fabric. Recognizing this fact about minds, I hope to have argued, is an important step in the process of changing them.

Notes

This paper is largely the unchanged transcript of an essay delivered at the "Is Feminist Philosophy Philosophy?" conference in 1993. Four years later, only minor alterations have been made to suit the printed page and to accommodate gross errors in fact and theory. I would wish to do much more (such as including some more recent references in the philosophy of mind), but the venue makes that seem inappropriate. Some more recent and I think subtler work that touches on the matters raised here can be found in my "Rethinking Philosophy in the Third Wave of Feminism," *Hypatia* 12, no. 3 (Summer 1997), 100–15; "Quine's

Ambivalence," *Cultural Critique* 38 (Winter 1998), 5–38; "Against Universality," *differences: A Journal of Feminist Cultural Studies,* forthcoming; and "Quine, Derrida, and the Question of Philosophy," *Diacritics,* forthcoming. Rebecca Bach, Lisa Bates, Emanuela Bianchi, Lynn Hankinson Nelson, Naomi Scheman, and Suzanne Daly provided invaluable comments on earlier versions of this paper.

1. "Individualism and the Objects of Psychology," in Sandra Harding and Merrill B. Hintikka, eds., *Discovering Reality: Feminist Perspectives on Epistemology, Metaphysics, Methodology, and the Philosophy of Science* (Dordrecht, Holland: D. Reidel Publishing Company, 1983), 225–44. After this paper was delivered, I learned from Naomi Scheman of the existence of her "Types, Tokens, and Conjuring Tricks," a masterful 1982 essay that extends the analysis of the "Individualism" essay, and whose failure to appear at the time speaks painfully to the institutional issues with which this essay is concerned.

2. See "Is Water Necessarily H$_2$O?" in Hilary Putnam, *Realism with a Human Face* (Cambridge, Mass.: Harvard University Press, 1990), 60.

3. Tyler Burge, "Individualism and the Mental," in *Midwest Studies in Philosophy, Vol. IV: Studies in Metaphysics,* Peter A. French, Theodore E. Uehling, Jr. and Howard K. Wettstein, eds. (Minneapolis: University of Minnesota Press, 1979), 73–121, and "Individualism and Psychology," *The Philosophical Review* 95, no. 1 (January 1986), 3–45. Also see the more recent "Individuation and Causation in Psychology," *Pacific Philosophical Quarterly* 70, no. 4 (December 1989), 303–22, and "Wherein Is Language Social?" in *Reflections on Chomsky,* Alexander George, ed. (New York: Basil Blackwell, 1989), 175–91. For work in psychology that bears directly on certain aspects of these problems, and especially as it relates to issues of gender, see the essays in *Making a Difference: Psychology and the Construction of Gender,* Rachel T. Hare-Mustin and Jeanne Marecek, eds. (New Haven, Conn., and London: Yale University Press, 1990) and the bibliographies they contain. I would want elsewhere to discuss at length why the sort of psychological research performed there has had so little impact on philosophy of mind, whereas cognitive science and other "mechanistic" forms of psychology have had so much influence; but the direction of the argument I would want to make there can be detected in the present paper.

4. Hilary Putnam, "The Meaning of 'Meaning,' " in *Mind, Language, and Reality: Philosophical Papers,* vol. 2 (New York: Cambridge University Press, 1975), 271.

5. Jerry A. Fodor, *A Theory of Content and Other Essays* (Cambridge, Mass. and London: The MIT Press/A Bradford Book, 1990), xii. The connections Fodor makes between holism and relativism are somewhat complicated, but they hinge on an interpretation of language familiar in analytic philosophy at least since Quine—namely, the view that the meaning of a word or sentence is determined to some degree by its context. This holistic view of Quine's is said by Fodor to lead to a relativism about content that is part and parcel of a more general relativism. For more on the issue from Fodor's perspective, in addition to *A Theory of Content,* see Fodor and Ernest LePore, *Holism: A Shopper's Guide* (Oxford and Cambridge, Mass.: Blackwell, 1992).

6. For some of his more recent views, see Jerry Fodor, "Replies," in *Meaning in Mind: Fodor and His Critics,* Georges Rey and Barry Loewer, eds. (Oxford and Cambridge, Mass.: Basil Blackwell, 1991), 255–319.

7. Jerry A. Fodor, *Psychosemantics: The Problem of Meaning in the Philosophy of Mind* (Cambridge, Mass., and London: The MIT Press/A Bradford Book, 1987), 132.

8. *Psychosemantics,* 129.

9. See "Against Universality."

10. For the record, a recent definition by Fodor of Intentional Realism is the position that "there are mental states whose occurrences and interactions cause behavior and do so, moreover, in ways that respect (at least to an approximation) the generalizations of commonsense belief/desire psychology" and "that these same causally efficacious mental states are also semantically evaluable" (*A Theory of Content,* 5).

11. For more on this position and criticism of it, see Putnam's works on the topic, especially those in *Realism with a Human Face, Reason, Truth and History* (Cambridge, England: Cambridge University Press, 1981), *Realism and Reason: Philosophical Papers,* vol. 3 (Cambridge, England: Cambridge University Press, 1983), and *Renewing Philosophy* (Cambridge, Mass., and London: Harvard University Press, 1992), all of which also contain important reflections on the philosophy of mind issues discussed here.

12. Although I lack room to justify it here, such a reading clearly depends on the understandings of science developed from sources as diverse as philosophers of science such as Paul Feyerabend and Putnam himself; sociologists of science such as David Bloor, Barry Barnes, Stephen Shapin, and Simon Schaffer; and feminists and other cultural theorists such as Michel Foucault, Donna Haraway, Sandra Harding, Helen Longino, and Evelyn Fox Keller.

13. For more on this point, see my "Rethinking Philosophy."

16

Replies to Hass and Golumbia

Nickolas Pappas

Reply to Marjorie Hass, "Can There Be a Feminist Logic?"

Professor Hass's paper has opened up a number of useful new topics for me. I applaud her clarifications of the idea of alternative logic—an idea that has often proved as murky as it is enticing—and her effort to find a profitable middle ground between the veneration of classical logic and the call for its abolition. Thanks to Hass's development of these options for feminist logic, alternative logic strikes me now as more plausible than it had.

However, I still don't know whether a genuine middle ground exists for new logics. Just how much can feminists do who want to get away from the traditional variety? Toying with logic is notoriously tricky. Make the changes too modest and they may be absorbed without a trace, leaving the essence of logic unchanged, in the way that denatured versions of revolutionary social proposals trickle into the political mainstream. Make the changes too bold and there comes a point at which you are no longer doing logic at all; for not everything that happens in the place of logic is alternative logic. These are familiar, even exhausted objections, but there is also a third to consider: If some new system constitutes a distinct alternative and continues to count as logic, it may also carry on performing the more unpleasant role of logic, namely its role of legislating in advance what is and what is not a legitimate statement, or a legitimate inference from such a statement.

Some of Professor Hass's suggestions face the first of these threats. They call for modifications in logical methodology and lexicon that will leave logic as usual unchanged. For example, I suspect that the problem over singular terms and Leibniz's Law of Indiscernibles may find an answer within the structure of classical logic, if we eliminate all individuals (that is, singular terms) from our logical vocabulary. This is not hard to do. Logic permits us to replace individuals with the unique holders of their properties. We drop the proper noun "London" and replace it with "the unique object that Londons." The phrase "the unique object" can be rendered logically with only quantifiers and predicates; thus we are left with no individuals presupposed by our logical lexicon and no problem with indiscernibles.

The opposite danger is more commonly invoked with alternative logics that arise outside a feminist context. Too radical and they cease to be logics at all. A system in which a sentence and its negation are both true is, according to this objection, not an alternative system, any more than thinking kind thoughts is an alternative way of writing a letter. (Kind thoughts may serve as a guilty alternative *to* writing, just as accepting blatant contradictions is an alternative to being logical.) The result is not an open, free-wheeling logical structure but no logical structure at all. Along these lines of criticism, some partisans of Fregean logic have ruled modal logic out of the running on the grounds that it simply adds two English words, "necessarily" and "possibly," to traditional logic, to form an unclassifiable mongrel.

The truth is that this dismissal of alternative logics is often deployed too quickly. It is rarely easy to judge in advance which reconstructions of logic are so radical as to cease being logic, and I can imagine a well-designed formal system that accepts both a sentence and its negation as true while still deserving the name of "logic." This does not ruin the objection to radical logics; it only means that proposed alternatives, such as versions of "many-valued" logic, have to be examined separately.

Consider, in this context, Professor Hass's most provocative proposal, that logic might take to exploring the nature of presupposition instead of the nature of entailment. By itself this idea already points to several ways in which classical logic might be opened up to new inquiries. Among other things, the focus on presuppositions may break the spell that indicative sentences have held over logic, because questions and commands also carry presuppositions. For instance, the question "Whose wallet is this?" presupposes

    a. that wallets have owners; hence
    b. that ownership is a real relationship.

(Compare "Whose rainforest is this?") Similarly, the command "Put on a hat" presupposes

> a. that the hearer is not wearing a hat;
> b. that the speaker is in a position to know that the hearer is not wearing a hat;
> c. that the speaker feels authorized to instruct the hearer to put on a hat;

and so on.

These presuppositions take some trouble to unearth. A logic of presupposition will have to include the word "whose" and "put on" in its lexicon, and some more complex description of imperatives and questions than our present logic does. To use Hass's example, we can say that "The woman walks quickly" presupposes that there is a correct speed for her to be walking *only if* "quickly" has a place in our logical framework that ties it to the concepts of "correct" and "speed," for only then will logic tell us of its implicit presuppositions. This is not a problem if we are willing to expand the rules and vocabulary of logic. Indeed, a number of such expansions, though their status as logic are still controversial, have already been carried out under the name of deontic logic, the logic of imperatives, and the logic of speech acts.

The problem is that two commands, at first sight structurally identical, may admit of different readings of presuppositions. Whereas "Put on a hat" presupposes that a hat is off, "Put on a show" presupposes not that the show is off, but that it does not yet exist. So "hat" and "show" need to be defined within the formal system along with "put on." Now we have a number of concepts requiring rigorous definition, where logic as it exists contains only a few sharply defined concepts ("exists," "all," "not," perhaps also "true," "possibly," and "necessarily").

Again, the size of the lexicon is itself not a telling objection against Hass's proposal. There is no self-evident reason to insist either that Frege identified the right primitive concepts of logic or that he correctly saw how long the list of such concepts should be. But recall Hass's definition of logic: it is "the formal study of truth-preserving thought, or inference." We have, by hypothesis, given up the quest for understanding inference, as that procedure is commonly understood, in a logic of presuppositions. This leaves only formality as the defining characteristic of logic. Is the system I am imagining still a formal system?

It may be. There are no a priori rules, as far as I'm concerned, about which elements of a natural language constitute its form and which ones its content. But for the concept of a formal system to make any sense at all, as I understand it, there must be some elements left undefined or undescribed within the system, elements that then will work as the raw material to plug into the logical structure of sentences. The symbolic sentence "Fa" in classical logic serves equally well to capture the predication in "This apple is a fruit" and "This ant is a formicid," just because "is a fruit" and "is a formicid" are taken to play equivalent logical roles in their sentences, and hence keep their roles when translated into symbolic language.

We thus come to the question that the examples about presuppositional logic force. Will the system being proposed contain some list (however long) of formal elements? It seems required to, to be a formal system; but if it contains some elements as formal, it will leave out others, in the way that classical logic treats "exists" as a formal element and leaves out "necessarily." I suspect that the act of separating out the formal elements, whatever they are or however many, will always be an act which in the long run legitimates certain modes of speaking and outlaws, or at least problematizes, others.

For let us not delude ourselves that logic is only a technique for thinking reflectively or critically. This pedagogical benefit of the subject, the reason it is typically taught in colleges, has been a spin-off of logic's main function, which is to provide a conceptual foundation for one of the sciences. Despite all the important differences between Aristotle and Frege, both expected the logic they developed and described to serve as the most general possible structure of a branch of the sciences. Aristotle took his analysis of subjects and predicates to demonstrate the privileged character of substance, and thereby to underwrite the structure of scientific explanations. Frege expected his symbolic system to lead to an axiomatic foundation for arithmetic. Because they wanted validation for their scientific enterprises, both of them thought their logics revealed something important about the structure of truth, of thought, and of the rational use of language. It is no wonder that, in the classical traditions of logic, modes of reasoning or means of expression that fell outside the strictures of logic were deemed irrational, incomplete, or essentially obscure; as long as logic represented the nature of all truth, any statement that deviated from its formal requirements would have to be found wanting in some way.

Consider one case from Frege. Fregean logic contains two quantifiers, the existential and the universal. (Actually, either quantifier may be translated into the other, so it is better to say that having one means having both.) Thus, a sentence like "All cats on the mat are wearing hats" falls neatly and simply into its constituent parts. But a sentence like "*The* cat on the mat is wearing a hat" turns into a problem. Russell had to invent the structure of definite descriptions to accommodate this English sentence, to all appearances as simple and clear as the last one, in Fregean syntax.

We may well ask whether the tail is wagging the dog: Does logicians' commitment to the grammar of classical logic turn a perfectly simple sentence into one of dubious meaning? This is only the most harmless example of how commitment to a logic can lead us to delegitimize certain forms of utterance.

But if all logics must be formal systems, as Hass seems to think, and if, to be formal, they must all treat certain elements of the natural language as essential to true reasoning and others as inessential, it seems to follow that every logic would come to legislate a proper way of proceeding. I suspect that for me, as for Nye, every logic (understood here as what logic has, most generally speaking been) is bad logic, because every logic lends itself to the exclusionary treatment of some forms of expression.

Is there a way to keep the unquestionable practical benefits of logic—its help in clarifying and testing arguments, and in developing computer programs—without falling under its exclusionary spell? The answer may be to demote logic to one language among many. Then logic ceases to capture the laws of thought and serves instead to make specific ways of thinking more conscious of themselves.

Rather than say that all logic is bad logic, I should say that the only good logic is a dead one; dead, I mean, in the sense that no one continues to hope that it will provide a foundation for scientific inquiry or even lay out the laws of thought. A dead logic, like a dead language, retains only some of its original functions: It serves inquiry rather than determining its course in advance by describing the patterns of certain forms of language use.

Reply to David Golumbia, "Feminism and Mental Representation"

I expect that the tone of my comments will make clear the deep sympathies I feel with Golumbia's treatment of his subject. The place of the mental in meaning continues to call for explication, and a feminist explication promises to bring new life to the old conversation.

The only questions here concern how the debate within analytic philosophy can find common ground with overtly political attacks on individualism. To identify that common ground, we first have to agree about what an attack on analytic theories of meaning really amounts to and how much it can accomplish. What is Hilary Putnam arguing for in "The Meaning of Meaning"? Where can his argument lead? In the first place, Putnam does not claim that "water" does not really mean "H_2O," for in fact it does mean that, and he asserts it to. Putnam will even say it *necessarily* means "H_2O"; hence, he is committed to preserving the reality of meaning(s). His point is specifically that meaning something by a word is not an act that one performs, whether consciously or unconsciously, whether in the physical brain or in the supernaturalized mind. Meanings may not be in the head, but Putnam does take them to be somewhere and does take the job of philosophy to be the hunt for them.

So, although it is true that Putnam's position works effectively against an individualistic theory of meaning—and all credit to him for that—I doubt whether it points the way to a legitimately *social* theory of meaning (or of mind). Although he closes "The Meaning of Meaning" with a call for more attention both to other people and the environment, I believe that in that paper his deeper agenda concerns the latter, the so-called world, which—once we learn to read it rightly—will point us toward theoretical and general principles of meaning. (This suspicion is to some extent borne out by Putnam's subsequent alliance with Saul Kripke in trying to spell out a causal theory of reference.) Putnam wants a foundation for meaning, and especially for that special traditional interest of philosophers, *necessity*. Only instead of looking for it in the head, he is looking in the physical universe, which is to say, of course, the universe of physics.

The problem, if I am right, will be that Putnam is still implicated in what Golumbia calls "attempts to tell just what are the 'ultimate' constituents of the universe." Although he is a much more self-conscious and self-critical philosopher than Jerry Fodor, Putnam continues to try, in his own way, to combat relativism. Doesn't his project implicate him in the problem that Golumbia is combating? Golumbia says, "Western culture continually seeks to establish a canon of cross-cultural and atemporal human truths, truths which do and will obtain regardless of our social and political contexts." But a theory of meaning that locates linguistic necessity in the nature of the physical world, regardless of which (kinds of) people occupy that world, and when, ought to come under Golumbia's attack in the same way. Because this Aristotelian conception of meaning, indebted most anciently to *De Anima*'s theory of perception, calls for critique at least as incisive as does any individualistic myth.

I have a second reason for suspecting that Putnam's line of thinking will not overcome the insidious assumptions that lie behind some analytic theories of meaning. "The Meaning of Meaning" takes a polemical stance, but not against analytic philosophy considered as a whole. For while Putnam *is* arguing against a current within analytic philosophy, he is not (in that paper) arguing against the tradition, which contains several prominent predecessors who likewise wanted to keep mental representation out of the theory of meaning. In the name of a newly "scientific" philosophy, Frege labored to keep his analyses of logic, mathematics, and meaning from being infected with what he called "psychologism," as represented for him, for instance, by Husserl. Partly in response to Frege, Wittgenstein, early and late, attacked the mental, where that is construed as a secret realm of consciousness, and questioned its efficacy and explanatory power in descriptions of meaning. And Quine, who still serves as the exemplar of analytic philosophy's neopositivist tradition, only admits referential meaning into his ontology where it steers clear of mentalism. This is not to say that Putnam faces no real opponents; not even that his opponents are isolated voices within analytic philosophy. But certainly there is no unified voice in the tradition according to which meanings are the work of reified minds, gendered or not.

In later works Putnam distances himself more sharply from certain projects of analytic philosophy, including those projects of his own represented by "The Meaning of Meaning" (see, for example, *Representation and Reality* [MIT Press, 1988]; *Realism with a Human Face* [Harvard University Press, 1990]; and *Renewing Philosophy* [Harvard University Press, 1992]). But even here, his clear opposition to other analytic philosophers does not bring him to embrace a fully social theory of meaning and mind. If such a social theory is implicit in his earlier critique of certain meaning-theories, Putnam does not draw the implication himself.

Putnam and his philosophical allegiances aside, I wonder whether such a social theory will necessarily prove more congenial to feminism than an individualistic theory does. After all, the conception of linguistic meaning as social might be taken to legitimate a white male paradigm of meanings: X means Y because the (white, male) power structure has taken it to mean Y. Certainly more than one neoconservative defender of "culture" has argued against pluralistic inquiries into meaning and mind on the grounds that our culture, as it has been (dominated), ought to preserve its past unity. "The social" can be as opaque, hence as susceptible to strategic manipulations, as "the mental."

But I have no arguments to back up that suspicion, and anyway the subject lies outside our present discussion. My concern has been to suggest that looking for a sympathetic figure within this analytical debate may be harder work than it first appears. An attack against one myth that establishes the usual power structures of knowledge may lead to another myth that establishes the same structures.

Note

I am indebted to Juliet Floyd for her corrections to an earlier version of these comments.

PART 5

FEMINISM BEYOND METAPHYSICS?

17

Leaping Ahead: Feminist Theory without Metaphysics

Leslie A. MacAvoy

s feminist theory philosophy? Ought feminists to engage in philosophical discourse? These questions reflect a concern that philosophy is inherently dominating. One might consequently argue that philosophical discourse is not only inappropriate for feminists to adopt but that it is also insufficient for articulating the oppression which women experience. The contemporary debate surrounding the inability of "mainstream" feminism to represent the voices and viewpoints of all women reflects the concern that this discourse may be inadequate to the needs of feminism.

Although I am sympathetic to this worry, I do not think that philosophy is inherently problematic for feminism. Rather, traditional philosophical discourse has been dominated by a particular style of metaphysics which thematizes human subjectivity and the relations to the other which are bound up with it in a way which is problematic from an ethical perspective. For the sake of simplicity, I will refer to this style of philosophizing simply as "metaphysics," and in elaborating this thought, I will make use of some of Heidegger's insights from *Being and Time* (*SZ*).[1] In particular, I will argue that the domination which plagues feminist theory bears close resemblance to the solicitous mode of *leaping in* (*einspringen*). By contrast, *leaping ahead* (*vorausspringen*) involves more authentic relations with the other. But these modes of solicitude are in turn related to the self-understanding that accompanies them. That is, the authenticity of one's relations to the other is implicated with one's own authenticity, and this pertains to how one's being has been phenomenologically disclosed. If we are to develop a philosophical discourse which is not dominating, it must take its point of departure from an epistemological model which avoids this as well. If we are to *leap ahead* instead of *leaping in,* our theory must do so too.

Feminists have good reason to be wary of metaphysics. Much has been written about how such concepts have traditionally displayed phallocentric biases which serve both to deny women voice and to relegate them to positions of subservience and inferiority. However, the problem with metaphysics runs deeper and involves the stance which metaphysicians assume with respect to the entities they discuss. Though no doubt well-intentioned, they tend to formulate essentialist claims, sometimes conferring universal status upon experiences which are far more context dependent. These dubious generalizations can be used to make often invalid inferences about the experiences of others.

Through engaging in this kind of philosophical practice, theorizers fail to respect difference and deprive others of voice. This problem has serious repercussions, particularly as metaphysical assumptions influence other areas of philosophy. Consequently, it often happens that others are deprived of voice, not only in the field delimited by the term "metaphysics," but also in epistemology, social and political theory, and ethics. Any practical measures which take these as their foundations will similarly be affected.

Many have noted that this problem manifests itself in feminist theory and practice. In particular, mainstream feminism has been accused of making claims about "women's" experiences and "women's" lives which in fact reflect the rather narrow experiences of the white, straight, middle-class women who do the theorizing. Among the practical implications is a possible misalignment among the political priorities of feminist groups, the activities they organize, and the needs of many women who experience oppression.

To the credit of feminist theorists, they are aware of this problem and are concerned to address it. But does avoiding metaphysics require avoiding philosophy altogether? I don't think so. If philosophy and metaphysics were coextensive, then it would seem that we would have to abandon both. However, I see little reason to suppose that they are coextensive. The term "philosophy" denotes a practice of thinking in which we try to understand ourselves, the world and the entities therein, and our relationship to the world and those entities. Presumably there are a number of ways of so understanding ourselves, and metaphysics is simply one of them. As such, there should be other ways of philosophizing which are not metaphysical, and so there should be ways of doing philosophy which are not problematic for feminist theory.

However, I don't want to make light of the question. It is important to understand the nature of this domination if we are to devise means to avoid it. I claim that metaphysics is dominating because it rests upon an inauthentic understanding of the human being, an understanding which itself disregards the importance of difference and of respecting difference. To demonstrate this point, I will explore the understanding of human being upon which metaphysics rests, how it tends toward domination, and how this is characteristic of inauthenticity. Having done this, I will begin to articulate what a more authentic understanding might be and the implications it might have for the way in which we construe relations with others. It is the last part of this discussion that I believe may be of particular use to feminism.

Metaphysics is a discourse, and any discourse may be characterized as an articulation of thought or understanding. When a discourse focuses on human nature, this implies that what is articulated is a particular self-understanding. As a discourse, metaphysics is distinguished by the particular self-understanding which grounds it, and this includes the understanding which we have of other entities encountered in the world and the relations which we bear to them.

There are two related assumptions upon which metaphysical discourse and the self-understanding which accompanies it are based.[2] First, the being of the subject lies in its ability to represent. Second, the being of an object lies in its being represented by a subject. These assumptions suggest that an object cannot properly be said to "be" until it has been made the object for some subject. Furthermore, the being of the object is reduced to the way it appears to the subject. This puts the subject in a position of relative power with respect to the object. First, she can define the being of the object in accordance with the way it appears to her. Second, anything which doesn't appear to her isn't acknowledged as having being. Either way, when a person is objectified in this way, she isn't given the opportunity to disclose her own being and to express herself, and it is to these situations that I refer when I speak of domination.

Within metaphysical discourse this scenario isn't generally construed as a problem because it is assumed that subjectivity is universal in the sense that we are all capable in principle of abstracting from our particular contexts and assuming the perspective of the subject to whom objects appear. Consequently, *who* assumes the universal stance is not an issue. The concern is rather with the view which it affords, and it is assumed that from this viewpoint everyone can and will see the same thing, namely, the essence of the object under consideration. However, if situatedness and context are irrelevant to epistemological considerations, it is redundant for everyone to engage in theoretical analysis. A few theorizers can assume a universal stance and consequently be appropriately positioned to speak objectively and for all.

This scenario is related to problems in feminist theory and practice.[3] In this case, the subject is the theorizer. If the problems of a particular group of women are not "seen" by the theorizer, she may assume that they do not exist or that she is justified in universalizing her own experiences. Alternatively, if she does "see" certain problems, she may assume that they are the way she perceives them to be, even though she may not be familiar with the context within which they arise. As such, her subsequent analyses may be of limited use in eliminating real oppression. We may fault the assumption of universal subjectivity, which implies that where one is situated with respect to a problem is of no relevance in analyzing it. This assumption has legitimated patronizing attitudes on the part of theorizers toward those about whom they theorize, attitudes which in the case of feminism have deprived other women of voice.

The subject's privilege to define the being of the object can be construed as dominating, and it is the understanding of human being as metaphysical subject which permits the perpetuation of this privilege. We are faced with two related difficulties here. The assumption that there is something like a universal stance and that it is possible for theorizers to abstract away from their own situatedness in order to take it up is questionable. The first problem, then, is that the particular viewpoint of the theorist is generalized and granted universal validity. The second part of the problem derives from the first. Because it is assumed that anything which might bias the objectivity of the theorist is left behind in the assumption of the universal stance, it is assumed that what appears from that position is also universally valid. This opens up the possibility for the formulation of problematic essentialist claims. A kind of homogeneity can be impressed upon the object under consideration which leads to the suppression of difference with regard to the object. As such the situatedness and context of both the subject and object poles of the epistemological relation are disregarded.

The traditional epistemological model assumes that something is what it is independent of context. It also assumes that the best way to get at true knowledge of objects is by bracketing those factors (such as context, but also emotions, particularities, and so on) which might compromise the objectivity of the subject. The subject, then, is understood to stand complete within itself, over and against the world to which it subsequently relates. And subjectivity, then, would be the reaching out of the subject toward the object across the void which separates them.

What is completely overlooked is the idea that subject and object are situated relative to one another within a context upon which they each have a particular perspective. It is from out of our situatedness, our already being related to other entities in the world in a meaningful way, that our understanding of them issues. Traditional metaphysics fails to appreciate that human subjectivity is a Being-in-the-world. If it is a condition of authenticity to disclose one's being to oneself, then at the very least authenticity requires a disclosure of that Being-in-the-world. If metaphysics overlooks this or is inadequate to this task, then the understanding of oneself which is generated through it represents an inauthentic disclosure of human being. It misconstrues human subjectivity and reduces the relations to others implicated in that subjectivity to the subject-object relation just described, and this leads to inauthentic relations to the other.

Understanding one's Being-in-the-world involves understanding world and the relatedness among entities which exists due to the phenomenon of world. This implies understanding one's Being-with-Others. In articulating this, I will make use of the distinction Heidegger draws between the two positive modes of solicitude, *leaping in* and *leaping ahead*.[4]

According to Heidegger, when one encounters another, there is always the sense that the other is "there too."[5] This implies that we have a sense that the other shares a world with us, and this impression or understanding is taken to be originary, challenging the notion that our pretheoretical understanding of ourselves is constituted by disembodiment or alienation from world and others. This is not to say, however, that we are always physically located with others in close proximity. *Mitsein* and Being-there-too pertain to being in the same world, and this means being implicated with one another in terms of significance and meaning. Consequently, one can be with those who are physically absent as well as be alone in the midst of a crowd.

There are various modes of solicitude, and Heidegger names a few. Among these are Being-alone, Being-missing, and Being-away, "Being for, against, or without one another, passing one another by, not 'mattering' to one another."[6] These modes can be most aptly characterized as negative modes in that they primarily suggest an absence of involvement, but Heidegger also calls them deficient and indifferent and claims that they are typical of average everydayness. These characterizations imply that these modes are also inauthentic.[7]

Heidegger's discussion of the two positive modes is more interesting for our purposes. The first, *leaping in,* is clearly characterized as less authentic than the other, *leaping ahead.* In *leaping in,* one

> takes over for the Other that with which he is to concern himself. The other is thus thrown out of his own position; he steps back so that

afterwards, when the matter has been attended to, he can either take it over as something finished and at his disposal, or disburden himself of it completely. In such solicitude the other can become one who is dominated and dependent, even if this domination is a tacit one and remains hidden from him.[8]

Heidegger goes on to say that what in effect happens in *leaping in* is that the other is denied her being as care. That is, I do not disclose the other as an entity for whom its being is an issue nor as an entity possessed of possibility. This is to treat the other more as a thing than as a fellow. If I disclose the other primarily as a "thing" devoid of possibility and behave toward her accordingly, this will have repercussions for her own self-understanding. It will likely become more difficult for her to authentically disclose her own being to herself.

There are some strong similarities between *leaping in* and the domination which occurs through feminist and other theories that are grounded in metaphysics. A theorist who assumes that she has an epistemological privilege which justifies her claim to speak for all women devalues concrete input which other women could offer to assist in overcoming their oppression. Patronizing attitudes can discourage the other from disclosing her being as such and can limit her ability to do so. Failing to see that they are possessed of possibilities which can lead to empowerment, such women can develop a fatalistic attitude through which they internalize their oppression. Although some women may respond to this challenge by redoubling their efforts to be heard, surely many are discouraged from speaking at all and remain disillusioned with feminism, convinced that it really isn't concerned with their problems.

Leaping in dominates the other outright, but it also has a second, more subtle, effect. Recall that sometimes the other can be dominated without even knowing it. This can occur when those who *leap in* sanction particular modes of expression as acceptable for theorizing or provide the conceptual tools "necessary" for conducting a proper analysis. These restrictions will have an effect upon the way in which theory is constructed and can end up diffusing another's voice. Feminists have noted the problems associated with using traditional philosophical concepts and methodology in analyzing women's experiences. These problems recur when mainstream feminist theorists establish similar criteria within their own discipline. Some feminists become marginalized and find it difficult to meaningfully express themselves within the accepted mode of discourse. They run the risk either of being unable to articulate themselves or of having their work dismissed as irrelevant and insignificant if they experiment with alternative approaches.

The domination which characterizes *leaping in,* subtle though it may be, resembles the kind of sway that the subject exercises over the object in traditional metaphysics. The other is objectified and rendered passive before the subject who defines the situation, and determines its meaning and the position of the other within it. The possibilities which are available to the other are not ones which she has herself disclosed, but those which have been disclosed and chosen for her through the projection of the other. Failure to disclose the other as an entity for whom possibility is constitutive contributes to domination and hinders the ability of the other to disclose her being to herself.

Moreover, the individual who dominates, who *leaps in,* is responsible, at least in part, for the other's not disclosing her being. That I inauthentically comport myself toward the other is a reflection of the fact that I have not disclosed her as an entity who is like me, namely an entity whose being it is to be engaged in that being.[9] As such, I fail to respect her being, I misunderstand what it means to "be-with" others, and insofar as this *Mitsein* is also constitutive of my being, I misunderstand myself and compromise my own authenticity.

Authentic *Mitsein* implies a genuine intersubjectivity in which the other is not disclosed as a voiceless thing. Instead, my understanding of myself as Being-in-the-world allows me to remain open to the other, and this facilitates a more mutual engagement on the part of both participants. In domination, on the other hand, one entity is compelled, intentionally or not, to assume a passive stance with respect to the other. This relation, which is not one of mutual participation, can be contrasted with *leaping ahead,* the mode of solicitude which is most authentic.

Heidegger says even less about *leaping ahead* than he does about *leaping in.* But in this mode of solicitude, one

> leap[s] ahead of [the other] in his existentiell potentiality-for-Being, not in order to take away his "care" but rather to give it back to him authentically as such for the first time. This kind of solicitude pertains essentially to authentic care—that is, to the existence of the Other, not to a "*what*" with which he is concerned; it helps the Other to become transparent to himself *in* his care and to become *free for* it.[10]

In this case, one comports oneself toward the other in such a way that the other is not denied her being as care. Here, one does not antecedently decide what is most important for the other, independent of her considered input, and then proceed to provide her with those objects or products. On the contrary, the point is that in *leaping ahead,* one discloses the other as an entity who is concerned and engaged with its being and who has possibilities. That is, the other has an openness to possibilities just as I do, and those possibilities must manifest themselves to her as such if she is to be able to authentically choose her path. Though we all have possibility as part of our being, the horizons of significance in terms of which concrete and specific possibilities manifest themselves are not identical across all individuals. I cannot choose for the other, nor can I assume that the possibilities which disclose themselves to me in a given situation are the same ones that disclose themselves to the other.

Concretely, *leaping ahead* could take many forms. At the very least, I think it would have to involve a serious commitment to grassroots political movement and a commitment to being open to all points of view. It may involve fostering an atmosphere in which women are encouraged to ask questions without fear of appearing ignorant or of being ignored. It may involve learning to be good listeners, learning when to be quiet and when to be vocal, and it may involve not being so quick to look for similarities between one's own views and experiences and that of an other, thereby overlooking important differences.

Central, then, to the idea of authentic solicitude is the importance of letting the other be. However, this should not be confused with a doctrine of straightforward noninterference in which I am obviated of all responsibility with respect to the other, in which I am permitted to ignore my relatedness to the other and to simply leave her alone. First, to do so sounds dangerously similar to the deficient and indifferent modes of Being-alone or passing one another by. Second, to do so would be to ignore my own *Mitsein* and Being-in-the-world, and would represent an inauthentic understanding of my own being. And finally, authentic solicitude specifically entails my involvement. After all, I am the one who must *leap ahead;* I am the one who must encourage the other to explore her being so that she may discover herself. In *leaping ahead* one comports toward the other so as to elicit responses from the other through which she may disclose her being as possibility to herself. *Leaping ahead* is a type of engagement which draws the other out, challenging her to express herself and awaiting her answer.

In many ways, this kind of comportment resembles that of a mentor, pedagogue or parent, and some might argue that this is paternalistic. However, I would maintain that being supportive and nurturing differs from being paternalistic, and this difference is precisely the one which exists between *leaping in* and *leaping ahead*. In *leaping in,* I make determinations as to what is in the other's interest which would be better left for her own consideration because I fail to respect her as an entity whose being is one of possibility. This is paternalistic. However, in *leaping ahead,* I encourage the other to explore her possibilities and to pursue those which she surmises will allow her to develop and express herself. And this feature is an important element of friendship.

As far as feminist theory and practice is concerned, then, approaching the other in authentic solicitude is to respect difference. It is to respect that the other has a distinct viewpoint and distinct experiences which she herself can analyze and articulate if given the opportunity and the tools. It is to recognize that the possibilities for overcoming oppression must be possibilities which the specific women involved can disclose for themselves from within their situations. It is also to recognize that we all have a role to play in assisting one another to achieve this level of self-awareness so that we become more attuned to our situatedness and the differences which this implies.

A discourse which is based upon a self-understanding which recognizes *Mitsein* and Being-in-the-world is one which will be more sensitive to metaphysical domination of the other and will be better able to recognize the inauthenticity of this relation. This, of course, does not guarantee that domination will not occur,[11] but it does provide the conceptual tools necessary to identify and analyze it. Metaphysics, as a discourse based upon a problematic conceptualization of human subjectivity, may be ill-fated from the start. It is ill-equipped to recognize, and even reinforces, the domination which our experience tells us exists, both that which I experience at the hands of phallocentric metaphysics and that which other women experience at the hands of feminist metaphysics.

One might argue that if the objections that have been made against metaphysics have their root in a particular understanding of human nature, then we need only change this understanding to correct the problem. We could construct a metaphysics of interrelatedness which rests upon a conception of human nature which takes this element into consideration. Wouldn't this solution be sufficient to accomplish the goals that I'm arguing for here?

It isn't clear to me that a metaphysics of interrelatedness would be any less oppressive than a metaphysics of presence. The key to understanding this issue lies in the essentializing tendency of metaphysics. Determinations about the essence of something depend upon our observations of that thing. But the way in which we perceive and interpret our observations is influenced by our prior beliefs and commitments which vary with culture, training, and so on. So a particular apprehension of the "essence" of something is going to be context bound and temporal, but when we engage in "essentializing" we attribute universality and atemporality to these appearances.

For example, suppose that I were to say that the essence of human nature lies in rationality. If I were asked how I arrived at this claim, I might say that I have only ever observed rational behavior in humans and never in other animals. This assumes that I must have antecedently had a conception of what counts as rational behavior in order to be able to identify human behavior as rational. My understanding of rational behavior is probably a product of my culture and my times, yet if I choose to treat that understanding as a universal essence, as the essence of rational behavior, then I treat it as if it were an absolute standard of rationality.

Metaphysics tends to privilege a particular disclosure within the world as the "right" or "true," and this implies an insensitivity to the phenomenon of world, suggesting an understanding of human subjectivity which again fails to grasp human Being-in-the-world. Metaphysics fails to appropriately grasp the object which it seeks to analyze, in this case human being, but this is only part of the difficulty. The larger point is that the notion of a metaphysical subject and the subject-object relation with which it is implicated are problematic. To maintain that human beings are essentially related to other entities in the world without appreciating the difficulties this poses for the traditional epistemological model is to overlook the complexity of the problem with which we are dealing.

In my view, the main difficulty is that our standard metaphysical and epistemological models are very egocentric, placing the subject at the center and the object or other at the periphery in a position of subservience and passivity. This is implicated in the domination which I have described. But this view of human subjectivity assumes that the ego is first and foremost separate from the world, that it does not first exist in a matrix of relations to the other which define and constitute it as who or what it is. It is from out of this entanglement of involvements that "subjects" approach "objects" or that objects draw near to subjects in a meaningful fashion. Human subjectivity, I would argue, doesn't much resemble the subjectivity of the metaphysical subject. Instead, it is far more embedded, far less rational and dispassionate, far more receptive and responsive to the world and others than is typically described.

A more phenomenological understanding of subjectivity preserves this sense of openness to entities in the world and affirms our essential relatedness to the other. One of the more striking features of such a subjectivity, in contrast to more traditional models, is the ambiguity between activity and passivity which characterizes it. The subject doesn't simply project significance onto a passive object; rather, the object appears to the subject in a meaningful way. The object gives meaning to the subject, and this, I think, decenters the subject somewhat and emphasizes the extent to which subjectivity involves an openness to the other.

When we consider the implications of this other subjectivity for the ethical aspect of our relations to the other, the shift is considerable. Where the metaphysical subject determines and defines the being and meaning of the other, the phenomenological subject is open to the meaning which the other gives. This openness to the other translates into an openness to the difference of the other, a difference which reflects, among other things, a difference in our relative situations.

In the context of Heidegger's work, the authentic solicitude of *leaping ahead* is the mode in which I am open to the other in a way which allows the other to disclose herself to me and to herself as a Being-possible, and this goes hand in hand with an authentic disclosure of one's being. When I disclose my own being as one of openness—to the world, to others, to possibility—I become more open to letting others disclose themselves. The air is cleared for a greater sharing and exchange.

Feminist theory has a dual role to play in fostering this disclosure. First, as a discourse, feminism can articulate an understanding of ourselves as Being-in-the-world and all that this implies. Second, in so doing, feminism can facilitate further understanding by creating space for others to disclose their being to themselves.

It is important that feminism continue to engage in philosophical activity, because critical reflection on how we understand ourselves and our relation to the world and others is crucial for any kind of social change. Yet it is also important that feminism appreciate the extent to which certain theoretical frameworks may implicitly reinscribe a very subtle domination.

Notes

1. Martin Heidegger, *Sein und Zeit* (Tübingen, Germany: Niemeyer, 1960); *Being and Time,* John Macquarrie and Edward Robinson, trans. (San Francisco: Harper & Row, 1962). I will reference this text using the abbreviation *SZ*. All page numbers will refer to the German edition.

2. Considerations of space prevent a more detailed explanation of this. However, what follows is the kernel of what appears in postmodern critiques of a "metaphysics of presence." Although I am more influenced by Heidegger's thoughts on the subject, the spirit of what I am arguing is consistent with the concerns raised by postmodernism. See also Martin Heidegger, *Nietzsche,* David Farrell Krell, trans. and ed. (San Francisco: Harper & Row, 1982).

3. See especially Linda J. Nicholson, ed. *Feminism and Postmodernism* (New York: Routledge, 1990).

4. Despite the fact that many hold that *SZ* has not made a sufficient break with metaphysical discourse, I would argue that one should attend to Heidegger's critique of the present-at-hand and traditional, particularly Cartesian and Kantian, theories of subjectivity.

5. Heidegger, *SZ,* 118.

6. Ibid., 121.

7. Ibid., 120–21.

8. Ibid., 122.

9. What I am in effect saying here is that if I disclose the other as like me, I will disclose her in a way which respects her being, that is, respects her *difference.* How is this possible? Isn't it rather the case that disclosing the other as "like me" is the root of the whole problem? Doesn't it encourage me to assume that whatever holds true for me is also true for the other? These are points which it is important to clarify. To authentically disclose the other as "like me" is to disclose the other as having the same ontological status as oneself. This means recognizing that she too has a being of possibility, which itself implies recognizing that she has a relationship to her being which only she can have. This, I think, is to respect that she is unique, that one cannot "stand in" for her, as it were. This is to respect difference. Metaphysics, insofar as it overlooks Being-in-the-world and the care which is implicated with this, may support and promote a very different sort of comportment in the face of a disclosure of ontological similarity.

10. Heidegger, *SZ,* 122.

11. If one agrees that we are always vulnerable to falling, it is inevitable that absolute authenticity will remain elusive. Arguably this is simply part of being human. However, it is still valuable to keep these pitfalls in mind, so that we can at least be sensitive to them and guard against inadvertent domination.

Bibliography

Barnes, Hazel E. *An Existentialist Ethics.* Chicago: University of Chicago Press, 1978.

Benhabib, Seyla. *Situating the Self: Gender, Community and Postmodernism in Contemporary Ethics.* New York: Routledge, 1992.

Bethold-Bond, Daniel. "A Kierkegaardian Critique of Heidegger's Concept of Authenticity." *Man and World* 24 (1991): 119–42.

Borgmann, Albert. "Cosmopolitanism and Provincialism: On Heidegger's Errors and Insights." *Philosophy Today* 36, no. 2 (1992): 131–45.

Caputo, John. "Disseminating Originary Ethics and the Ethics of Dissemination." In *The Question of the Other: Essays in Contemporary Continental Philosophy.* Arleen B. Dallery and Charles E. Scott, eds. Albany, N.Y.: SUNY Press, 1989.

Card, Claudia, ed. *Feminist Ethics.* Kansas City: University of Kansas Press, 1991.

Cole, Eva Browning, and Susan Coultrap-McQuin, eds. *Explorations in Feminist Ethics: Theory and Practice.* Bloomington: Indiana University Press, 1992.

Dallmayr, Fred R. *Twilight of Subjectivity: Contributions to a Post-Individualist Theory of Politics.* Amherst: University of Massachusetts Press, 1981.

Frings, Manfred. "The Background of Max Scheler's 1927 Reading of *Being and Time:* A Critique of a Critique Through Ethics." *Philosophy Today* 36, no. 2 (1992): 99–113.

Heidegger, Martin. *Sein und Zeit.* 9th ed. Tübingen, Germany: Niemeyer, 1960; *Being and Time.* John Macquarrie and Edward Robinson, trans. San Francisco: Harper & Row, 1962.

———. *Nietzsche.* David Farrell Krell, trans. and ed. San Francisco: Harper & Row, 1982.

Hekman, Susan. "Reconstituting the Subject: Feminism, Modernism, and Post-Modernism." *Hypatia* 6, no. 1 (1991): 44–63.

Miles, Murray. "Heidegger and the Question of Humanism." *Man and World* 22 (1989): 427–51.

Nicholson, Linda J., ed. *Feminism and Postmodernism.* New York: Routledge, 1990.

Nuyen, A. T. "A Heideggerian Existentialist Ethics for the Human Environment." *Journal of Value Inquiry* 25 (1991): 359–66.

Pheby, Keith C. *Interventions: Displacing the Metaphysical Subject.* Washington, D.C.: Maisonneuve Press, 1988.

Phelan, Shane. "The Jargon of Authenticity: Adorno and Feminist Essentialism." *Philosophy and Social Criticism* 16, no. 1 (1990): 39–54.

Plumwood, Val. "Nature, Self, and Gender: Feminism, Environmental Philosophy and the Critique of Rationalism." *Hypatia* 6, no. 1 (1991): 3–27.

Spelman, Elizabeth. *Inessential Woman: Problems of Exclusion in Feminist Thought.* Boston, Mass.: Beacon Press, 1988.

Walker, Margaret Urban. "Feminism, Ethics, and the Question of Theory." *Hypatia* 7, no. 3 (1992): 23–38.

18

Philosophy Abandons Woman: Gender, Orality, and Some Literate Pre-Socratics

Cornelia A. Tsakiridou

I t is not easy to speak in gender in English because in English things are not always spoken in their gender. There are no feminine, masculine, or neuter nouns as there are, for instance, in my native language, Greek. In Greek, being feminine, masculine, or neuter is part of what something is. Of course, one is not aware of this modality as one speaks or writes, except in a grammatical sense. But it is there, in the words, as a substratum and an orientation that become more visible when the language is used poetically—to say, for instance, that *he philosophia einai gynaika* (philosophy is a woman) or that she is *physis poetike* (a being of poetic or creative nature). There is also the poetry of proper names, which always makes me think of my late great-aunt Theologia (Theology), a farmer in a Greek village, whose name never struck me as odd or inappropriate for who she was.

Now, if we examine the meanings of feminine nouns like *Ge* (*Gaia*), *glossa* (tongue or embodied speech, as distinguished from the abstract, masculine *logos*), *physis, polis, psyche, philosophia, poesis, thalassa* (sea, a more contained body of water than masculine *okeanos* or ocean), we will notice relationships of inclusion, internalization, growth, animation, creation—patterns that have natural equivalents or analogs in female physiology, sexuality, and in behaviors that derive from them. To give an example: feminine nouns *kyesis, physis, poiesis* are terms of generation and formation suggesting respectively the state and process of gestation, birth (or generation including the born being or creature itself), and composition (both natural and artificial). *Psyche* (soul) is a related term of animation, suggesting life itself and its observable signs, such as breath or movement.

A remarkable fourth-century example of analogy between maternity and letter writing is noted by Jesper Svenbro in his original study of reading and writing in ancient Greece. It is a riddle from a comedy by Antiphanes entitled *Sappho* that begins with this line: "There is a feminine being (*esti physis theleia*) who, within the folds of her dress, keeps her babies who, although without voices, emit a cry that resounds across the waves of the sea. . . ." It is given the following explanation: "The feminine being is a letter (*theleia men nyn esti physis epistole*); the babies that she carries with her everywhere are the letters [of the alphabet] (*grammata*)."[1] Antiphanes's comic intentions aside, the fragment is remarkable for the correspondence between grammatical pattern and content: *Physis* and *epistole* are feminine; *vrefi* (babies) and *grammata* (alphabetical letters) are neuter. The analogy works grammatically, visually, and performatively. The letter gathers and keeps its words together the way a mother gathers and keeps her children close to her body. When the letter is being read, living creatures (the spoken words) emerge from the sheet like children emerge from their mother's body and dress.

A similar relationship between speech and world informs the archaic figure known as ring composition. It involves the repetition at the beginning and end of a passage of a phrase or word which then works as a frame or enclosure for the unit. In many instances, ring composition has the effect of mimicking anticipation and closure in human events, especially where the poet, as in Homer, portrays vivid characters and their actions. But it also works with the description of inanimate objects, as for example in Hesiod's account of the shield of Heracles[2] where, as William G. Thalmann has observed, the verbal description, by its form, embodies the composition of the picture that we are to imagine.[3] Hesiod's verse:

> And on the shield was a harbour with a safe haven from the
> irresistible sea, made of refined tin wrought in a circle,
> and it seemed to heave with waves.
> . . . .
> And round the rim Ocean was flowing,
> with a full stream as it seemed,
> and enclosed all the cunning work of the shield.
>
> (207–9, 313–14)

These examples suggest an iconographic, iconological[4] language that is semantically and syntactically oriented toward sexual difference.

The ontological possibilities that it creates for its speakers with graphic transparency outline a world that is manlike, womanlike, and childlike (with the implication of sexual immaturity or promise). To the extent that, to borrow a metaphor from Jacques Derrida, language is a place where one lives but where also one is inhabited; to speak Greek is to speak and be spoken in sexual difference and based on that, to conjugate, to strive to couple and pair world and word, speaker and spoken, the inside and outside, same and other.[5] Thus, Greek is—*is* because it has been spoken and poeticized continually for the last three thousand years— a language predicated on difference and unity, but one which resists extinction and ossification by failing to either differentiate totally or unify totally; to bring, in other words, a logic of closure or sexual indifference upon itself.

To say, therefore, that Greek is gendered is not to speak of a linguistic accident (that is, something of which the language can be rid or cleared). Rather, gender is at the root of that unique geography that Greek occupies and engenders in human space: the geography of philosophy itself—of the orientation, the movement that becomes philosophy.

The idea of gender as an ontological structure within at least some of our natural languages raises an issue that concerns the very ground of the philosophical enterprise and the role of the feminine in it. To be more specific, given not only the absence but the distortion of woman in philosophical thought over the past 2,500 years, it is reasonable to ask why philosophy proceeded in this way. What, in other words, compelled it in that direction? Now, the Greek of Homer, Hesiod, and the pre-Socratics is philosophy's native language. If, as we have suggested, this language gave the feminine a significant portion of the cosmos and its reflection, what happened that upset that condition? How and why did feminine declinations of world and speech become less relevant and authoritative against the very logic (and ontology) of the language that hosted them? What forced the eclipse of the woman-world? If man, somehow, came to dominate language or to instrumentalize it to his needs, desires, and self-reflection, by what mechanism did he do it? And what gave him power over language to begin with?

This last question is tempting to answer in violative terms, thinking of language as a body or *topos* that one can invade and occupy. But language, as we have seen, inhabits; it geographs and for that matter logographs its speakers—language inscribes and engenders its own and their own modalities, even those that seem to gravitate toward an independent, external authority (such as that of an ego).

From this perspective, the recession of the feminine must be sought within the very logic of the Greek language, as an event not derivative but constitutive of its identity. This event, I suggest, coincides with the emergence of a new modality of articulation: the modality of inscription or writing. As we shall see later, the parameters at work in Greek literacy were to affect not just the execution of speech, that is, its transcription and metaphorical death, but the very act of speaking itself, the physiological voice and the body that constituted it.[6] If literacy meant a new sense of presence (and present), a new way of declining time and space—for example, as Derrida has suggested, the unconsciousness and aphasia of the (writing and written) subject—it also meant a new way of centering sexual difference, a redeclination of man and woman. This development, as we shall see, underwrites pre-Socratic and Platonic metaphysics.

I

The idea that the suppression of the feminine was a Greek phenomenon and a philosophical one has already been suggested in feminist literature. Luce Irigaray has maintained that the language of feminine desire was submerged by the (masculine) logic that has dominated the West since the time of the Greeks.[7] This logic is supposed to reflect and favor male anatomy (that is, phallomorphism) and as a result to impart value on concepts with a presumably phallomorphic logic such as individuality, exhibition (extroversion), and definition.

On the other side, female anatomy is predictably suppressed and devalued and its logic is restricted to a set of opposite and inferior (lesser) concepts, such as introversion, plurality, and indefiniteness. Irigaray is unclear about whether this happens naturally within certain languages, in this case Greek, or it is the result of the particular use of a language by an ideology. Her willingness to treat language in an abstract, speculative sense makes it difficult to test the idea that syntax and grammar are phallomorphic structures. Are they in French? Were they in classical Greek? Are they in all human languages? And if so, why and how, by what operation or mechanism, did they become so?

Equally troublesome is the idea that a feminine syntax will be a syntax only in a metaphorical sense, as will be things like proper names or grammatical subjects and objects. This rather romantic notion seems to overlook the fact that the plasticity and ambiguity inherent in all natural languages are not independent of the inherent structures that give a language its unity and distinct identity. These structures are intuitively sensed and operated by native speakers and in fact constitute the very modality of native speech. Thus, when she explains that (feminine) syntax would involve nearness, proximity, but in such an extreme form that it would preclude any distinction of identities, any establishment of ownership, and thus any form of appropriation, it is difficult to establish what kind of language, if a language at all, could display these characteristics and still manage to communicate or make sense.[8] With the exception of sheer nonsense, all word formations, even the most poetic (that is, creative in scope), assume a certain order and rule; in fact they are creative precisely because they deviate from or improvise on standard semantic and syntactic arrangements and on the expectations associated with them.

Thus, we may follow Irigaray in the general direction of her insight that the suppression of woman (as sex and person) in the West is Greek in origin. But we cannot follow her in her claim that all language is essentially phallomorphic and masculine. For one, Greek language is not. And, I would guess, neither is French. They are naturally gender-inclusive languages.

Depending on their construction, natural languages have their own idiosyncratic ways of suggesting orientation to their native speakers, and certainly the allocation of gender can be one of them. When I speak Greek, for instance, the feminine is not only a grammatical structure. It is also a certain intuition of world and a way of directing myself in it—functions which extend to gestures, facial expressions, body-language, and of course, speech. In that context, it makes sense to say that the masculine becomes a limit, an encompassing intuition of otherness in things—similar to what the phenomenologists like to call a horizon. Within that horizon and its dynamics, a multiplicity of relations is possible which invokes but also challenges that limit. The same applies to the other side: the function of the feminine as a horizon for the masculine. The interaction of these two horizons produces the space delineated by the total reality of the Greek language—I can put this in a somewhat poetic way by calling that reality the Greek cosmos.

We may find a relevant image in Hesiod's mythological account of masculine *Ouranos* (the god Sky) spreading himself over feminine *Gaia* (the goddess Earth) in order to create the totality of the visible to the Greeks—there will be more on *Ouranos* and *Gaia* later. This archaic metaphor has an obvious iconographic function that recalls, as in most ancient cosmologies, ritualized perceptions and narratives of sexual intercourse and union. The same theme in classical context could define the relationship of masculine logos to feminine *sophia* (wisdom)—which, as we shall see, Plato appropriates. One example, from Plato's *Phaedrus,* is Socrates's description of the archaic poetess Sappho as "wise" in matters of oracular and erotic possession. Socrates appears to revel in her passion and is moved by her poetry to compose his own reasoned lyric (*logos*) about erotic arousal and the possession of the soul by abstract universals.[9]

Of feminine gender, *sophia* is an interesting word to study for the naturalism of Greek nouns. It comes from the root -*saf*—*sapor* or *sapere* (in Latin)—which means the taste of a fruit's juice and possibly the ability to tell a fruit by its taste. In Homer and Hesiod, *sophia* refers to craftsmanship and knowledge of how a thing works; in Hesiod it refers to how to sail a ship.[10] The feminine gender most probably reflects an association with access to the interior of a crop, with the ability to know intimately but also to receive nourishment and pleasure from that knowledge.[11] The archaic association with a trade or skill maintains the idea of close contact such as, for example, that which an iron smith has with his tools or a sailor has with his boat and the sea. Later classical and philosophical usage shows a marked change. For example, Herodotus, in *The Histories,* defines *sophia* in terms of *theoria* (viewing, spectacle, reflection) and recalls that the Persian king Kroisos admired Solon for his love of learning from sights (*philosophia theories*) of distant travel.[12] Similarly, in 145e of Plato's *Theaetetus,* the term is associated with the abstract, speculative knowledge of the forms, a meaning also found in Aristotle's *Metaphysics* where *sophia* is identified with "first philosophy."[13]

The etymology of *sophia* suggests an original meaning of intimate, sensual contact between knower and known probably, but not exclusively, based on sexual union and reproduction—for example, being able to tell whether a child could be conceived, under what conditions, and whether it would be healthy, and then by analogy whether fruit was ripe for collection, whether a field would yield a good crop, and so on. A certain elasticity, then, in the gender of the word would be predictable because associations that originally favored a female archetype could be reversed or transferred to male characteristics—both physiological and sociological (for example, that men farmed but women weaved)—or shifted back and forth according to context. In philosophical context, of course, such two-way reversals were rare, with the notable exception of Plato's Diotima, as we shall see later. Women were generally excluded from philosophical circles, so it would be reasonable for the term to shift in the direction of masculine activities while formally retaining its feminine declination. Thus, Plato linked *sophia* with the method of division, and Aristotle followed by making a similar connection to definition by genus or difference(s).[14] In 259 of the *Sophist,* the feminine metaphor of weaving seems to suggest the very opposite view from the one that Plato maintains: Although divisible, speech (*logos*) is impossible without an interweaving (*symploke*) of all kinds of things and of the words (*eide*) that correspond to them.

The association of *sophia* with gender reversal has implications for the perception of male and female realities within world and language. Philosophy was preceded in Greece by the discourse of theater, and in that theater and its concomitant ritual crossings of sexual identity or fusions of sex were commonplace. Dionysos, the hermaphrodite patron and object of pantomimic dance and song, seems to be one such archetypal form, despite the fact that his feminine nature was gradually subdued by his masculine attributes. Fusions or plasticity of sexual identity and by implication of gender are quite consistent with primitive *sophia*. They are not, however, consistent with its philosophical meaning. The well-known Aristotelian definition of the female/feminine in terms of lack or deficiency in male/masculine nature, and its adoption by Christian thought in theorists like Thomas Aquinas, are good examples of how the equation of analytical and taxonomical speech with true speech can restrict and ultimately distort the natural unity implicit in a language.

This is an appropriate point to move into the main body of our discussion. It will develop in four additional parts. First, I examine two compelling examples of sex and gender manipulation in Plato, specifically in the *Phaedrus* and the *Symposium*. Second, I give an argument that identifies resemblances between Plato's subverted feminine and the feminine in feminist subversion. Third, I make some general observations about archaic literacy and a hypothesis concerning the recession of the feminine in prephilosophical Greece. Fourth, I explore a study of certain fragments of Anaximander, Heraclitus, and Parmenides that show evidence of a simultaneous shift toward sexual indifference and literate perception in Greek language. I will conclude with reflections on language, gender, and the destiny of feminine voice in philosophy.

II

In histories of Greek philosophical language, *elenchos* is associated with the name of Socrates and his interrogative way of doing philosophy. Practiced like a drill on those who either failed or neglected to discipline their speech, *elenchos* put Socrates in the position of an authority not unusual in Greek tradition. From the time of Homer, *elenchein* was used to induce shame, to discredit, belittle, or diminish a person or persons in the presence of others. If we follow the term's etymology, the recipient of *elenchos* became the least of all present—the meaning of *elachus-elachistos*—the closest to absence that one could be in the midst of a company or gathering of peers.

On one occasion, Homer uses it to describe men that presumably behaved like women by refusing to take action in their own interest against the orders of their generals.[15] The context is an inflammatory speech by Thersites, a man described in the most unfavorable terms as a lowly and hateful character without measure in speech or mind.[16] It is clear that the description *elencheia* is meant as an insult to the gathered soldiers that directly questions their sexual identity and perhaps implicitly their prowess or manliness.[17] Although this kind of talk is explicitly disapproved of by Homer as base and vulgar, the use of *elencheia* does suggest the existence in rhetorical contexts of a form of gender manipulation that worked by evoking in an audience or individual a sense of obligation to and solidarity with their sex.[18] Plato understood the psychological power of this practice on a male audience and adopted the elenctic rhetoric of Socrates in his earlier dialogues. But he also used the practice in far more sophisticated and, we could say, theatrical ways than his teacher in order to create visually and sensually compelling imagery for his abstract universals (*eide*).

The *Phaedrus* gives an impressive example of this development in its study of erotic or divinely inspired speech. As Plato describes it, the Eros that lifts the soul toward the immortal realities is a masculine force directed to a masculine body. Passionately spoken by Socrates—who was known for his dry, detached discourse—the great palinode of Eros[19] works with an irreverence to sexual difference that turns the pederastic subtext of the dialogue into a solemn travesty.[20] The pains and delights of sexual arousal, so vividly described by Socrates, culminate in a vision of abstraction which can become memorable only by a somatic recollection of pleasure and rupture in which the feminine is markedly absent.

The idea that abstract thought needs erotic metaphor to carry it through memory reflects in part Plato's experience of oral mnemonics and its practice of affective and physiological recollection (by voice, body-rhythm and motion, pleasure, movement, perspiration, and so on). But it also reflects, especially in this context, the gravitation of Greek imagination and language toward the erotic and procreative aspects of human sexuality—the logic and rhetoric of sexual difference. As we shall see later, in the *Symposium*, Plato was confronted with a language compellingly declined in two genders, drawing its ontological force from that difference and therefore imposing on him feminine being, feminine desire, and speech. But he was also confronted—and seduced—by a language that could feign sexual indifference and fictionalize its own logic, its own articulate body. Plato's was a poetic intrusion within the language-corpus, within the imaginary of Greek speech that was increasingly writing itself out, showing its powers of diversion, of silence, withdrawal, and return.

Plato followed his native language to its own defeminizing, deeroticizing possibilities and was enchanted to discover a world that could reproduce and redesire itself without woman. The *Phaedrus* provides a good illustration of this discovery.

Early in the dialogue, Socrates is taken out of his ordinary masculine self and put on stage. Plato has him driven outside the city—to the very location where according to myth the nymph Oreitheia was brutally raped—and once there makes him delight in flowers, trees, and fresh water, things that are real, sensual, and in this context ostensively feminine.[21] He also twists and turns like a flattered but embarrassed virgin and later, just before he delivers his first discourse, he covers his head in shame, a characteristically feminine gesture for that time.[22] In so doing, he seems to be insulting as feminine the speech that he is about to present according to which universality and its Eros-like fantasies are threats to the social and procreative order.[23] But the speech is also masculine because it has been forced on Socrates by Phaedrus, and Socrates has received it like a woman, like the violated Oreitheia.

Socrates will complain that the speech which so pleased Phaedrus is vulgar and should be avoided by all philosophers.[24] Part of its crudeness comes from its literal and cynical view of sexual intercourse and its benefits: children from a woman, pleasure from a youth.[25] Plato is ready to dismiss the logic of Eros, of the sexual difference that poeticized Greek language and thought. Philosophy's pleasures and progeny will require of language only a metaphorical femininity; the philosopher will continue to decline names in the feminine but only in a grammatical and rhetorical sense. The neuter beings of Platonic metaphysics, forms like *to agathon* (the good), *to kalon* (the beautiful), *to dikaion* (the just), will be incubated in the philosopher's dialectical and elenctic mind without the presence of woman—even as an attendant. This is noble procreation and Plato goes on to contrast it with the vulgar reproduction of animals and other inferior, nonphilosophical souls which only know how to mount and sow children.[26]

This view is given a more explicit discussion in the *Symposium,* where Socrates recalls the "wise" (*sophe*) woman Diotima in order to clarify and advance his argument about the nature of Eros.[27] In the *Symposium,* the feminine, sensual, aspects of Eros and their corresponding feminine nouns are subsumed under an abstract, masculine aspect that is deemed superior.

At the introduction of the story, the verb "to alienate" is used by Socrates to identify his intellectual authority over Agathon—who states that he cannot counter Socrates's arguments[28]—with that which Diotima supposedly exercised over him in an earlier time when he was subject to her authority.[29] Socrates then proceeds to recall that Diotima directed him away from the view of Eros as a god or something divine. Instead, she taught him to see Eros as a "wise demon-like man" whose wisdom had to do with vulgar and utilitarian (*vanausos*) things like the crafts and professions, and who in that capacity served to mediate communication between gods and mortals.[30] She compared his status to that of "correct opinion" which also mediates the relationship between knowledge and ignorance,[31] and described him as a seducer, a sophist, and a sorcerer, the son of a wise and wealthy father (named Resource) and a foolish and poor mother (named Poverty).[32]

The denigration of Eros reflects Plato's own appropriation of the god's traditional Homeric identity in which he typically mediated the union of men and women. As in the *Phaedrus,* that identity must be renegotiated in the context of a new kind of reproduction. Encased in the dialogue with Diotima are abstract neuter nouns like *agathon* and *kalon* which allude to Plato's ultimate objective. To explain their relationship to Eros, Diotima delivers an explicitly feminine discourse, a speech which Socrates, in jest of course, attributes to her "awesome wisdom" (*ethaumazon epi sophia*).[33]

Diotima's speech[34] is the first and last presence of a female voice in Greek philosophy—and perhaps in all canonical philosophy until our times. Its sad irony lies in the fact that a woman is made to deliver a speech that will deface the feminine in Greek language and philosophy. It is a speech that is full of the feminine nouns of animation, creation, gestation, and birth/generation that we mentioned earlier in our discussion: *psyche, physis, kyesis, genesis.* All human beings, Diotima's argument runs, desire the beautiful (*to kalon*) for the purpose of giving birth (*tokos*) to a being that will survive them.[35] This birth can be either of a physical or a mental nature and so, of course, is its offspring. Eros is a desire for beauty in an other, man or woman, for the purpose of immortality in the bodies of one's offspring and their descendants. But Eros is philosophical only if the lovers and their offspring are mental, asomatic, beings of masculine and neuter gender, respectively.[36] Diotima's language in this passage clearly refers to the forms: "What is lost, and what decays always leaves behind a fresh copy of itself."[37]

As she approaches the conclusion of her speech, she describes a young man's overlooking vision of a sea of good, plentiful, and magnificent discourses (*logoi*). The verb for that great sight is *theoron*—the same word used by Herodotus to describe Solon's *sophia.* It reaches its highest and most splendid form in the neuter spectacle of the beautiful (*to kalon*) with which Diotima ends her entire discourse. With that discourse woman disappears from the position of the subject and object of Eros. Her body, speech, beauty, and wisdom are now the subject of an imaginary gender. In Greek, she could be called an *atopic* or *o/utopic* being. Both words mean the absence of place and by implication the absence of existence (*ou topos*).

III

The reduction of woman to imaginary interlocutor and, if I may say, interactor in man's intellectual, spiritual, artistic, and sexual pursuits is a Platonic or more rightly a classical Greek invention whose grip on the masculine imagination is still powerful and creative today. Fashion, film, and in general visual experience in European and American society are dominated by this myth. So are the vast bodies of literature, art, and theater in which typically we find the unconscious reflections of human experience and belief.

In the second half of our century, feminist study has begun to expose the presence of this myth in all areas of human representation. In philosophy, this enterprise is especially challenging because what feminist investigation is facing there is the distinction between true and ideologically based argument. Hasty and sweeping generalizations that either identify the two or dismiss the entire practice of critical reason as the product of ideological preference make it difficult to demand accountability from those who practice the discipline on either side (feminist or masculinist). And yet, when rid of its misconceptions and universalized in the full inclusive sense, philosophy makes man and woman equally accountable for fact and reason. Thus, the problem arises not with reason itself but with the pseudo-realities justified and perpetuated in its name.

Feminists are not exempt from such influence. There are instances in which philosophy that describes itself as feminist resolves to consider woman as the negative and false other of all philosophical discourse— the very qualities that have been used to exclude her from the discipline since its inception.[38]

An example of this tendency is the call for the subversion of all categories and arguments associated with universality, ideality, and abstraction. Presumed to be exclusively masculine, these modalities are to be undermined by a constant rejection (or mockery) of their authority. There are at least three serious problems with this view. First, the classification of reason and its functions as masculine perpetuates the fallacy that women are essentially irrational and as such unphilosophical beings. Second, it implies that philosophy is incapable of correcting itself, a notion that puts feminist philosophy in the rather odd position of a practice without a subject. Third, the idea of feminine resistance by irony and laughter on the one hand, and fragmentation or dispersion on the other, assumes the existence of a sterile and destructive opposition between feminine and masculine. Subversion denies to woman and man equal and complementary functions in the reflection and representation of language and reality. It also denies to woman a positive, creative function within philosophy and knowledge, thus reinforcing the age-old stereotype of her inherent anarchy, negativity, and deficiency. We need only think here of Aristotle's claim in the *Politics* that though rational and capable of deliberation (*vouleutikon*), woman lacks authority (*akyron*)—a description that refers either to women's lack of civic power and rights or to their lesser nature (if we go by Aristotle's biology).[39]

In a contemporary context, a good example of the power of this stereotype can be found in Jean Baudrillard's argument that sexuality is essentially masculine and that feminine sexuality exists symbolically only, as a parody or theater of male desire and fantasy.[40] We may imagine feminist philosophies of subversion in the same condition, as pretenders to a discipline which needs them in order to continue being itself and for this reason has given them license to be disorderly and irreverent. This means that within the frame of an essentially masculine discipline, the feminine continues to project itself as a destitute, an *atopon*. It cannot lead anywhere because it cannot be placed anywhere. It can only displace what the masculine has created. A woman philosopher in this view is never a real thing; she is never a thinker of consequence. But this is not to say that she is powerless. Baudrillard states:

> The feminine is not just seduction; it also suggests a challenge to the
> male to be the sex; to monopolize sex and sexual pleasure, a challenge
> to go to the limits of its hegemony and exercise it unto death. Today
> phallocracy is collapsing under the pressure of this challenge (present
> throughout our culture's sexual history), and its inability to meet it.[41]

For Baudrillard, male authority over sexuality ends in fantasy and perpetual desire. The one follows from the other. The power of a spectacle lies in the fact that unlike its physical object it cannot be possessed—the ideal woman is on the screen, in the pages of a magazine, on a billboard, never at home. A feminist philosophy of subversion is in a similar position. It is never at home in philosophy; it refuses to be part of its history and its present. It is powerful because, like a fantasy, it cannot be refuted. In this sense, it may be said to "exhaust" those who try to engage with it in critical dialogue by issuing propositions that cannot be met (for example, those of Irigaray on language).

Baudrillard's insistence that woman's relation to power is negative and that it is acquired—or ought to be acquired—at the expense of the reality and creative presence of her sex, is, of course, ill-conceived. But it is especially helpful in reminding us that feminist subversion is constructive only when it remains aware of its own unreality, of the fact, in other words, that in subverting masculine practices and discourses it is also subverting the myths that they have created about woman and her speech, and foremost the myth of her destructiveness, anarchy, and negative (as in "sinful") presence in creation. The danger for feminist philosophy, as I see it, is what Plato saw in one of his best moments: the hatred of or contempt for reasoned (language ordering and creating) discourses when they fail the goals or expectations of their speakers—what he called *misologia*.[42]

There are feminist philosophers, of course, who will argue that misogyny (the hatred of or contempt for woman) is good reason for misology. The problem with this view is that it assumes mistakenly that reason and woman are incompatible or that woman's relationship to reasoned speech can only be one of resistance or censure. This is far too narrow a view of the feminine's presence in human language. Philosophical languages, from the traditional Greek and Latin to the more modern French and German, are too rich in feminine nouns to be discarded as the mere artifact of male domination.

As in other aspects of significant human communication from antiquity to the present, so too in philosophy; woman and the feminine are vitally present though not always conspicuous realities. I may cite in this context the exemplary work of Caroline Walker Bynum on the fluidity of gender in medieval hagiography, which demonstrates how feminine imagery permeated the language, imagination, art, and theology of male-dominated Christian Europe.[43]

Closer to our study, we have seen this presence in the *Symposium*, in which despite the irony and condescension of the Socratic narrative, Diotima's language overflows with feminine nouns and imagery. It is now time to consider why Plato found it necessary to appropriate and suppress the feminine in his speech, what this development owes to the thought of some of his pre-Socratic precursors, and how both relate to the emergence of written communication.

IV

Discussion of orality and literacy in the context of Greek philosophical beginnings continues to center on Eric Havelock's thesis that philosophy emerged when the translation of oral communication into writing (around 750 B.C.) made it possible to treat speech and by implication thought as objects that could exist independently of the speaker's body, voice, gesture, and lived space.[44] In very general lines, Havelock's argument runs like this. The separation of speaker and spoken word in literate practice resulted in the perception of speech as language (*logos*): an ordered, structured system of meaningful units that could be studied in a variety of sequences and formations. With attention directed away from the physiological and affective context of speech, another level of communication experience emerged that modeled the experience of *noetic* (cognitive) space.[45] The visual, two-dimensional representation of meaningful gesture and voice in writing gave words a dimension of abstraction and interiority that they did not have in oral communication. Eventually, writing brought about a new kind of consciousness, one that experienced and ordered the world in terms of intangible and invisible units of meaning not subject to the temporal and spatial limitations of oral discourse. With this turn inward toward a more private and abstract sense of communication, and outward toward a world of timeless and unchanging objects, Greek philosophy (and metaphysics) was born.[46]

Havelock's sharp distinction between orality and literacy has been criticized, in part because a "literate" consciousness in the pre-Socratics and even in Plato is by no means as evident as he has suggested, and in part because the "oral" intellect that informs Homeric epic shows compelling signs of linguistic awareness and skill that Havelock considers inconsistent with orality.

If we follow Arthur W. H. Adkins, who in defense of this last point cites, among other examples, that of Odysseus, in *Odyssey* 9, using the name "No-One" to introduce himself to the Cyclops—who subsequently has to cry out to his neighbors that "No-One" is trying to kill him—we can say that philosophical Greek was the result of syntactical and semantic shifts within the Greek language itself, shifts which included and actually built on the existing, prephilosophical literature but which cannot necessarily be tied to the appearance and practice of writtten communication.[47]

A similar view is adopted by Thalmann in his study of thought patterns and organization in archaic poetry, specifically in his observation that far from being deficient (or primitive), the epic mind was actually capable of detecting and representing complex logical and psychological unities. These unities invariably mapped (geographed) realities in the physical and human world. Thalmann states:

> The poem at once exhibited the world's fullness and variety and discovered its essential order. But it also represented that order by virtue of its existence as a pattern in the mind. By embodying the forms of

thought habitual to poet and audience, the poem evolved in the course of the performance as a model or mental image of the world that it sought to elucidate.[48]

I suggested earlier that Greek is ontologically transparent to the material, libidinal, and symbolic denominations of sexual being; that it is, in other words, iconologically and iconographically oriented toward the declination of sexual difference. It can speak from the body's other and from the difference of its desire toward the whole world. Thalmann's study does not seek that difference and the grammar it engenders, but it clearly brings to surface the iconological power of archaic orality. Although not as radical (or terminal) as Havelock has suggested, the translation of sexual denomination from vocal to graphic space could not have come without consequences. In fact, if we view speech and writing as modalities of alterity and difference within the body of language itself— a notion that follows Derrida's observation that the very problematic of literacy and orality presupposes a more complex, interdependent ground of articulation[49]—we may see in the phenomenon of Greek literacy an indigenous suppression of sexual difference: a shift toward sexual indifference and neutrality that oriented the language toward its philosophical and metaphysical possibilities.

Gender was at the epicenter of that movement, though not in the articulate, visible way in which it is being arranged today. We may think of latency or repression or simply, in more organic terms, of the gestation of that centrality from an archetypal ground to the eccentricity of a feminist moment in philosophy—a moment destined to violate the presumed neutrality (sexual indifference) of philosophical discourse.

As Greek began its ascent toward literacy, words such as *logos* and *glossa, okeanos* and *thalassa,* which in oral communication were denominated to man and woman by natural and performative resemblance, lost in their written experience the visual and physical connection to their objects. These words became asexual and asomatic beings, lacking the tactile, audial, and sensual impact of oral iconography. The sense of intimacy and power with which, as Walter Ong has pointed out, oral peoples experience the naming of things—naming is an event, the one who names also makes something happen or become what it is—was shaken.[50] If we recall a point made earlier about the function of gender as a sensual catalog of the human lifeworld, we may begin to see in these two developments the origins of the recession and subsequently the suppression of the feminine in Greek language.

There is a common premise to begin with. Literacy required the experience of, and eventually created the reality of, a new kind of body.

The emergence of a form of communication that projected in nonsomatic space not only the visuality and sensuality of the spoken word but also its voice, its living physiological connection to the speaker's body and lifeworld, made the body itself a sort of specter—a projectual reality. The written word or text was an image that projected a different kind of living function: It did not grimace, gesticulate, or for that matter utter itself. Unlike its oral equivalent, it had no libidinal and physiological efficacy—except, perhaps, in the activity of inscription itself, a task characteristically relegated to slaves (lesser bodies).[51]

Literacy shifted attention away from the sensual, lived body and in so doing challenged the authority of its creative, reproductive function, an authority centered in and disposed by the female body.[52] Writing was more lasting than one's offspring. It put one's own voice in a body, the text, which could live forever. Women who could write or have their words recorded, like Sappho, seemed aware of this new kind of immortality.[53] But they were unaware that its literate logic was slowly depriving them of that option.

There is linguistic evidence to help us imagine how language gradually shifted to the masculine and to its philosophical ideal, the neuter. One of the earliest metaphysical words, the feminine noun *arche,* is a cognate of a verb (*archo*) which means both "to begin" and "to rule."[54] A variant of *archo* is the masculine noun *orchamos,* which means the first of a row (for exampl, in a chorus) and whose cognates are the masculine noun *orchis* (testicle) and the feminine nouns *orchesis* (pantomimic dancing) and *orchestra* (place for dancing) from which, of course, we get our word "orchestra." There is, finally, one more word, the verb *huparcho* (*hupo — archo,* under-begin/rule), which means "to make a beginning," "to exist" (as in "come into being") but also "to lie under" (a superior in battle) or "to belong" (to someone).

Now, if we consider all of these words together as a cluster of overlapping referents and meanings, the way they could only be seen if someone actually put them in writing, one thing becomes very clear. They could easily, though not necessarily, be perceived and ordered in a masculine, disciplinary, and hierarchical orientation. There is, in other words, a logic implicit in these words that would make possible this kind of arrangement. Yet, it is not the only logic. One may choose to intuit in *arche* meanings associated with male physiology and therefore to speak and write in that direction, for example, with male-centered and -oriented analogies among masculinity, authority, and origin.

But one can equally shift direction toward the word's ostensively feminine nature and intuit patterns and forms of authority and origin recognizable in female physiology, understanding *arche,* for example, as *genesis, kyesis,* or *physis.* Thus, the language in and of itself is not restrictive or biased toward one of the three genders. Rather, it can be restricted by those who use it without awareness of its indigenous elasticity or with the express aim of violating its natural inclusiveness. Now, clearly a writer is a more observant and careful user of language than a speaker—at least a practiced, trained writer. It would make sense therefore to associate writing with the systematic application (and exploitation) of language— a strategy which continues to underwrite philosophical discourse today, including that of feminist philosophy.

Yet, despite an emerging sense of authority over language and world, writing must have brought with it considerable anxiety. It was, after all, as we have already suggested, replacing the sensuality and transience of oral speech with the asomatic and yet evocative (if not explosive) permanence of the written sign. A new way of experiencing body, speech, action, and world was on the horizon. And so was the effort to explain its origins and tell its stories. Literacy was in need of its own mythology. A new cosmogonical story had to be told using signs and abstract impressions rather than voices, bodies, and gestures. The iconographic logic of the Greek language was shifting toward new possibilities.

But the process was slow and by no means uniform. The culture was still predominantly oral (as it remained in the time of Plato and as it remains today in some of its most significant expressions).[55] Literate storytellers had to evoke heroic imagery from their oral past in order to explain their new lifeworld. It was a challenging inheritance: voyages in unknown seas, great feats that put one's body and endurance to the test, the honor of having been the first to undertake the journey and find the way back. These images had to be repainted and relived. It would make sense for the new poets to think of *arche* because they were becoming masters of a new beginning. But would they have to see this as a masculine task? The question is anachronistic—such an epiphany of gender and language is a sign of our times. Knowing this, we can still speculate an answer.

We recall from Greek mythology that dangerous journeys were not exclusive to men. There are stories of goddesses, nymphs, and mortal women in Greek mythology that make this quite clear (the adventures of Ariadne, Danae, Persephone, Demetra, and so many others). There is archaic Sappho and her circle who were eloquent, daring, and creative in both verse and life (for example, Sappho lived for some time as a political exile in Sicily).[56] There are also fifth-century women poets like Myrtis of Anthedon and Korinna who were famed to have competed with men poets and won (for example, Korinna defeated Pindar), and who also recorded themselves as storytellers of heroes, both male and female.[57]

Now, we have seen in the *Phaedrus* and in the *Symposium*, indisputable memory of female presence and authority in significant communication—a memory which Plato the metaphysician had to appropriate and transform. Despite his protestations against writing's violation of living speech,[58] Plato could see that writing was already speaking for itself. Perhaps his allusion to Sappho was meant to identify a common insight. Writing Greek dissociated posthumous remembrance from the living bodies and memories of one's offspring and from the maternal body of their origin. Man could now produce descendants alone without woman, without her (and his) natural sexuality. He could make his own *arche*, be himself the principle and source (womb) of a new reality, a new corpus. More than just a technology, writing oriented Greek speech toward a new conception of body, sexuality, progeny, and immortality. Somewhere between Thersites's elenctic insults and Plato's simulated woman, the voices of the few women writers were silenced and feminine speech was relegated to the mortal, ephemeral and confining space of an orality whose words and world were deemed perishable—and indeed have perished.

To summarize: I am suggesting that woman disappeared from significant communication when the new language of abstraction that writing generated out of Greek orality gradually eroded her natural and archetypal bonds to speech. Thus, her powerful presence in Greek language was simulated, parodied, and reordered in order to accommodate an emerging masculine (and neuter) cosmos whose parameters, though universalized in other languages, remained archetypally Greek. Over the centuries, *arche*, orchestra, monarchy, hierarch(y), became incompatible with feminine presence and speech, even though Greek continued to decline the words in feminine gender.

V

In histories of Greek philosophy, the early pre-Socratics have been principally viewed as the first rational cosmologists and naturalists. Our perspective is different. In the proto-literate investigations of Anaximander, Heraclitus, and Parmenides, oral forms that derived from natural analogies to sexual anatomy and performance, from the rituals that represented and celebrated sexual difference, began to unravel.

In the early part of the sixth century, Anaximander proposed that what orders things must itself be invisible, and called that mysterious substance *arche*. *Arche* was comprehensive, in that it included all substances, and dynamic because it regularly absorbed and generated all matter out of its endless, limitless (*apeiron*) body. Anaximander's world was largely shaped by an oral consciousness which fused human, heroic, and divine action and centered its reality on the binding rituals of human community (story-telling, sacred dance and meal, marriage, death, and so on). The world that he tried to describe and order "in accordance with the ordinance of time [*kata tou chronou taxin*]," was a very different place.[59] It was by comparison a wasteland, recognizable as part of the human experience only because of its material constituents (*stoicheia*) like water, air, fire, and earth, and their orderly relationships which resembled those of law-governed communities. Trespassings between the elements would be identified and punished and restitution made to the rightful owners (for example, trespassing day was made to yield to night). Terms like the feminine noun *taxis* that denoted military formation and rank, and *dike* that denoted right and custom—later Plato's abstract *dikaiosune* (justice)—described the regulation of conflicts and their resolution. *Arche* functioned as supreme judge and authority. She ruled concealed and absent from the world.

Now, if we proceed on the assumption that *arche, taxis, apeiron* (being without end or indefinite), *chronos*, and *dike* are Anaximander's own language (and not that of later commentators), there is good reason to be impressed with his choice of terms. Without exception, all five words in this case communicate order and extension in space and time. They are about boundaries, limits, measure, order, rank, judgment, duration, authority, and judgment. These terms do not have for Anaximander the abstract sense that they have for us. They are closer to describing actions and events, such as someone failing to see the end of a line or seeing it very clearly. Like words in oral experience, they coincide with events, not with thoughts. Thus, they describe both the object of Anaximander's inquiry and his activity: He inquires into order but he also orders words, things and his own speech.

What we see in his vocabulary is in part what Paul Ricoeur calls "interpretation" or "the act of the text," a process by means of which language actually directs the reader's thought rather than follows it.[60] But Anaximander is not only being written; he is also writing, and his speech now follows him. He is its *arche*—a male father, named by a feminine noun, discovering a new dimension of speech, body, and gender.

Next to Anaximander's incorporeal *arche*, we have Heraclitus's (fl. 504–500 B.C.) fascination with the identity and unity of opposites, which he called *logos*. Those who agreed with that unity—which actually spoke for itself—were "wise" (*sophoi*): "Listening not to me but to the *logos* it is wise to agree that all things are one."[61] Here, too, transcribed speech, or *logos,* speaks for itself the way that Anaximander would were words coming out of his body. *Logos* is Anaximander's bodiless, uprooted voice—his voice as text. The text is a creature; a strange, living-dead thing, a thing that collects all voices and makes them one. Heraclitus can see the creature, what he calls *physis* (later to mean "nature"). He can study it like one does a corpse, a thing lying down.

Understandably, then, *keimenon* becomes the later Greek word for text—it is speech that lies down (as if) destroyed, withered away (like a corpse exposed), idle, or neglected. Lying down and laying in order are also two of the meanings of the verb "*legein*" of which *logos* is a cognate.

Now, if we assume that *logos* is the unifying power of the vocalized text and therefore what implicitly brings it to life—gives it its *physis*— then the reading speaker is a new kind of cosmologist, a taxonomer of signs rather than actions. By his own account, Heraclitus "divided up each thing according to the creature (*physis*),"[62] a creature which in a famous fragment he describes as loving to hide from him: "*physis* likes to hide."[63] The creature of course is the written language facing him like an animal faces its hunter. A feminine noun, she may also tempt and taunt him to take her in a tacit sexual metaphor. Or she may be a playful daughter, an immortal child whose play he can direct and dictate. Here the analogies of orality are still at work. But those of literacy are taking over. The text lying before him is his own (masculine) logos. It is dead; he is alive. He makes it speak (when he reads it). He is its voice. *Logos* dominates *physis.* The creature taunts him but she is voiceless without him. In Fragment 104, favored by Havelock for its contempt for orality, Heraclitus accuses his compatriots for reveling in worthless song, dance and cult festivities while, presumably, he spends his time recording his voice for posterity.[64]

Like Heraclitus, Parmenides (b. 515–510 B.C.) struggled to keep written and oral speech separate. Fragments like the following have been read in metaphysical terms, as if Parmenides had in his grasp centuries of literate cognition and abstract thought: "It is all one to me where I begin; for I shall come back there again in time."[65] This fragment is describing the experience of going back time and again to one's own transcribed speech. His text needs no reminders, no audience, no interlocution. It is there waiting for him, a kind of surrogate home and familiar body that needs his presence and voice in order to speak again.

A new perception of being must have been associated with that experience. Spoken things were now fixed in time and space (the writing space) and could come to life in a way that other *keimena* (for example, corpses) and *logoi* could not. Whereas spoken words could be lost in time and space—their echoes fading—what one put in writing remained in its place, whole, unchangeable, and one.

Thus, Parmenides observed: "The same thing can be thought as can be," or "for it is one and the same to think (*noein*) and to be."[66] And again on the permanence and recalcitrance of literate language: "That which can be spoken [written or read] [*legein*] and thought needs must be; for it is possible for it, but not for nothing, to be; that is what I bid thee ponder."[67] Parmenides' *logos*, like the *logos* of Heraclitus, is literate speech. It is its literate, textual being that makes it incorruptible, undeniable, and alive (every time one reads it). In his own words:

> One way only is left to be spoken of, that it is; and on this way are full many signs (*semata*) that what is is uncreated and imperishable, for it is entire, immovable and without end. It was not in the past, nor shall it be, since it is now, all at once, one, continuous; for what creation (*gennan*) wilt thou seek for it? How and whence did it grow?[68]

From the standpoint of the reader, this is a cosmogony that does not need the other sex—except perhaps for rhetorical purposes. This passage too is typically read in terms closer to twentieth-century concerns (about metaphysics and predication) than to those of Parmenides' time. Yet, if we read it in the context that I have been suggesting, it becomes a description of the experience and nature of written text and of the writer's or reader's fascination with it. If this passage has ontological implications, it has them in two ways. One is the ontology of text and its experience; the other is the ontology of gender in written communication. When Parmenides marvels at the ungenerated stillness of "that which is," he feels the need to speak of a *genna*. *Genna*, a feminine noun, which means both the end product and act of giving birth (that is, genesis), is what a written text, unlike a speech, cannot have. Speeches have bodies with mothers and fathers; they have life stories and lifeworlds. Words are spoken by children, by adults and old men and women. This kind of speech grows, ages, and dies.

But something motherless (and fatherless) has no origin and no end. At the end of the fragment, he claims that his way is the end of all genesis. We should correct him and suggest that it is end of the unitive, natural genesis by male and female. This genesis is of a different kind; it is not unitive and though fatherless, it does have a father: the writer, master of his speech.

Parmenides provides a compelling example of how the emerging literate consciousness appropriated not only the language of orality but the full gamut of masculine and feminine beings that it had created. In his proem to what is known as the *Way of Truth,* he presents the image of a youth being led by maidens (*korai*) to the secret abode of the goddess of justice (*Dike*) where he receives a revelation of a "well-rounded" or "circling" truth (*Aletheies eukykleos*).[69] The entire narrative is a rhetorical device, directed at the persuasion of Parmenides' oral audiences. The proem's female deities are decoys for his largely oral audience, the people that he calls "two-headed," (*dikranoi*) with "roaming" or "misled" minds (*plagkton noon*), "deaf and blind at once, altogether dazed, hordes devoid of judgment" who believe that oral and written speech are one and the same, reversible (*palintropon*) sides of the same thing.[70]

Used to a world evenly distributed between male and female beings, Parmenides' confused listeners become philosophy's first others. Despite the fact that orality's power and authority are still to be reckoned with— "do not let custom (*ethos*) force you (*viastho*)," the goddess advises the youth—Parmenides is confident that he is on the winning side. Through the mouth of the goddess, he invites his audience to put aside their gazing, "aimless eye" (*askopon omma*), their "echoing ears and tongues (*glossan*)," all of which are images of oral communication, and instead to follow him in the *elenchos* made possible by written speech (*logos*).[71] It is clear in this context that *elenchos*, the dismissal of oral speech and the reprimanding of those who consider it either equal or superior to written speech, has also as its target the receptive and richly sensuous way in which oral sensibility encountered the world.

In view of what he sets out to accomplish, Parmenides' language is understandably condescending and casts oral consciousness in a position of inferiority that we still ascribe to oral or "primitive" cultures today. In considering how this reorientation affects woman, we should be careful not to overextend ourselves. Clearly, certain important feminine nouns take their place on the side of orality—such as *glossa* and *physis*. Certain important masculine nouns find their way on the side of literacy—such as *logos* and *elenchos*. But the distribution is not conscious. Rather, language seems to record minute changes and rearrangements that only later and in a diachronic sense would define a reality—that of the feminine's recession in significant speech.

Similarly, the appropriation of female deities and their revelatory powers is undeniable, but it does not seem to be based on a derogatory judgment against the feminine itself. In this area too, we are still in the course of a development that will begin to reach consciousness and articulation in classical times. What is, however, striking about these first pre-Socratics (and certainly we have not exhausted the group or the issue), is that they experience in literacy the conditions for the discovery of an alternative cosmogony and with it of alternative forms of being and life. What these forms have in common is an independence from graphic analogies, from the regularities, rhythms, and vital forms (the forms of ritual, of marriage, birth, death, and so on) in which oral consciousness discovered, lived, and imagined its reality.

It was, as I have been suggesting all along, the departure from this iconographic mode of representation that gradually undermined the feminine as the masculine's complementary and necessary real other and introduced the imaginary, parodied, and outcast woman of later philosophical discourse.

The classical reconstruction of the myth of Oedipus, a myth in which the discovery of the real maternal body is punished with a permanent life in the imaginary—a life of blindness to what is other than oneself— may signify, in the destiny of the self-blinded Oedipus, the deep anxiety of living with an imaginary body and despising its ephemeral other. Perhaps a trace of this anxiety exists in Hesiod's proto-literate (c. eighth-century B.C.) *Theogony,* in the account of the primordial couple, the goddess Earth (*Gaia*) and the god Sky (*Ouranos*). In narrative sequence, Sky is first Earth's offspring. She creates him out of her body as an "equal to herself" so that he can "cover her on every side" and host the stars and the gods forever in his luminous body. Later, he becomes her consort and together they create deities like Thetis (of custom-law) and Mnemosyne (of memory and remembrance) and one-eyed creatures like the Cyclops whom Sky hates and secretly destroys. Together with the bravest of her sons, Kronos, Earth punishes Sky with castration for destroying his offspring.[72]

The child turned consort turned victim is the logic that constitutes the Oedipal drama in the cycles of Aeschylus and Sophocles. Like Jocasta, Gaia is the real, physical body with which the lover son cannot reconcile. This is why the castration of Ouranos gives birth to Aphrodite. As Hesiod describes her, she rules "the whisperings of maidens and smiles and deceits with sweet delight and love and graciousness."[73] She is feminine desire but cast from the side of the one who desires her; one who is part mystified, part seduced by the deceit in which he likes to imagine woman. Aphrodite is the fictional body of man's desire. Plato's Diotima may be her philosophical analog, alluding to the philosopher's yearning for reason in the feminine voice.

VI

Considered as an emerging moment within the body of Greek language, writing triggered the suppression of feminine speech and world at the same time that it shifted orality toward its philosophical possibilities. The idiom that was going to become Greek philosophy built on an ideal of sexual indifference that poeticized Greek language across masculine and neuter lines, leaving the feminine silent or at best prone to cacophony and disorder. The relocation of body and voice in transcribed speech, the absence of woman from that experience (with the exception of the few women poets whose fragments survive today), the association of writing with a surrogate corpus rivaling biological progeny and its promise of immortality, engendered a peculiar parity.

Together with woman, man became silent, a silence which philosophy in our century is beginning to recognize and articulate. In the case of gender, its natural distribution in Greek language survived the philosophical imagining of women as inferior and incomplete beings, estranged and adversarial to any positive ontology. We saw in Plato how feminine iconology challenged his efforts to speak of universals through neuter nouns and at the same time made his discourse memorable. In one respect, it would be right to say that the eclipse of the feminine was the price we had to pay first for the engendering of the written body and voice and then for the reasoned calculus that it gave us in the logic of Greek language—the fact that such was the way in which Greek could think and show itself as language.

This is neither to justify the suppression and silencing of woman nor to ennoble it. But we are following a movement of human voice in history, and history, to recall Hegel, is not invariably kind to the human being— especially when it must speak the absolute.[74] Philosophy's voice, with its elenctic cadence and immortalized neutrality, drove Greek language to favor the masculine but by no means destroyed its indigenous openness to femininity. Poetry and demotic (folk) song—both expressions of more total speech (with powerful oral and literal impulses)—continued to decline the world in both genders. In names like *Theologia,* orality preserved an iconography—the woman who in that name bore children, farmed the fields, baked bread, fed the men, buried the dead, and lit candles in prayer—that brings theological reason to an awareness of its monocular, truncated vision of God and human.

In feminist philosophy, philosophy too is recollecting woman. In the area of prephilosophical and philosophical Greek, there is much that deserves further study and discussion. I include the logics and poetics of sexual difference, the semantic and syntactical shifts that made writing speech and speaking in writing possible, and especially, the dynamics of gender distribution and alignment in philosophical space—such as the alignment of neuter and absolute form (*eidos*) in Plato.

To the extent that philosophy's first language has not yet been spoken fully or seen in its full ontopoetic force, philosophy, in whatever

CORNELIA A. TSAKIRIDOU

language it now finds and disperses itself, continues to articulate a Greek riddle. Perhaps that riddle can be discovered in other languages, like Latin or German or French. Perhaps it will surface unpredictably in a language so far silent or too "oral," too unaware of itself as "language," to be philosophical. Or perhaps it will remain a riddle.

Whatever the future, the emergence of woman in philosophical space is neither an accident nor an event external to the discipline, a mere ideological or social shift in its practice. Woman has been in philosophy from the beginning because she has always been in language. The task of feminist philosophy is to decipher and rethink that presence in full gender.

Notes

This paper is dedicated to the memory and life of Marianthi V. Georgoudi, Ph.D. (1957–85). It is based on a presentation at the 1993 Conference "Is Feminist Philosophy Philosophy?" organized by the Graduate Faculty Women in Philosophy, New School for Social Research. I am grateful to an anonymous reviewer and especially to my editor, Emanuela Bianchi, for insightful and constructive comments on earlier versions of this paper. My thanks also to Gabriel (Villy) Ulkeroglou and Carolina Bogdanou for keeping my mind tuned to the voices and images of Greek language.

1. Jesper Svenbro, *Phrasikleia: An Anthropology of Reading in Ancient Greece,* Janet Lloyd, trans. (Ithaca: Cornell University Press, 1993), 158–59; hereafter *PA.* Svenbro uses this riddle to argue that Sappho's fragment 31 is an allegory for the act of reading or animating a written poem.

2. Hesiod, *The Homeric Hymns and Homerica,* H. G. Evelyn-White, trans. (Cambridge, Mass.: Harvard University Press, 1982), 140–325.

3. William G. Thalmann, *Conventions of Form and Thought in Early Greek Epic Poetry* (Baltimore, Md.: The Johns Hopkins University Press, 1984), 10–11; hereafter *CFT.* Basing his work on a detailed study of similar patterns in epic poetry, Thalmann has concluded that archaic thought had its own distinct patterns of organization and structure different from but by no means inferior to those of classical antiquity. The logic that he assigns to the epic mind seems especially congenial to the physiology of the female body, of sexual union and reproduction, and deserves to be studied in that connection: "This manner of viewing things is a particular sense of form as enclosure, wherein antithetical extremes define what lies between them and the whole consists of juxtaposed but interrelated parts," 3.

4. "Iconographic" refers to the creation or inscription of images; "iconological" to the syntactic and semantic disposition of a language toward iconography. An iconological language like Greek has a high degree of plasticity: an impulse for word making. The adjective *glossoplastes* (one who shapes speech/*glossa* or tongue

favors orality but not at the exclusion of writing) is used to describe a poet or writer who can bring more language out of what is originally given to her. On this quality of Greek in philosophical context, see Arthur W. H. Adkins, "Orality and Philosophy," in *Language and Thought in Early Greek Philosophy*, Kevin Robb, ed. (La Salle: Monist Library of Philosophy, 1983), 225; hereafter *LT.* The iconological nature of Greek is exemplified during Hellenistic and Byzantine antiquity in the rhetorical genre of *ekphrasis* or pictorial writing (that is, description that rivals the actual perception of memorable objects or events). This is from the second-century treatise of Hermogenes on the genre: "it [*ekphrasis*] is visible, so to speak, and brings before the eyes that which is to be shown. . . . The special virtues of *ekphrasis* are clarity and visibility; the style must contrive to bring about seeing through hearing. It is equally important that expression should fit the subject: if the subject is florid, let the style be florid too, and if the subject is dry, let the style be the same." *Ekphrasis* reached Italy in the fourteenth century and had a profound influence on the art and theory of Renaissance humanism. See Michael Baxandall, *Giotto and the Orators: Humanist Observers of Painting in Italy and the Discovery of Pictorial Composition 1350–1450* (Oxford, England: Clarendon Press, 1971), 85; especially chapter II.3.

5. Derrida's context is different but still related and his argument favors a natural versus a universal language/idiom for philosophy. Fundamental concepts of philosophy inhabit and are inhabited by the languages that articulated them (such as Greek, German, and Latin): "Once one realizes the fact that philosophy inherits a language or is inhabited by a language, the most lucid choice one can make, and the freest, is not to avoid this problem, but to write with this language, to push as far as they can go the philosophical experience and the poetic experience of the language." *Points . . . Interviews, 1974–1994,* Elisabeth Weber, ed., Peggy Kamuf and others, trans. (Stanford, Calif.: Stanford University Press, 1995), 375.

6. The voices that Derrida hears or strives to release in a philosophical text, for example, in order to make language think, echo the Greek way of thinking language. They are also women's voices, especially when he attempts to order them. It is as if he does philosophy out of a feminine that he cannot articulate. Elsewhere, it seems that he wants philosophy to do what it cannot (such as in *Points,* 375). The reference to women's voices also occurs in *Points,* 394.

7. Luce Irigaray, *This Sex Which Is Not One,* Catherine Porter and Carolyn Burke, trans. (Ithaca, N.Y.: Cornell University Press, 1985), 25; hereafter *TS.*

8. Irigaray, *TS,* 124.

9. *Platonis Opera II,* I. Burnet, ed. (Oxford, England: Oxford University Press, 1953), 235bc. Sappho is described first as wise—"for the wise men and women of old"—and then as "beautiful" (*kale*), a quality that she was reputed not to have had. But she is not directly called wise. The fragment that describes Sappho as "quite ugly, being dark in complexion and of very small stature" is Fragment 1 from her biographies; in David A. Campbell ed., *Greek Lyric I: Sappho and Alcaeus,* David A. Campbell, trans. (Cambridge, Mass.: Harvard University Press, 1982).

10. Hesiod, *Homeric Hymns*, 649.

11. It is inevitable to associate this with orality in an originary way (for example, in Freudian terms). The import of *sophia* is also plurisensual; tactile, visual, audial, kinetic, and affective/somatic states are included, suggesting a dispersion of orality beyond its somatic center. This plurality may account for the term's tacit creative (poetic) sense—such as in the *Phaedrus*, where Sappho, skilled in eroticizing language, is called *sophe*. It is significant that in the dialogue Plato will deeroticize *sophia* and the feminine. The reference to Sappho is therefore ominous. (The association with Freud was pointed out to me by Emanuela Bianchi.)

12. In I 30, Croesus says to Solon: "Stranger of Athens, we have heard much of thy wisdom and of thy travels through many lands, from love of knowledge and a wish to see the world." *Herodotus, The Histories*, George Rawlinson, trans. (Rutland: J. M. Dent & Sons, 1992); and *Histories I*, A. D. Godley, trans. (Cambridge, Mass.: Harvard University Press, 1944). I am indebted for this reference to Nikos Vardiambassis's *Istoria Mias Lexis* (*History of a Word*), (Athens: Livani Press, 1996), 37–39 (in Greek).

13. *Platonis Opera I*, J. Burnet, ed. (Oxford, England: Oxford University Press, 1973); Aristotle, *Metaphysics* I-IX, Loeb Classical Library, Vol. XVII (Cambridge, Mass.: Harvard University Press, 1980).

14. One example is *Sophist* (218d-221c), *Platonis Opera I*.

15. Homer, *Opera I*, Iliad II, Thomas W. Allen, ed. (Oxford, England: Oxford University Press, 1963).

16. Ibid., 210–15.

17. Thersites actually says: "Come on you soft and shameful ladies [*kak'elencheia, Achaides, ouket' Achaioi*], let's board our ships and go home." The Greek is more emphatic (i.e. using the feminine *Achaides* in place of masculine *Achaioi*). Rendering this in English can be awkward.

18. Ibid., 245–50.

19. Plato, *Phaedrus*, 244a–57b.

20. The palinode is the third speech delivered in the dialogue and the second by Socrates.

21. Plato, *Phaedrus*, 229–30bc.

22. The speech is given on the same theme of the Lysian-type speech delivered by Phaedrus earlier. The argument is that eros is an evil because of the loss of mind and good judgment that it brings about. The opposite, friendship (*philia*) is the basis for stable, lasting relationships.

23. Plato, *Phaedrus*, 237–41d.

24. Ibid., 243cd.

25. Socrates attributes this kind of behavior to sailors and unfree men.

26. Plato, *Phaedrus*, 250e–51a.

27. *Symposium of Plato*, Tom Griffith, trans. (Berkeley: University of California Press, 1989), 201d–12b. Socrates specifically says: "I said Eros was a great god, and a lover of beauty. Diotima proved to me, using the same argument by which I have just proved it to Agathon, that, according to my own argument, Eros was neither beautiful nor good."

28. Ibid., 201c.

29. Ibid., 201e.

30. Ibid., 202.

31. Ibid., 202a.

32. Ibid., 203de. Masculine *poros* and feminine *penia* are treated as proper names. Eros is their masculine offspring.

33. Ibid., 206b. Here Griffith translates: "I find your knowledge so impressive."

34. *Symposium*, 206b–12a.

35. *Tokos* is a feminine noun; a female being's act of bringing forth.

36. *Symposium*, 209bc.

37. Ibid., 208a.

38. Alice Jardine maintains that women "will most certainly welcome the demise of Truth—Man's Truth." This kind of statement is compelling only in a rhetorical sense as a more philosophical way of saying that women will welcome the rejection of many false claims made about women. Its problematic nature becomes apparent when Jardine continues: "It is not enough to oppose Man's Truth; the very conceptual systems that have posited it must be undermined. And finally she will begin to recognize that many of those conceptual systems are intrinsic to feminist thinking whether or not openly declared: systems of defining the self, perception, judgment, and therefore, morality." It is hard to see how any kind of thought, feminist or otherwise, can operate in the conceptual and historical vacuum suggested here. Failure to discriminate between ideological and nonideological aspects of theories and arguments is another problem; see Alice A. Jardine, *Gynesis: Configurations of Woman and Modernity* (Ithaca, N.Y.: Cornell University Press, 1985), 153.

39. Aristotle specifically writes: "For the slave has no deliberative faculty at all; the woman has, but it is without authority, and the child has but it is immature" (1260a). (Richard McKeon, ed., *The Basic Works of Aristotle* [New York: Random House, 1941] (*Politics* translation by Benjamin Jowett). Aristotle may be arguing from the status of women in his society which does not let them exercise their reason. If he argues from his understanding of female physiology, the other reading of *akyron* (that is, less important or minor) seems appropriate. Ernest Barker prefers "inconclusive." See his *Politics of Aristotle* (London: Oxford University Press, 1958); also Aristotle, *Politics*, H. Rackham, trans. Loeb Classical Library, vol. XXI (Cambridge, Mass.: Harvard University Press, 1994).

40. Jean Baudrillard, *Seduction*, Brian Singer, trans. (New York: St Martin's Press, 1979), 6; hereafter *S.*

41. Ibid., 21. See also chapters 1 and 2, 5–27.

42. Plato, *Phaedo*, 89d–90d. Phaedo recalls what Socrates told him in jail: " 'The danger of becoming misologists or haters of argument,' said he, 'as people become misanthropists or haters of man; for no worse evil can happen to a man than to hate argument.' " *Platonis Opera I.*

43. Caroline Walker Bynum, *Fragmentation and Redemption: Essays on Gender and the Human Body in Medieval Religion* (New York: Zone Books, 1992), especially chapters V and VI, 151–238.

44. For this argument, the formative text is *Preface to Plato* (Cambridge, Mass.: Harvard University Press, 1963); hereafter *PP;* especially chapters VII, VIII and IX, 115–64. For subsequent argument with regard to pre-Socratic orality, see Havelock's, "The Linguistic Task of the Presocratics," in Kevin Robb, ed., *Language and Thought in Early Greek Philosophy* (La Salle, Ill.: The Hegeler Institute, 1983), 7–82.

45. Havelock, *PP,* 198–201.

46. Ibid., 218–19. See also Walter J. Ong, *Orality and Literacy: The Technologizing of the Word* (New York: Methuen & Company, 1982).

47. Robb, *LT,* 220–21, 224.

48. Thalmann, *CFT,* 32.

49. "If language were not already, in that sense, a writing, no derived 'notation' would be possible; and the classical problem of relationships between speech and writing could not arise." Jacques Derrida, *Of Grammatology,* Gayatri Chakravorty Spivak, trans. (Baltimore, Md.: The Johns Hopkins University Press, 1976), 56–57, 62–63.

50. "For anyone who has a sense of what words are in a primary oral culture, or a culture not far removed from primary orality, it is not surprising that the Hebrew term *dabar* means 'word' and 'event.'" By contrast, "deeply typographic folk forget to think of words as primarily oral, as events, and hence as necessarily powered: for them, words tend rather to be assimilated to things, 'out there' on a flat surface." Ong, *Orality and Literacy,* 32–33.

51. For a study of the relationship between writing and reading and the *erastes* (lover)-*eromenos* (beloved) relationship in pederastic context (specifically analogies between sexual penetration and writing) see Svenbro, *Phrasikleia,* 187–216.

52. The Attic vase inscriptions and paintings studied by Svenbro in which writing is clearly eroticized may register a reflexive response to this new form of speech based on oral experience. The fact that the eroticized bodies (both literal and textual) are masculine is consistent with the view that I am taking. Plato's problematic in the *Phaedrus* is all the more urgent from this standpoint (that is, the pairing of Eros and writing). Consider the parallel to the archaeological evidence examined by Svenbro. "Socrates: 'You know, Phaedrus, writing shares a strange feature with painting. The offsprings of painting stand there as if they are alive, but if anyone asks them anything, they remain most solemnly silent. The same is true of written words" (275d). This translation from Plato, *Phaedrus,* A. Nehamas and P. Woodruff, trans. (Indianapolis, Ind.: Hackett, 1995). An example of a vase painting in which a youth is shown reading a stele in the position of an *eromenos* is in Svenbro, *Phrasikleia,* 194.

53. Sappho's Fragment 147 can be brought as evidence of experience with literacy: "Someone, I say, will remember us in the future." See Svenbro, *Phrasikleia,* 154–59. Svenbro believes that in 147 Sappho is reflecting on immortality through her written poem. He concentrates his argument about a literate Sappho on the famous poem, Fragment 31: "He seems to me the equal of the gods." Sappho's male rival is the future reader of the poem, symbolized by the young woman to

whom both Sappho and the suitor are attracted. He will read the poem when she (Sappho) will no longer be alive. Svenbro uses the fragment of Antiphanes discussed above to support his interpretation. Fragment 2 of her biographies claims that she "wrote" nine books. See Campbell, *Greek Lyric I.*

54. For the meanings of the various Greek terms here and elsewhere in the paper, I have relied on H. G. Liddell and R. Scott, *Greek-English Lexicon with a Revised Supplement* (Oxford, England: Clarendon Press, 1996).

55. On Plato's response to orality see Havelock, *PP,* especially chapter XIII, 234–53.

56. Fragment 5 from Sappho's biographies makes this claim. She sailed from Mitylene to Sicily probably between 605/4. See Campbell, *Greek Lyric I.*

57. On women poets in antiquity and these two poets in particular see Jane McIntosh Snyder, *The Women and the Lyre: Women Writers in Classical Greece and Rome* (Carbondale: Southern Illinois University Press, 1989), 40–54.

58. Plato, *Phaedrus,* 275–78.

59. All fragments of the pre-Socratics from G. S. Kirk and J. E. Raven, *The Presocratic Philosophers* (Cambridge: Cambridge University Press, 1957). This example is from Fragment 103.

60. Paul Ricoeur, "What Is a Text? Explanation and Interpretation," cited in *Mythic-Symbolic Language and Philosophical Anthropology,* David M. Rasmussen, (The Hague: Martinus Nijhoff, 1971), 148.

61. Heraclitus, in Kirk and Raven, *Presocratic Philosophers,* Fr. 50.

62. Ibid., Fr. 1.

63. Ibid., Fr. 123.

64. Havelock, *PP,* 16.

65. Parmenides, in Kirk and Raven, *Presocratic Philosophers,* Fr. 5.

66. Ibid., Fr. 2.

67. Ibid., Fr. 6.

68. Ibid., Fr. 8.

69. Ibid., Fr. 1.

70. Ibid., Fr. 6.

71. Ibid., Fr. 7.

72. Hesiod, *Homeric Hymns,* 120–35.

73. Ibid. 200–205.

74. This view of history is articulated with particular clarity in Hegel's *Introduction to the Philosophy of History,* Leo Rauch, trans. (Indianapolis, Ind.: Hackett, 1988). For example: "The process of development, so quiescent in the world of nature, is for Spirit a hard and endless struggle against itself. What the Spirit wants is to arrive at the concept of itself; but it itself hides this concept from itself—and it is even proud and filled with joy in this self-estrangement," 59. The suppression of woman is one form of self-estrangement, perhaps the most significant for philosophy because the concept "human" entails both genders. This is not to suggest that Hegel saw gender as a factor in world history.

Notes on Contributors

Emanuela Bianchi, a Ph.D. candidate in the Department of Philosophy at the New School for Social Research, is a visiting scholar in the Department of Rhetoric, University of California, Berkeley.

Teresa Brennan is Schmidt Distinguished Professor of Humanities and a professor of philosophy at Florida Atlantic University. She is the author of *The Real Third Way*, on alternative economic strategies.

Drucilla Cornell is a professor of law, political science, and women's studies at Rutgers University. Her most recent book is *At the Heart of Freedom: Feminism, Sex, and Equality*.

Jacques Derrida has taught for many years at the École des Hautes Études en Science Sociales in Paris and has held visiting appointments at leading universities in Europe and the United States, including New York University, the New School for Social Research, and the University of California, Irvine. He has written extensively in philosophy and literary and political theory. His most recent concern has been the question of the animal, explored in "L'Animal que donc je suis," in *L'Animal autobiographique: autour de Jacques Derrida*.

Ruth Ginzberg taught philosophy and women's studies at a number of colleges and universities through the end of 1997. She resides in southeastern Wisconsin and co-owns a small video-production company specializing in custom educational videos for nonprofit organizations.

David Golumbia is an independent scholar who gained his Ph.D. in English from the University of Pennsylvania. Some of his recent work appears in *Cultural Critique, Hypatia,* and *Postmodern Culture.*

Marjorie Hass is an associate professor of philosophy at Muhlenberg College in Allentown, Pennsylvania. She works on issues in philosophy of logic, philosophy of language, and feminist philosophy and is writing a book about the difficulties of representing negation.

Virginia Held is Distinguished Professor of Philosophy at the City University of New York, the Graduate School, and Hunter College. She has published widely in social and political philosophy and feminist ethics and is working on a number of essays on the ethics of care and the challenge its theories present to standard moral theories.

Leslie A. MacAvoy is currently a visiting assistant professor of philosophy at McGill University.

Patricia S. Mann teaches philosophy at Hofstra University. She writes on a variety of social issues, from assisted suicide to gendered aspects of globalization. She is working on her next book, *Interrogating Autonomy: Agency in the Twenty-first Century.*

Marjorie C. Miller is an associate professor of philosophy at Purchase College, SUNY. She was a coeditor of *Contributions and Controversy in Feminist Philosophy,* a special double issue of *Metaphilosophy.* Her recent articles address issues of race, gender, and class in the contemporary United States.

Lynn Hankinson Nelson is a professor of philosophy at the University of Missouri, St. Louis. She is the author and editor of several works on W. V. O. Quine, feminism, and philosophy of science and is working on *Scientism Well Lost, Evidence Regained: The Case for Social, Naturalized, and Normative Philosophy of Science.*

Nickolas Pappas is an associate professor of philosophy at City College and the Graduate School and University Center, City University of New York. He is the author of the *Routledge Guidebook to Plato and "The Republic"* and a number of articles on topics in ancient philosophy and aesthetics.

Matthew R. Silliman teaches philosophy at Massachusetts College of Liberal Arts. His recent publications include essays on the philosophy of law, epistemology, and political theory.

Cornelia A. Tsakiridou is an associate professor in philosophy at La Sall University, Philadelphia. She has published work in aesthetics, recently a volume on the art and cinema of Jean Cocteau, and specializes in the study of visual and textual analogies in photography, sacred art, and literature.

Alys Eve Weinbaum is an assistant professor in the Department of English and a member of the Critical Theory Faculty at the University of Washington. She is presently working on a book on representations of race and reproduction in transatlantic modern thought.

Iris Marion Young is a professor of public and international affairs at the University of Pittsburgh, where she teaches ethics and political philosophy. Her most recent book is *Intersecting Voices: Dilemmas of Gender, Political Philosophy, and Policy.*